Tangled Yarns / Angela Harris and Tony Harris

TANGLED YARNS

The Lives of James Finlayson and Margaret Wilkie

Angela Harris & Tony Harris

MADGE
BOOKS

First published in 2024
by Madge Books
Edinburgh, Scotland

Cover image: Map of Europe circa 1800.
Cover design by Richard Bowring

Publisher's Note: This is a work of non-fiction.

Publishing services provided by Lumphanan Press

Tangled Yarns/ Angela Harris & Tony Harris. – 1st ed.
ISBN 978-1-7384792-0-7

Printed by Imprint Digital, UK

Contents

An invisible red thread connects those who are destined to meet, regardless of time, place, or circumstance. The thread may stretch or tangle, but will never break

CHINESE PROVERB

Introduction

A Scottish 'Icarus' of the Middling Sort[1]

We could portray James Finlayson (1770–1852) as a tragic figure. He and his wife Margaret Wilkie lived in an age of revolution of social order, industrial innovation and religious dispute. In setting the Finlaysons in their context, this book includes references to a tumultuous history, from the French Revolution to the Napoleonic wars. We mention relevant evangelical divisions of the churches: Quakers, Burghers, Antiburghers. We also explore Imperial Russian and Finnish sources for contextual information about the couple. The history of the company Finlayson Oy has already been well covered in twentieth and twenty-first century accounts and our emphasis has been on the Finlaysons' earlier lives and later years.

James developed his mechanical skills in the textile centre situated in Glasgow and the west of Scotland. He went on to transfer those skills in wool, linen and cotton manufacture to the less developed industries in St Petersburg and Finland. James was born into an Antiburgher family, the son of a philandering tailor. Nowadays many people have a limited understanding of what the Antiburghers stood for but they formed a strict, puritanical Presbyterian sect that separated from the established Church due to its stance against patronage.

Why do we cast him as tragic? Aristotle wrote in *Poetics* about archetypal tragic figures and plots. A tragic hero is defined as a character who makes a judgement error that inevitably leads to their own destruction – usually death but this could be expanded to include financial ruin. Aristotle specified certain characteristics that the tragic hero usually possesses, which includes *hubris*, or excessive over-confidence. The plot of a tragic life story includes *hamartia* (an error in judgement that leads to their downfall), *peripeteia* (a reversal of fate), *anagnorisis* (the heroes recognising that their own actions caused their situation), *nemesis* (punishment the hero cannot avoid), and *catharsis* (feelings of pity and fear felt by the audience towards the character).[2]

James was a talented mechanic throughout his career, but rather like the mythical Icarus who flew too close to the sun and melted the wax of his wings, falling to his death, James overreached himself. James' character flaws were *hubris* (or excessive pride) and ambition. He could be described as a man who aspired to be a successful businessman and in terms of the well-known Peter Principle,[3] repeatedly reaching levels of incompetence. If only James had accepted his strength in mechanical engineering, he might have had a less turbulent and precarious life. Ambition and drive can be positive qualities. However, as with Shakespeare's Macbeth, they can be destructive and lead many to stray from their true strengths and show poor follow-through.

> The Icarus syndrome characterises leaders who initiate overly ambitious projects that come to naught, causing harm to themselves and others in the process.[4]

The conscious mind can trick us to select goals that reflect the internalised expectations of others and lead to ill-fitting career paths. Sometimes these goals conflict with our 'true purpose' that can lie under the threshold of awareness. What are we good at and what gives us joy? Zachary Phillips, poet, author, and mindset coach, helps people by promoting self-knowledge and alignment.

> Unless you are completely honest with yourself, your actions will be out of line with your true purpose. By 'true purpose' I am not referring to anything religious or spiritual. I am referring to what you as an individual, given your unique set of genetics and environmental influences, is best set up to do.

> If you can align your lifestyle, words, actions and pursuits with your true purpose, a deep sense of meaning will follow.[5]

James replayed the problematic behaviour again and again – perhaps because he was not completely honest with himself and was not aware of his true purpose. Sigmund Freud called this pattern the *repetition compulsion*. These mistakes in career led to his ruin (*hamartia*). It is plausible that he modelled himself on successful business or religious mentors such as John Napier (1752–1813), an iron founder in Glasgow; William Dunn (1770–1849), a Scottish agriculturist, machine maker and mill owner; John Paterson (1776–1855), Bible Society pioneer; and Daniel Wheeler (1771–1840), a British Quaker, minister, teacher and missionary in Russia and the South Pacific. These men were his contemporaries but they were either luckier, were more self-aware, had more support from family or were more aligned with their ambitions.

Through misfortune or his own character flaws, James

suffered financial reversals when he lost everything (*peripeteia*). Living in straitened circumstances must have been humiliating (*nemesis*). Many middling sort of people lived a precarious existence aspiring to move up the social ladder of class. Their security was based on provision of credit and this was often out of their control.

Just before he died, James appeared to recognise some of his own role in his problems and sought reconciliation with the local Quaker meeting (*anagnorisis*). However, there is no evidence that James ever acknowledged his own role in business failure. He might have died attributing failure to external events outwith his control. We can perhaps feel pity for James and also fear that this could so easily happen to us (*catharsis*).

An alternative view of James is that he showed resilience after each setback and he was prepared to migrate to St Petersburg in Russia and then Tampere in Finland. He kept trying and his attempts aligned with the beliefs of the famous inventor Thomas Alva Edison (1847–1931), inventor, who said:

> Our greatest weakness lies in giving up. The most
> certain way to succeed is always to try just one more
> time.

Margaret Wilkie – the wind beneath his wings[6]

One of the objectives in writing this book was to bring Margaret Wilkie out of the shadows and into the limelight and this has proved to be difficult as she was a middling sort of woman and little is recorded about women in the eighteenth and nineteenth centuries. Matthew Peek, the Military Collection Archivist for the State Archives of North Carolina, wrote:

> As an archivist, I live in the incomplete. We always
> know there are records or perspectives missing, which
> makes describing the materials challenging.[7]

The only fact we have discovered is that she was buried in the same grave as James, although there is no mention of her on the headstone. We also located some one-sided correspondence to her. Descriptions about her refer to her entrepreneurship in Finland. We have included informed but possibly incorrect conjecture into our narrative. We concluded that Margaret was a true hero with the strength to support James 'for better for worse, for richer, for poorer, in sickness and in health, to love and to cherish, till death them do part'.[8]

What prompted us to write this book?

Angela and Tony retired in Edinburgh. Angela had been a Chartered Counselling Psychologist and academic in the faculty of the Psychology Department at Glasgow Caledonian University. In her retirement, she completed the Postgraduate Certificate in Scottish Family and Local History at the University of Dundee to inform her genealogical research. Tony was a water engineer at the consulting firm of John Taylor and Sons. He received an OBE in the 1985 Queen Elizabeth II Birthday Honours for 'services to civil engineering in the People's Democratic Republic of Yemen.' One of his voluntary pursuits was to start a Friends group for the Newington Cemetery which was involved in identifying interesting men and women buried there.

The headstone erected for James Finlayson triggered our interest and James Finlayson was one of the first to be highlighted for the Edinburgh Doors Open Day – Scotland's largest free festival that celebrates heritage and the built environment and offers free access to over a thousand venues across the country each September. The Finlaysons' story might have finished there but we visited the Finlayson area in Tampere and became re-invested in the project. Any visitor looking up from the centre of Tampere will see how the Finlayson sign dominates the skyline. Finlayson is a famous trademark as a manufacture of textiles. To further our research, from Finland we took the train to St Petersburg and gained a better idea of the Finlaysons' migration.

We both enjoy historical research but differ in our perspectives – Tony reads about the history of wars and Angela is more interested in social history that investigates local people. Both of us are curious and question the material with *'so what?'* Sometimes information is given almost as an aside, such as the note that James and Margaret had no children. Angela's experience in counselling older men and women who were childfree led us to question what this barren state might have meant to the Finlaysons at different stages of their lives. The Finlaysons migrated to Russia and Finland. Anyone who has migrated might have experienced the effect of different climates and topographies on their wellbeing and so this book includes information on local climate conditions.

Where we stay provides an excellent base for research on the Finlaysons. Edinburgh hosts the National Records of Scotland (NRS) and the National Library of Scotland (NLS) that includes the National Map Library. In addition, Glasgow is close and the City Archives are housed in the Mitchell Library and the Archives & Special Collections of the University of Glasgow Library is located in the city. There is also the Trades House of Glasgow archive. The rest of our research was carried out in correspondence with archivists in England, St Petersburg, Russia and Finland.

We describe James as a tragic figure and this might be contested. As Jack Gilbert (1925–2012), the American poet, wrote in 'Failing and Flying':

Everyone forgets that Icarus also flew

I believe Icarus was not failing as he fell,
But just coming to the end of his triumph.[9]

NOTES

1 'Middling sort' is a term that commentators use to socially categorise British society from Tudor to Victorian times in imprecise and variable terms. The middling sort is the social ranking between the labouring working class and the gentry and nobility class

2 Aristotle and Heath, M. (1996) Poetics, London: Penguin Books.

3 Peter, L. J. and Hull, R. (1970) The Peter Principle, London: Pan Books.

4 Vries, M. F. R. de, (2019) This quote by Manfred F. R. Kets de Vries is from a 2019 INSEAD Knowledge article entitled "The Icarus Syndrome: Execs Who Fly Too Close to the Sun": https://knowledge.insead.edu/ leadership – organisations/icarus-syndrome-execs-who-fly-too-close-sun. Used with permission

5 Phillips, Z. (2018) How to Get Your Sh!T Together. [Kindle version], Independently published. http://www.amazon.co.uk. p. 224. Used with permission from Zachary Phillips.

6 Adapted from Silbar, Jeff and Henley, Larry (1982) Wind Beneath My Wings.

7 Peek, M. (2021) Comment on Lois Leveen, "Best Guess or Worst Doubt: What's the Role of Conjecture in Writing Biography and History?" in David Prior, et al., The H-CivWar Author's Blog, 24 August. https://net-works.h-net.org/node/4113/blog/h-civwar-authors-blog/8089270/best-guess-or-worst-doubt-whats-role-conjecture/ : accessed 19 November 2023. Used with permission from H-CivWar Authors' Blog.

8 Cranmer, T. (1549) Traditional Marriage Vows. In: Book of Common Prayer.

9 Gilbert, J. (2005) Failing and Flying. In: Refusing Heaven: Poems by Jack Gilbert. pp. 16–17 © 2005 by Jack Gilbert. Used by permission of Alfred A. Knopf, an imprint of the Knopf Doubleday Publishing Group, a division of Penguin Random House LLC. All rights reserved.

— CHAPTER ONE —

Newington Necropolis
or 'Ekkie Bank'

Death announcement on 24th February 1855:
Margaret Wilkie, relict of the late Mr James
Finlayson – 8 Nicolson Square, 15th inst.

[Transcript of *Edinburgh News and Literary Chronicle*,
24 February 1855]

On 14 February 1855, the renowned homeopath, Dr
Dionysius Wielobycki, made his way from his
premises in Queen Street, Edinburgh to attend the
bedside of a dying woman in her home at 8, Nicolson Square.
Margaret Finlayson was drowning in her own fluids from
bronchitis and died the following day.[1] It was an unusually
cold day and during the earlier part of that week there had
been occasional showers of snow accompanied by frost. Dud-
dingston Loch and other ponds in the vicinity became frozen
and were used by skaters and curlers.[2] Margaret was a woman
in reduced circumstances with a small pension. Although
Wielobycki attended wealthy patients, he also provided
obstetric services to poor women in their confinements. He
was fluent in Polish, German, French and English and this
linguistic facility might have been attractive to Margaret due
to her familiarity with multilingual friends, such as Ferdinand

Uhde and Jane Paterson. We know that her husband, James Finlayson, had gained some linguistic skill as he started to translate *Grounds of a Holy Life* by H. Turfurd.[3] Kaisa Koskinen thought it probable that James had also learned some Russian from his years living and working there.[4] We have no evidence of Margaret's linguistic ability but she might have learned Russian and Finnish to a rudimentary level and even some German through her friendship with Ferdinand Uhde, a friend from St Petersburg who later became the manager at the Finlaysons' mill. Margaret's friend, Jane Paterson was fluent in 'Russ':

> She took a most lively interest in the prosperity of the
> Bible Society; and from her knowledge of the Russ,
> and other languages much spoken in Petersburg, was,
> on numberless occasions, serviceable in conversing
> upon its affairs, writing, and translating letters, and in
> various other ways assisting in the work.[5]

There is no record that Margaret's bronchitis was treated by Wielobycki with homeopathic medicine. He was a popular doctor with the ladies; however, the trust in him was proved to be ill-founded when two years later, in 1857, he was convicted and sentenced for the forgery of a will and defrauding two elderly wealthy spinsters under his care.[6]

When in 1849 James Finlayson paid 11 shillings (£0.55) for a lair in Newington Necropolis, as Newington Cemetery in Edinburgh was then known, he had a wider choice of last resting place than in earlier times when his non-conformist views may have been at odds with an established church burial.[7] In the 1840s there was a boom in joint stock companies or other commercial ventures establishing cemeteries for profit, replacing in healthier and more attractive surroundings the insanitary and overcrowded kirkyards attached to churches. Outbreaks of cholera and typhoid in 1830s Edinburgh led to demands to open up the old core of the city, in time creating new infrastructure such as George IV Bridge and Victoria Street. Medical and public health reforms followed these outbreaks, such as quarantining the sick and fumigating their fever-stricken dwellings, but all these changes came much later.

The continuing insanitary and unhealthy conditions were exploited to the full in the publicity material and prospectuses for the new cemetery ventures, emphasising the problems of the old burying grounds and the benefits of the new. Typical is the prospectus for the Edinburgh Western Cemetery Company for Dean Cemetery, which stated that graveyards were sadly lacking, because,

> .... the pernicious exhalations from the ground were
> as prejudicial to the general health as the spectacles
> presented in turning up graves for new interments
> were revolting to the better feelings of the age, and
> the exposure of the grounds to the public gaze of
> parties passing through the neighbouring thorough-
> fare had deprived these churchyards of that seclusion
> and privacy which should ever form a main character
> of the last resting places of humanity.[8]

Just over a mile from his home in 8 (now 12) Nicolson Square, James could have taken up the offer from 1847 of the Edinburgh Southern Cemetery Company at the Grange Cemetery, laid out by David Bryce, which benefitted from the 'amenity and beauty of situation', 'proximity to the City' and 'the highest attainable security that the remains therein deposited shall continue undisturbed'.[9]

Slightly further away, on farmland obtained from the Dick family of Prestonfield, the Metropolitan Cemetery

Figure 1: Newington Necropolis brochure.

Source: Metropolitan Cemetery Association. 'Newington Necropolis'.
Brochure. Edinburgh, 1844. National Library of Scotland.

Association had from 1846 offered lairs in the Newington Necropolis, off Dalkeith Road, Echo Bank at competitive prices.

The front page of the Newington Necropolis brochure lists the Company Directors and David Cousin as Architect (see Figure 1). David Cousin (1809–1878) was born in North Leith, the son of John Cousin, a joiner to whom David was articled. He then secured a place in the architectural office of William Henry Playfair, leaving there in 1831 to start his own practice from his father's house at 24 Fettes Row. In 1841 Cousin was appointed Assistant to the elderly Edinburgh City Superintendent of Works, taking over when he retired, and only retiring himself as Superintendent in 1872. Cousin retained the right to continue his private practice, which from about 1843 was based at 43 Princes Street.

Cousin's prolific output included the feuing layout of the Grange Estate, Mayfield Gardens, Waverley Park, Craigmillar Park and West Savile Road, but he is perhaps best remembered for his designs of the Warriston, Dean, Dalry, Rosebank and Newington Cemeteries. The latter in particular is an example of the Victorian 'garden cemeteries movement' with its emphasis on planting and an informal fluid layout, an early example being the Père Lachaise cemetery in Paris. Monuments, statuary and classical style lodges, vaults and catacombs were a feature of this style of cemetery and Newington was no exception, catacombs being in the original concept as envisaged. Cousin's layout included the neo-Norman west-facing catacombs and terrace in the middle of the cemetery and the Victorian gothic lodge and gates at the Dalkeith Road entrance.

The Newington Necropolis brochure of November 1845 goes on to state:

> In the selecting and laying out of this Ground, the
> Directors have endeavoured, they trust successfully,
> to meet the improved taste and feelings of the
> Community, with regard to places of Sepulture. The
> situation commands extensive and beautiful views,
> and is perfectly secluded, and at the same time of easy
> access to the Inhabitants, not only of Edinburgh, but
> of Liberton, Duddingston, etc, while the soil is deep
> and dry.[10]

The brochure continues:

> The Price of a perpetual and exclusive right to One
> Space, seven feet long by 3 feet broad, will vary from
> £1, 11s. 6d. to £4, 13s. 4d., according to situation.

And further on:

> A range of beautiful and substantial Catacombs, well
> lighted, airy and dry, has been erected on the most
> approved plan, which affords the means of Sepulture
> to a large extent, in leaden coffins, above ground, at
> the following rates, viz:
>
> A Single Private Catacomb for one coffin £5-10-0.
> Vault capable of holding 18 coffins £90-0-0. Ample
> space is afforded in the front of the Terrace Wall for
> Mural Monuments, for which the charge will be
> £3-10-0 or £3 each according to situation;

The first interment in the new cemetery was of James
Muirhead, who died at 53 Clerk Street, Edinburgh of scrofula
aged 15 years and 9 months and was buried on 29 March 1846
in plot G160 (G53 in the 1846 Lair Book). The lair purchased
by James Finlayson in 1849 is in the middle of Section P, away

from the more expensive plots adjacent to the roadways and not listed in the quoted prices. Poverty in old age may have combined with a Quaker lack of ostentation in burials and avoidance of headstones to influence this economical decision, although he was not then a practising Quaker. The Glasgow Quakers two monthly meetings in August 1846 confirmed his earlier resignation from the Society of Friends and, despite an attempt at reconciliation in early 1852, membership had not resumed before his death. James would not therefore have been entitled to burial in the Quaker Burying Ground in the Pleasance Edinburgh. Gravestones only began to be used in Quaker Burying Grounds much later, in the mid-nineteenth century.

Cousin's layout of the first phase of the cemetery, shown in Figure 2, is from the 1846–7 Edinburgh and Leith Post Office Directory. The same Directory also includes a different lithographic view from that fronting the Company Prospectus and Newington Necropolis brochure. Although still somewhat idealised, this later lithograph shows more realistically what was built and the same lithograph was also used for the Company's share certificates. The Newington catacombs as built include formal stone terracing, a staircase at each end and a small central vault (see Figure 3). However, attitudes to vault interment changed and these catacombs were not commercially successful, only two burials there being recorded to 1909, but there may be more.

Newington was also known as Echo Bank cemetery, (locally spoken of as 'Ekkie Bank'). Bounded to the west by the Pow Burn and to the east by Dalkeith Road the initial area of 3.35Ha (8.28 acres) was extended in two stages towards Cameron Toll to the extent we see today, in all amounting to 5.64Ha (13.93 acres). In the late 1860s a carriage drive was built from a new entrance in Craigmillar Park to the cemetery. This

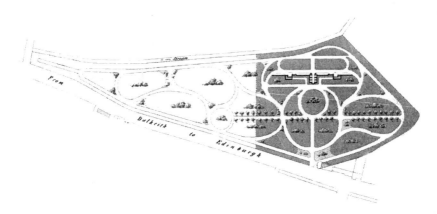

Figure 2: Ground Plan of Newington Cemetery

Source: Lithograph by F. Schenck, in 1846–47 Edinburgh and Leith Post Office Directory, p.468. National Library of Scotland.

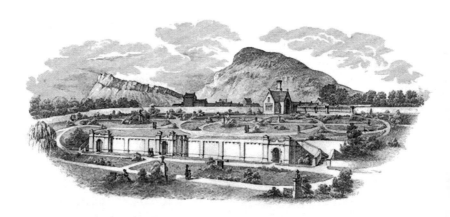

Figure 3: Catacombs of Newington Cemetery

Source: Lithograph by F. Schenck, in 1846–47 Edinburgh and Leith Post Office Directory, p.467. National Library of Scotland. Enhanced and cropped by Magnus Hagdorn.

drive was later closed in the twentieth century and the land sold, part of which now forms the rear of Ventnor Terrace & Place. In the 1880s the South Suburban Railway was built alongside the Pow Burn, and Newington Station together with its adjacent tram stop offered another convenient access to the cemetery.

The Lodge at the Dalkeith Road entrance, an integral part of Cousin's original cemetery design, continued as the Cemetery Superintendent's residence and was originally quite a small building. Features are the gabled porch with a tall roll-moulded pointed arch and the fish-scale slated roof surmounted by the prominent central chimney with four tall stacks.

James Finlayson died at home in Edinburgh on 18 August 1852 and was interred in lair P125 on 21 August to be followed by his wife Margaret (Wilkie), who was interred with him on 19 February 1855. They had no children. The Newington Cemetery Burial Book records the cause of death for both of them as 'decline of life'.

The Finlayson textile factory, which James had founded in Tampere, Finland in 1820, continued after his departure from the business in 1835 to expand throughout the nineteenth and twentieth centuries, investing in new developments in textile spinning and weaving and using modern materials. Tampere was Finland's first industrial town, for a time its second largest city and is now its third largest. In the aftermath of the October Revolution in Russia in 1917, Finland declared independence, 6 December being recognised as Finland's Independence Day.

In 1970 the Finlayson Company celebrated its 150th anniversary by producing a company history in three languages, Swedish, German and English. Anticipating that event, in 1969 the Finlayson Company enlisted the help of the cotton-spinning firm of J. & P. Coats of Paisley to find out what had happened to their founder after his return to Scotland. Following lengthy research, the unmarked Finlayson grave was found in Newington Cemetery and in 1970 the Finlayson Company arranged for a headstone, understood to be of Tampere granite, to be erected on lair P125, with upkeep of the grave overseen by J. & P. Coats. This headstone is shown in Figure 4.

In the summer of 1974 Brian Denoon, Teacher of English, writer and broadcaster from Inverness encountered the name 'Finlayson' while on holiday in Tampere. The name in enormous Gothic script was standing out, as it still does today, across the skyline above industrial buildings (now a museum complex) in the heart of Tampere. Intrigued as to how such an obviously Scottish name came to be so celebrated, in this and subsequent visits to Finland Brian set about trying to find out more about how it got there. Brian's published papers tell how his meticulous research led to a considerable expansion of the scope of the history of the Company and a better understanding and appreciation of James Finlayson's life and work. In Newington Cemetery, the Finlayson grave and headstone had become rather overgrown, but Brian was able to find it again after some initial difficulty and clearance. Efforts are now being made to keep the grave clear.

Brian's work on James Finlayson led to him writing the entry on 'James Finlayson of Tampere, Finland', in the Oxford Dictionary of National Biography. In the 1980s, he decided to mark Scottish/Finnish links by placing a plaque where the Finlaysons had lived in Nicolson Square, Edinburgh. After Brian obtained the necessary permissions from the authorities and funding from the Company, on 8 October 1988, in the company of invited guests, the Lord Provost of Edinburgh unveiled this plaque, shown in Figure 5.

Figure 4: James Finlayson's headstone in Newington Cemetery.
Note: Date of James' birth is now known to be 27 November 1770.

Source: Antti Liuttunen, 2023. Vapriikki Photo Archives.

In July 1992 Newington Cemetery was Category B Listed, including the Lodge at 222 Dalkeith Road, Vaults, Gates, Gatepiers and Boundary Walls (Reference LB27933).

In 1982 there was a fatal accident when a headstone fell on a teenager and this, with other factors such as its overgrown and neglected state, led to the cemetery being compulsorily purchased by City of Edinburgh Council (CEC) in 1994. The north-west part is set aside as a wildlife area and CEC staff limit the work they do to seasonal grass cutting, invasive weed control and safety maintenance, such as essential tree management and checking headstones.

In January 2014, following informal contacts at the cemetery, Friends of Newington Cemetery (FoNC) was set up as a sub-group of the Grange/Prestonfield Community Council. It holds monthly working parties, with activities to clear unwanted undergrowth, ivy removal where damaging to the

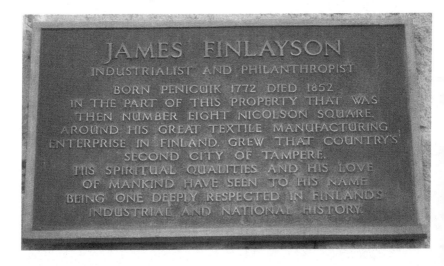

Figure 5: Photograph of James Finlayson plaque, Nicolson Square, Edinburgh

Source: Kim Traynor, 1 June 2012, available under a Creative Commons Attribution-Share Alike 3.0 Unported license fabric, bulb planting and weed control. Research into notable graves has been undertaken with the aim of trying to conserve and record the social, cultural and family history embedded in the artefacts. Information on what FoNC has done and is doing is published on the website www.newington-cemetery.org.uk.

Newington, along with many others in the care of CEC, is now classed as a non-operational cemetery. With the support of CEC, many other cemetery Friends Groups have now been established, with enthusiastic volunteers helping to look after this important City heritage. In 2021 CEC promulgated guidance to help Groups work safely.

Newington Cemetery was established in the nineteenth century in what was then open country as an escape from the overcrowded and insanitary city burying grounds. It is now a publicly accessible escape from noisy streets, a peaceful green lung in the midst of our city and a wildlife sanctuary, supporting biodiversity and a sustainable Edinburgh.

It was not long after we moved to Edinburgh that we became interested in Newington Cemetery and the wealth of natural, social and cultural history to be found there. Family visits to Finland, including Tampere, developed an interest in James Finlayson's grave and headstone. We wanted to learn more when we discovered that James's wife Margaret is buried with him, but not mentioned on the headstone. In the research into published papers on Finlayson, we kept coming across the name Brian Denoon and wondered who he was. Then fortuitously Brian got in touch with the Friends of Newington Cemetery and we were able to meet up and keep in touch. The detailed and original research which Brian carried out from the 1970s onwards for many years, enabled us to add more detail to the lives of the Finlaysons, sometimes using archive material not then available.

NOTES

1 Deaths (CR) Scotland. Castle and Portsburgh. 15 February 1855. FINLAYSON, Margaret. 685/3 124. http://scotlandspeople.gov.uk/ : accessed 25 January 2024.

2 Death announcements. (1855) Edinburgh News and Literary Chronicle. 17 February. FINLAYSON, Margaret. British Newspaper Archive. https://www.britishnewspaperarchive.co.uk : accessed 24 August 2023.

3 Finlayson, James (1832) Letter to Daniel Wheeler, 30 June. Daniel Wheeler Papers, London Society of Friends Library, TEMP MSS 366 Volume 1 Item 88.

4 Koskinen, Kaisa. (2014) Tampere as a Translation Space. Translation Studies 7(2). www.tandfonline.com/doi/abs/10.1080/14781700.2013.87 3876 : accessed 16 November 2021.

5 Swan, William (1823) Memoir of the late Mrs Paterson, wife of the Rev. Dr Paterson, St Petersburg, 2nd ed. Edinburgh: Waugh & Innes. p. 164.

6 Annual Register (1858). The Annual Register or a View of the History and Politics of the Year 1857. Chronicle: Conviction and Sentence for Will Forgery. London: F. & J. Rivington.

7 Newington Necropolis. Sales Book. James Finlayson 1772–1852.

8 Edinburgh Western Cemetery Company (Dean cemetery). (1845) Prospectus. Edinburgh Room, Central Library. YRA/630/43802.

9 Edinburgh Southern Cemetery (Grange cemetery). (1847) Prospectus. Edinburgh Room, Central Library YRA/630/43802.

10 Metropolitan Cemetery Association (1844) Newington Necropolis: A Brochure. National Library of Scotland. p. 6.

– CHAPTER TWO –

James Finlayson of Penicuik

Setting the scene

This chapter and subsequent chapters are about the places where James Finlayson and Margaret Wilkie lived, either separately or together as a couple, and the impact they had on them. We therefore include thoughts on the weather, climate, geography and revolutions, including the Industrial Revolution.

In the eighteenth century and earlier, monarchy, religion, economics and politics were considered drivers for change. In the late twentieth and twenty-first centuries, the social and environmental factors have gained prominence. For people who have migrated from one part of the world to another, they will notice differences in culture, terrain, astronomy and climate. The mammalian part of us responds to these differences. Munros in the Highlands of Scotland, the flat lands and large skies of Norfolk, the short twilight of the Tropics, the White Nights of St Petersburg, the chill winds in Edinburgh, the long winters in Finland – all these places can affect our moods. James and Margaret lived in different parts of Great Britain and the Baltic and, as part of their lives, these differences will have had a lesser or greater impact on them. Towns are mostly described as they existed during the Finlaysons' time, without mention of later buildings, infrastructure and events. However, when historic extreme weather did occur, it had a much greater effect then on local people, as they could not clothe, feed or house themselves as we now can. Prolonged bad weather could cause bad harvests, with hardship and starvation the lot of many people and their livestock.

Global warming and climate change largely caused by human activities, with increasing levels of carbon dioxide and other greenhouse gases in the earth's atmosphere, are measured from pre-industrial base levels, assumed for the UK to date from the late eighteenth or early nineteenth centuries. This is also the start of this narrative, but it is not its purpose to ascribe any weather or climate events mentioned to global warming or climate change.

The surroundings of Penicuik

Auchencorth Moss (55°47'36'N, 3°14'41'W) is an extensive area of peatland with its centre about 3 miles (5km) east of Carlops, a village on the A702 about 17 miles (27km) south-west of Edinburgh and 2.5 miles (4km) west of Howgate, a hamlet on the A6094 1.5 miles (2.5km) south of Esk Bridge in Penicuik. The Moss, at an average elevation of about 800 feet (250m approx.) above sea level (asl), is a natural reservoir draining the eastern slopes of the Pentland Hills and feeding the River Esk, which in the past powered Penicuik's flax, paper and cotton mills. Now Auchencorth Moss is a research centre monitoring environmental factors associated with its boggy origins and the carbon naturally embedded within it and also a World Meteorological Organisation (WMO) global climate monitoring station.

Howgate historically is within Edinburghshire, although the boundary with Peeblesshire is only 0.6 miles (1km) south on its east side along Kingside Edge. The lands around Howgate were known to be bleak and difficult, of barren bog cut through by treeless ravines, renowned for its inhospitable terrain, with the mire of Auchencorth Moss fit only for the cutting and drying of peat for fuel. This land did not escape the 'agricultural improvers' of the late eighteenth and nineteenth centuries, with land drainage enabling grassland and grazing and arable crops, but also reducing the peat-bog carbon sink. As well as water-power being developed downstream, limestone and coal were mined nearby. Also in the eighteenth century, Howgate was the first stop for stagecoaches out of Edinburgh *en route* south to Peebles and beyond, with horses changed and travellers fed at the Old Howgate Inn. Howgate Kirk, set up outside Penicuik in the 1740s as strongly Antiburgher, grew out of the Secessionist movements of the 1730s and the Covenanting traditions of the 1600s.[1] Antiburghers were member of a section of the Secession Church in Scotland which in 1747 separated from the other party in that Church (the Burghers) on the question of taking the Burgess oath.

Penicuik (55°49'51'N, 3°13'28'W) is about 600 feet (180m) asl and as much as 200 feet lower than the Moss itself, recognised historically as having the potential for water-power. Year-round precipitation across the area helped to keep watercourses flowing to the River Esk on the east side of the town. Both the Old Statistical Account of Scotland (1791–99) and the New (1834–1845) refer to Penicuik in the County of Edinburgh in some detail. Some extracts are shown in Tables 1 and 2.

Table 1: Population of Penicuik (1755–1793)

In 1755	890 individuals
In 1772	1132 individuals (200 were under the age of 8)
In 1779	1349 individuals
In 1793	1721 individuals (403 families)

The chief cause of the increase is the erection of a
cotton mill below the village, the first in Scotland,
and the spirit with which two paper mills have been
carried on for some time past. The cotton mill, at
present, employs about 500 hands, sometimes more.[2]

Climate, Minerals etc. – The changes of weather
are often sudden and violent; the winters are severe,
and the air is keen and piercing, with few of those
thick fogs from the E. that are so troublesome
and unwholesome on the coast. Of late, however,
the winters have been uncommonly mild, but the
summers have been cold, short, and unprolific. There
is not much rain through the year, but when it does
fall it is generally in heavy showers. At 12 noon, 5th
September 1788, Fahrenheit's thermometer rose to
73° in the shade and 80° in the sun at New Hall. In
the higher parts of the parish the crops are precarious,
and the grass luxurious …[3]

Climate – In its natural history the parish presents
but few phenomena deserving particular attention.
The most prevailing winds are the west and south.

The east is not felt here as keenly as in the neighbourhood of Edinburgh; but the west from blowing
across the extended moors between this and Linton
has but little of the blandness for which in general it
is celebrated. It is both cold and damp … The great
extent of wet moorland, together with the height of
the country, averaging about 800 feet above the sea,
necessarily produces cold and moisture.[4]

Civil History – The uniform quiet of a country
parish was, in the case of Penicuik, interrupted about
the year 1810, by the extensive paper manufactories
being turned by Government into *depôts* for prisoners

of war, and the peaceful cottages attached to them
into barracks for the military necessarily required.
The paper-mills of Valleyfield were on that occasion
fitted up for the reception of 6000 prisoners, whilst
those of Eskmills, then used as a cotton manufactory,
accommodated 1500 British soldiers. This occurrence
could not fail to produce results very unfavourable to
the social and religious well-being of the parishioners.
The peaceful artisan gave place to the soldier; and
the din of a camp, with its attendant irregularities ...
On the close of the war, however, in the year 1814,
the mills happily returned to their former proprietors
and purposes --- an event which was hailed by the
inhabitants with a general illumination, and other
demonstrations of their heartfelt joy.[5]

The *Gazetteer for Scotland* provides the following summary
of the climate for Scotland:

> Climate information for Penicuik: Winters in
> Penicuik are usually cold for Scotland, with January
> daily temperatures of about 5.6°C and nights cooling
> off to −0.2°C in the coldest month. Summers are very
> warm, with daytime temperatures in July typically
> reaching 18.8°C and nights dipping to 9.7°C. Rainfall
> in Penicuik is typical, totalling 986 mm in a typical
> year. Precipitation is distributed evenly, falling over
> about 156 days per year. Penicuik has low sunshine
> totals, with 1194 hours of sunshine recorded In a
> typical year[6].

The UK Meteorological Office provides information
about 30-year climate averages. Table 2 *(overleaf)* shows the
information for Penicuik.

Penicuik Village

Penicuik (Cymric pen-y-cog, 'hill of the cuckoo'), is a village and a parish in the south of Edinburghshire county (later changed to Midlothian). The village stands 600 feet above sea-level, on the west bank of the river North Esk, by road is 12 miles north by west of Peebles and 10 miles south of Edinburgh. It is renowned for its paper making industry at Valleyfield Mills that operated from 1709. However, it was also the site of the first cotton mill in Scotland.

In 1774, the Board of Trustees for the linen industry appointed Peter Brotherston[7] to manage a new cotton spinning school in Edinburgh containing twelve spinning machines and requested him to make carding and spinning machinery. In 1776 he and Bertram Gardner & Co, Bankers in Edinburgh, acquired the tack for five Scottish acres of land from Sir John Clerk of Penicuik with the use of water for mills and other machinery. Brotherston did not have the capital but provided the expertise and the bankers provided the finance. They built the first cotton mill in Scotland[8] at Esk Mill under the inspection and direction of John Hackett, who was an assistant to Richard Arkwright in Nottingham and an acquaintance of John Hargreaves. The large waterwheel powered machinery for the carding, roving and spinning of cotton. His mill was modelled on that of Richard Arkwright of Nottingham, who threatened to stop the operation. However, the Lord Advocate's opinion was that Arkwright's patent did not apply in Scotland. By 1794, 500 people were employed there. Peter Brotherston died in 1784 and was buried in Penicuik churchyard on 22nd November. His brother, John Brotherston, took over the tack or lease in 1786.

Table 2: 30-year climate averages 1991–2020 for Penicuik

Month	Max. temp. (°C)	Min. temp. (°C)	Days of air frost (days)	Sun-shine (hours)	Rainfall (mm)	Days of rainfall ≥1 mm (days)
January	5.86	0.31	13.10	34.79	98.13	15.53
February	6.53	0.38	12.55	65.49	81.49	12.87
March	8.75	1.37	10.08	99.61	68.26	12.10
April	11.71	2.75	5.73	129.74	58.01	10.73
May	14.86	5.07	2.58	170.93	62.27	11.83
June	17.18	8.06	0.10	143.49	81.66	12.26
July	18.92	9.79	0.00	146.01	85.85	12.88
August	18.47	9.65	0.00	135.32	88.37	13.07
September	15.92	7.68	0.37	111.99	74.29	12.40
October	11.93	4.90	3.28	80.80	98.77	14.47
November	8.43	2.27	7.92	55.24	93.22	14.58
December	6.04	0.20	13.03	34.29	102.95	15.02
Annual	12.08	4.39	68.74	1207.70	993.27	157.74

Source: UK Meteorological Office data. Note: Location – Meteorological Station Penicuik (55°49'51'N, 3°13'23'W, 188m asl). Contains public sector information licensed under the Open Government Licence v3.0

Penicuik was unique in Britain in having three prisoner of war camps: Greenlaw (from 1803); Esk Mills (from 4 February 1811); and Valleyfield (from March 1811). By 1803, the Finlaysons were living in Glasgow and James had left Penicuik behind. One can only suppose, however, that he maintained some contact with friends and family still living there. Ian MacDougall wrote a detailed account of the camps in Scotland in his book, *All Men are Brethren*.[9] He points out that given the polyglot and cosmopolitan nature of Napoleon's army, it is not surprising that the camps included prisoners from all over Europe and beyond. According to MacDougall, there were a few black prisoners or 'men of colour' in the camps.[10] If one could listen in to the conversations it would be a veritable Tower of Babel. Penicuik was a rural town and its inhabitants must have found exposure to different cultures both frightening and fascinating.

Howgate Village

The little hamlet of Howgate is situated between the Pentland and Moorfoot Hills, about 11 miles from Edinburgh and 2 miles from Penicuik village. In the eighteenth century it was a place of much greater importance than it is now as it was located on the old road from Edinburgh to Peebles. Prior to the formation of the present main road from Edinburgh to Peebles, a great part of the traffic between the metropolis and the south passed through it. The Carlisle and Dumfries coaches caused no little stir as their scarlet-coated drivers pulled up daily at the little inn for refreshment for man and beast. This hostelry is mentioned by Lockhart in the fifth chapter of his *Life of Scott*. While on a fishing expedition to West Loch, along with George Abercromby (afterwards Lord Abercromby), William Clerk of Penicuik and his friend Irving spent the night there.

In the Jacobite Rebellion of 1745, some of Bonny Prince Charlie's army passed through Howgate on its way from Edinburgh to Dumfries and Carlisle. Fortunately for the dissenting village, the army was divided into smaller groups and only those under the command of Lord George Murray passed through.[11]

Howgate Associate

A great split in the Established Church of Scotland occurred in 1733 over patronage. Dissenting attendees to the General Assembly stated that church ministers should be chosen by church elders and not patrons. Four ministers left and formed the Associate Presbytery (or Secession Church). Not long after, in 1746, the 'Breach' occurred over a religious clause contained in the oath taken by the burgesses in the towns of Glasgow, Edinburgh and Perth.

> The clause ran in the following terms: – "Here I protest before God, and your Lordships, that I profess, and allow with my heart, the true religion presently professed within this realm, and authorised by the laws thereof: I shall abide thereat, and defend the same to my lifes end; renouncing the Roman religion called papistry." The question, – What is meant by the "true religion presently professed within this realm," &c. gave rise to long and keen discussion. One party in the Synod interpreted these words to be of similar import with the true religion as presently professed and authorised, &c. – and maintained that swearing this part of the oath was equivalent to giving a solemn approbation of those corruptions that prevailed in the Established Church, and against which the Secession had publicly testified. Another party maintained that this clause of the oath bound the individual, who swore it, to approve of the true religion itself, as that which was settled and professed in this realm, but did not bind him to approve of the manner in which it might be settled and professed; and that, therefore, it did not require of him any approbation of the prevailing corruptions in either church or state.[12]

The Associate Presbytery split into two groups: The Associate (Burgher) and the General Associate (Antiburgher). The Howgate Associate congregation originated with members of the congregations of Dalkeith and West Linton who adhered to the General Associate Antiburgher church, while the majorities of these congregations adhered to the Associate Burgher Synod at the Breach that arose from the controversy over the burgess oath. A church was built in Howgate in 1751. A new church was built in 1856 as a replacement.[13]

The 1775 map in Plate 1 by cartographers, George Taylor and Andrew Skinner, was Plate 5 in their volume *'Survey and maps of the roads of North Britain or Scotland'* published in 1776. It was effectively Scotland's first road atlas. and shows the routeways from Edinburgh to Howgate and Penicuik. This map was published about five years after James' birth.

It was fortunate that both James and Margaret were alive in 1851 and were included in the UK census of that year. His birthplace was given as Penicuik in Peeblesshire. On the face of it, this is incorrect as Penicuik was always in Edinburghshire. However, it is possible he was born on the outskirts of Penicuik and in a hamlet that extended over the border into Peeblesshire. Alternatively, as Penicuik was the more significant place in the area, he may have given that as the birthplace name because it would be recognised. The 1851 census was held on 30th March and this means that an 80-year-old was born between 31 March 1770 and 30 March 1771.

Brian Denoon[14] recounts the research into James' birth date carried out by J. & P. Coats of Paisley, a textile giant, on behalf of the Oy Finlayson Ab management celebrations for the 150th anniversary of their founding. The researcher made the assumption that James was born in 1771 (1851 minus 80 years) and conducted a paper search at Register House of the

Old Parochial Registers of Births and Baptisms. The only baptismal record found for a Finlayson baby in Penicuik was an incomplete record that gave neither name nor gender:

> Finlayson (James) Taylor in Pennycook & his spouse
> Margaret McLairin had a child named ... born August
> 29th & baptised Septr 20th. Wit James Bammage &
> James ?[15]

In the absence of any other entry at the time, this seemed the likely date of birth and baptism. However, later this assumption was shown to be flawed. In Scotland, the established religion was the protestant Church of Scotland, or Presbyterian Church from 1560. An Act of Privy Council in 1616 ordered that a record of all baptisms, marriages and burials be kept in every parish. Statutory registration became compulsory in 1855 for all births and deaths and regular marriages for all religious denominations. The regulations came into force from 1 January 1855 following the passing of the Registration of Births, Deaths and Marriages (Scotland) Act 1854. Before that time the recording of baptisms was patchy, particularly for dissenting sects. Seceding believers were sometimes intractable and refused to comply with church bureaucracy. In addition, according to ScotlandsPeople,

> Registration in the Church of Scotland's registers
> was costly and unpopular, so many people did not
> bother to register events at all. Although details of
> some non-conformists can be found in Established
> Church registers, many members of other religious
> denominations chose to have events registered in
> their own churches. In addition, rapid urbanisation
> during the nineteenth century contributed to the
> diminishing influence of the Church and a decrease

in registration in these areas. It was estimated at the time that as few as 30% of events actually occurring were being recorded for some urban parishes.[16]

Fortunately, from 26 June 2017 the ScotlandsPeople website added other baptismal records including those of secessional churches such as the Howgate Associate. This church was a seceder Presbyterian church – the General Associate or Antiburgher sect formed in 1747. When the church registers were checked through ScotlandsPeople in 2020 as preparation for the bicentennial celebration, we found that the OPR baptism was a duplicate baptism of one in Howgate Associate, which provided more details for the child baptised on 20 September:

> James Finlison Margrat McLeran had a child born August 28 1772 and baptised September 20 by Mr Bunyan Minister at Howgate the child name is Isebel.[17]

In addition, there was an entry in Howgate for a James Finlayson born to the same parents:

> James Finilson and Margret McLeron had a child born November 27 and baptised December 16th by Mr Bunyon Minister of the Gospel at Howgate the child name is James.[18]

This baptism in Howgate falls within the age range of 80 in the 1851 Census and thus it seems very likely that this is the correct baptism and birth for James. This means that the date on the headstone for James' birth is incorrect.

These new baptismal records also gave details of other siblings:

- Jean (baptised on 23 February 1767 at Howgate Associate)
- James (born 27 November and baptised on 16 December 1770 at Howgate Associate).
- Isebel (born 28 August 28 and baptised 20 September 1772 at Howgate Associate).
- Mary (baptised March 1777 at Dalkeith Associate)
- Alexander (baptised 26 September 1779 at Howgate Associate)

The Finlayson family of Penicuik

The surname Finlayson has different phonetic spellings: Findlason, Findlayson, Findlaysoun, Findleyson, Finilson, Finlaison, Finlaisone, Finlason, Finlieson, Finlasone, Finlaysone, Finleyson, Finlison, Finlawson, Finlson, Fynlawsone, Fynlason and Fynloson. Prior to 1764, it is uncertain whether the people mentioned in baptism, marriage and burial church records in Penicuik were linked to 'our' James Finlayson. According to the Reverend Thomas McCourty's account in the Old Statistical Account of 1794, the population of Penicuik in 1779 was 1,349 individuals. It is possible, therefore, that the families were related.

The earliest church entry recorded in Penicuik was the baptism on 7 June 1657 of Agnes Findlason,[19] a daughter born to Robert Findlason of Nether Mosshouse in Penicuik Parish. The next entry is for John Finlason the son of James Finlason of Nether Moss, Penicuik, baptised on 24 September 1671. On 13 November 1669, James Finlason[20] married Margaret Scott and on 13 May 1676 a James Finlason[21] married Margaret Laurie. From the records we cannot be sure if they are different people or remarriages.

One James Finlayson was an elder in the parish church of

Penicuik. His role was included in the Kirk Session minutes of 11 July 1760, 13 July 1764, 17 January 1772 and 5 December 1772.[22] However, the date of his ordination as elder is not given. The role of elder lasted until retirement or death but there is no mention of either in the subsequent minutes. The burial records for Penicuik 1658–1854 were transcribed by Lothian Family History Society. Between 1673 and 1800, there were 19 burials of Finlayson. These records show that Robert Finlayson, the son of James Finlayson, Elder, was buried in January 1772 in Penicuik churchyard. In addition, his mother, last name Ketchen (no first name), was buried with him. James Finlayson married Marion Kitchen on 1 August 1740. Presumably this is all the same family.

The Kirk Session minutes also include the scandal of a married man, James Finlayson, who was a member of the congregation of Howgate and was disciplined for uncleanness with an unmarried woman, Margaret Fairbairn, of the parish of Penicuik.[23]

Pennycuik Kirk 6 July 1778

The session agreed to meet next Friday in the Church
to enquire into a scandal that had been raised
against Margaret Fairbairn an unmarried woman by
Jas Finlayson a married man and a member of the
Associate Congregation at Howgate of his being
guilty of Uncleanness with her when he & she were
servants to John Laurie of which crime he had made
confession before the Session of Howgate for which
he had been often rebuked before the Howgate
Congregation and was now dismissed from censure
by that Session. The Session appoint both the man &
the woman to be cited next Friday.[24]

Pennycuik Kirk 10 July 1778

This session being constitute the officer reported
that he had summoned James Finlayson to this Diet
but that he informed him that he could not attend.
Margaret Fairbairn, being called, compeared[25] and
upon her being interrogate whether James Finlayson
and she had been guilty together she peremptorily
denied the charge he had brought against her she said
that he had oftener than once made attempt upon
her chastity and upon her refusal, declared he would
give her a character, and his accusation all malice and
revenge. She was devoutly exhorted to an ingenuous
confession of guilty but continued still to deny his
having any criminal converse with her. The Session
delay the further consideration of this affair at five
weeks. [26]

Pennycuik Kirk 17 Dec 1778

The Session being met and constitute in consequence
of an agreement last Lord's Day in order to inquire
into the process betwixt James Finlayson and Margaret Fairbairn. They being cited called compeared.
James was asked if he had confessed himself guilty
of uncleanness before the Session of Howgate with
said Margaret Fairbairn answered he had and had
made satisfaction before that Congregation and was
absolved from scandal. He was seriously exhorted to
beware of scandalizing any innocent person through
malice or any other bad motive but still continued in
the strongest terms to assert the fact. Said Margaret
was asked if she owned the charge he had brought
against her. She answered that she never had carnal
dealings with him. She was seriously exhorted to
acknowledge the truth if guilty; but declared that tho'
he had frequently made attempts upon her chastity;

yet she had never been so far lost to herself as to
gratify his vicious desires and that it was altogether
out of revenge asperged[27] her character. They were
both dealt with at great length by the Session to
be ingenuous but to one purpose he continuing to
assert and she to deny in the most positive terms. The
session finding it impossible at present to discover the
truth agreed to delay the further consideration of this
affair to some future period.[28]

The claim of uncleanness was not resolved, and in 1781
Margaret made a petition to the Kirk Session and this was
referred to Dalkeith Presbytery for a judgment.

A reference from the Kirk Session of Pennycook was
produced and read setting forth that James Finlayson
a married man and Margaret Fairbairn an unmarried
woman compeared before them. James was asked
if he had confessed himself guilty of uncleanness
before the Session of Howgate with the said Margaret
Fairbairn, answered he had and had made satisfaction
before that congregation and was absolved from the
scandal. The said Margaret Fairbairn being asked if
she owned the charge brought against her answered
that he never had any carnal dealings with her and
declared that although he had made attempts on
her chastity yet she had never been so far lost to
herself as to satisfy his beastly desires and that it
was altogether out of revenge he had aspersed her
character. A petition was also given to the Kirk
Session of Pennycook praying them to consider her
disagreeable situation and to assoilzie[29] her from the
most malicious and groundless scandal and restore
her to full communion with the Christian Church.
The Session having done every thing in their power to
bring this process to an issue without effect referred it

to the Reverend Presby of Dalkeith for decision and
the woman was cited to attend this meeting of Preby.
She being called compeared and being interrogated
adhered to her declaration before the Kirk Session
of Pennycook. The above reference being read and
considered, the Presby after reasoning on the affair
found that it is now more than seven years since the
above scandal was raised, that there appears no other
ground or foundation for it than James Finlayson's
bare assertion, and that Margaret Fairbairn's character
both before and since the scandal was raised against
her hath been fair and irreproachable therefore did
and herby do absolve her from said scandal and
restore her to the privileges of the Church. [30]

It is interesting that this sentence refers to the scandal
as occurring more than seven years before 1781, which
would have been 1774. Unfortunately, there are no Kirk
Session records for Howgate Associate before 1790.[31] It is
noted above that James and Margaret's daughter Mary was
baptised in March 1777 at Dalkeith Associate and they were
residing in Loanhead. It is plausible that this short-term
move was triggered by the scandal – although by 1778, they
had returned to the Howgate congregation according to
Alexander's baptism.

It is possible that there was more than one James Finlayson
who was a member of Howgate Associate but it is more likely
that it is only the one — the father of our James Finlayson.

In the Penicuik Kirk session minutes, there is a reference on
30 June 1764 that James Finlayson, a tailor, married Margaret
McLaren (there are various phonetic spellings of this name)
in Penicuik. They appeared before the Church of Penicuik
session to register their marriage.

> Compeared before the Session James Fynlason and
> being asked by the Minr if he was married answered
> that he was married to one Margaret McClaron by
> one Peter Wilson who calls himself a Minr. The above
> persons did both compear and showed their Lines
> date June 30th 1764. The Minr exhorted them and
> declared them married persons.[32]

Finding records of such marriages can be problematic according to the National Records of Scotland.

> When a man and woman declared before witnesses
> that they were man and wife, that was a marriage.
> Many dissenters who were married by their own
> clergyman took this path. It was the type of marriage
> made famous at Gretna. Obviously in all these cases,
> there were no banns of marriage and, therefore,
> except where some dissenting marriages were noted,
> likely to be no record in the parish registers.' [33]

In Scotland a marriage was considered 'regular' after the reading of banns and if the marriage ceremony was conducted by a minister of the established Church of Scotland. We could not find a record of the celebrant, Peter Wilson, in the lists of students of the Theological Hall of the Associate Presbytery (Burgher) or the General Associate Hall (Antiburgher),[34] nor in the Church of Scotland records.

Apart from the baptisms at Howgate there are two other references: the call in 1795 for the Reverend William McEwan following the death of Rev Andrew Bunyan[35] and 1797 communion roll of Howgate, Antiburgher, Associate Session, United Presbyterian and United Free Church.[36] In the first, James Finlayson is a signatory. The second has the entry as a member of the congregation, as shown in Table 3.

Table 3: Communion Roll, Howgate Associate Session

#	Name	Residence	Occupation	Born	Bapt.	Place of death	Date of death
46	James Finlayson	Penicuik				Penicuik	1799
Congregation 237 men and women in the congregation							

Source: Howgate, Antiburgher, Associate Session, United Presbyterian and United Free Church. 'Communion Roll', 1826 1796. National Records of Scotland. © Crown copyright, National Records of Scotland, [archival reference]. Used with permission.

There is no burial for James given in 1799 in Penicuik. The nearest is on 4 May 1800 for a resident in Penicuik who was buried on 4 May 1800:

> Finlayson (James) Residenter in Pannycuick was interred in this Church ye 4th May 1800.[37]

It is difficult to be sure of James Finlayson's pedigree but the most likely is as shown in Figure 6.

James Finlayson's father was a tailor and the Reverend Thomas McCourty provides the wages for selected tradesmen in the Old Statistical Account, as in Table 4.

Where are James Finlayson's early years?

Apart from his baptism, we could find no records of James' early life in Penicuik, such as residence, education or employment. Although there are no extant apprenticeship records for the cotton mill, it is possible and even probable that James Finlayson gained his mechanical engineering skills there, before moving to Paisley. The National Archives at Kew's guide on Apprenticeship and Master records explains that it is not always possible to find records for common trades such as weaving or other eighteenth-century industries because:

- informal indentures became increasingly common with fathers often teaching sons and nephews
- the Statute of Apprentices only applied to trades which existed when it was passed in 1563.[38]

The most notable example of this was the cotton industry.

> Apprenticeship was a formal method of vocational training in crafts and trade that originated in the guild system of medieval times. Ideally, a master or mistress agreed to train a child in a trade for a specific term of years and in most cases to board and house the child. In return the master was paid an agreed premium and the child committed to serve faithfully and keep the secrets of the trade.'[39]

Apprenticeships were an intergenerational transmission of knowledge that was primarily tacit in nature. They usually lasted seven years and apprentices were typically indentured at 14 years of age. If James was an apprentice at Esk Mills, it would have been about the time of Peter Brotherston's death.

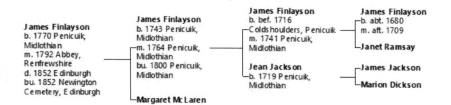

Figure 6: James Finlayson's possible pedigree.

Source: Angela Harris, personal files.

Table 4: Common wages in 1794 for Penicuik

Men servants	£5–7 per annum with bed, board & washing
Women servants	£3 per annum with bed, board & washing
Day labourers	1s without, and 8d with victuals
In harvest women	7d with victuals
In harvest men	8d or 9d with victuals
Carpenters	1s 6d
Masons	1s 8d per day
Taylors	8d with victuals per day

Source: Sinclair, Sir John. The Statistical Account of Scotland, Penicuik, Edinburgh, Vol. 10, Edinburgh: William Creech, 1794, p. 422. University of Edinburgh, University of Glasgow. (1999) The Statistical Accounts of Scotland online service: https://stataccscot.edina.ac.uk:443/ link/osa-vol10-p422-parish-edinburgh-penicuik

NOTES

1 Whittemore, C. et al., (2014) Stories from an Edinburghshire Village: Howgate. West Linton: Whittemore.

2 Sinclair, S. J. (1999) The Statistical Account of Scotland, Penicuik, Edinburgh, Vol. 10. The Statistical Accounts of Scotland online service: Edinburgh: William Creech; University of Edinburgh; University of Glasgow. Available at: https://stataccscot.edina.ac.uk:443/link/osa-vol10-p422-parish-edinburgh-penicuik. P. 422

3 Sinclair, S. J. (1999). p. 428.

4 Gordon, J. (ed.) (1845) The New Statistical Account of Scotland. Penicuik, Edinburgh (1999). Edinburgh: Blackwoods and Sons. p. 30.

5 Gordon, The New Statistical Account of Scotland. Penicuik, Edinburgh. pp. 33-34.

6 Gittings, B. M. (2023) The Gazetteer for Scotland. ©The Gazetteer for Scotland, 2023, used with permission from The Gazetteer for Scotland at htpp://www.scottish-places.info/.

7 Nisbet, S. M. (2003) The rise of the cotton factory in eighteenth century Renfrewshire. PhD Thesis. University of Paisley.

8 Fitton, R. S. (1989) The Arkwrights: Spinners of fortune. Manchester: Manchester University Press.

9 MacDougall, I. (2008) All men are brethren: French, Scandinavian, Italian, German, Dutch, Belgian, Spanish, Polish, West Indian, American, and other prisoners of war in Scotland, 1803-1814. Edinburgh: John Donald.

10 MacDougall, I. (2008) pp. 178–179.

11 Whittemore, et al., (2014).

12 McKerrow, J. (1839) History of the Secession Church. Edinburgh: William Oliphant and Son. pp. 273–274.

13 Mackelvie, W. (1873) Annals and statistics of the United Presbyterian Church. Oliphant and A. Elliot.

14 Denoon, B. (1991) James Finlayson of Penicuik 1772–1852: Industrial founder of Finland's second city. Aberdeen University Review, 65 (Autumn).

15 Baptisms (OPR) Scotland. 20 September 1772. (Birth: 29 August 1772). FINLAYSON. ScotlandsPeople 697/ 20 32. © Crown copyright, National Records of Scotland, [archival reference]. https://www.scotlandspeople.gov.uk, with permission from ScotlandsPeople.

16 Record guides, Church Registers. ScotlandsPeople, [archival reference] https://www.scotlandspeople.gov.uk/guides/church-registers. © Crown copyright, National Records of Scotland, with permission from ScotlandsPeople.

17 Baptisms (NCR) Scotland. Antiburgher Associate Session, Howgate. 20 September 1772 (Birth: 28 August 1772). FINILSON, Isebel. CH3/1363/12 43. http://www.scotlandspeopl.gov.uk © Crown copyright, National Records of Scotland, [archival reference], with permission from ScotlandsPeople.

18 Baptisms (NCR) Scotland. Antiburgher Associate Session, Howgate. 16 December 1770 (Birth: 27 November 1770). FINILSON, James. CH3/1363/12 39. https://www.scotlandspeople.gov.uk. © Crown copyright, National Records of Scotland, [archival reference], with permission from ScotlandsPeople.

19 Baptisms (OPR) Scotland. Penicuik. 07/06/1657. FINDLASON, Agnes 697/ 10 10 Penicuik. https://www.scotlandspeople.gov.uk, © Crown copyright, National Records of Scotland, [archival reference], with permission from ScotlandsPeople.

20 Marriages (OPR) Scotland. Penicuik 13/11/1669. FINLASON, James. 697/ 30 52 Penicuik. https://www.scotlandspeople.gov.uk, © Crown copyright, National Records of Scotland, [archival reference], with permission from ScotlandsPeople.

21 Marriages (OPR) Scotland. Penicuik. 13/05/1676. FINLASON, James 697/ 30 73 Penicuik. https://www.scotlandspeople.gov.uk. © Crown copyright, National Records of Scotland, [archival reference], with permission from ScotlandsPeople.

22 Kirk session minutes 1708–1812. Scotland. Penicuik. CH2/297/3. © Crown copyright, National Records of Scotland, [archival reference]. https://www.scotlandspeople.gov.uk, with permission from ScotlandsPeople. pp.222/223; 226/227; 242/243; and 248/249.

23 Kirk session minutes 1798-1812. Scotland. Penicuik. Scandal of Uncleanness Betwixt James Finlayson and Margaret Fairbairn CH00020297 – 00003-00261.jpg. © Crown copyright, National Records of Scotland, [archival reference]. https://www.scotlandspeople.gov.uk, with permission from ScotlandsPeople.

24 Kirk Session Minutes 1798-1812. Scotland. Penicuik. 6 July 1778. CH2/297/3. CH00020297 – 00003-00261. © Crown copyright, National Records of Scotland, [archival reference]. https://www.scotlandspeople.gov.uk, with permission from ScotlandsPeople.

25 Compear v., to appear before a congregation for rebuke or examination in court.

26 Kirk Session Minutes 1798-1812, Scotland. Penicuik. 10 July 1778. CH2/297/3 CH00020297 – 00003-00261. © Crown copyright, National Records of Scotland, [archival reference]. https://www.scotlandspeople.gov.uk, with permission from ScotlandsPeople.

27 Asperge v., criticise or cast aspersions.

28 Kirk Session Minutes 1798-1812. Scotland. Penicuik. 17 Dec 1778. CH2/297/3 CH00020297 – 00003-00263. © Crown copyright, National Records of Scotland, [archival reference]. https://www.scotlandspeople.gov.uk, with permission from ScotlandsPeople.

29 Assoilzie means to acquit or absolve.

30 Presbytery Minutes. Scotland. Dalkeith. 4 Dec 1781. CH2/424/15 CH0000200424 – 00015-00123.jpg. Page 122. © Crown copyright, National Records of Scotland, [archival reference]. https://www.scotlandspeople.gov.uk, with permission from ScotlandsPeople.

31 Free Church Minutes 1790-1880. Scotland. Antiburgher Associate Session, Howgate. CH3/1363/1. © Crown copyright, National Records of Scotland, [archival reference]. https://www.scotlandspeople.gov.uk, with permission from ScotlandsPeople.

32 Marriages (OPR) Scotland. Penicuik. 30 June 1764. FYNLASON, James and MCCLARON, Margaret 697/ 30 199 Penicuik. © Crown copyright, National Records of Scotland, [archival reference]. https://www.scotlandspeople.gov.uk, with permission from ScotlandsPeople.

33 Sinclair, C. (2000) 'Excerpt from Jock Tamson's bairns: A history of the records of the General Register Office for Scotland.' National Records of Scotland. © Crown copyright, with permission from ScotlandsPeople.

34 Mackelvie, W. (1873).

35 Call to William McEwan, Preacher of the Gospel in Kilmarnock to Be Pastor. (1795) Scotland. Associate Congregation at Howgate.

36 Communion roll 1796-1826. Scotland. Antiburgher Associate Session, Howgate. CH3/1363/14. © Crown copyright, National Records of Scotland, [archival reference]. https://www.scotlandspeople.gov.uk, with permission from ScotlandsPeople.

37 Burials (OPR) Scotland. Penicuik. 4 May 1800. FINLAYSON James. 697/30/332. © Crown copyright, National Records of Scotland, [archival reference]. https://www.scotlandspeople.gov.uk, with permission from ScotlandsPeople.

38 National Archives Research guide: Apprentices and masters. https://www.nationalarchives.gov.uk/help-with-your-research/research-guides/apprentices-and-masters/ Provided under Open Government Licence v3.0.

39 Zeev, N.B., Mokyr, J. and van der Beek, K. (2015) Flexible Supply of Apprenticeship in the British Industrial Revolution. Preliminary version. p. 35.

– CHAPTER THREE –

Margaret Wilkie of Paisley?

M any of the histories of the Finlaysons we have consulted are patriarchal in their selection of material. There are many accounts about James Finlayson and few about his wife, Margaret. Fortunately, in Scotland and some parts of Finland, women kept their maiden or father's surname after marriage – and, as such, women's maiden names are used throughout their lives. For example, unlike in England, children's baptismal records more likely include the mother's maiden name and funeral records for women often contain both married and maiden names.

Statutory registration of births, marriages and deaths in Scotland was introduced in 1855. Before then, the only records of milestone events were these: baptism, marriage banns, marriage ceremonial and death/burial records from the registers of a local church. The Scottish church played an important part in the lives of its parishioners beyond just marking births, marriages and deaths. Kirk or Church sessions were held to keep the congregation in check, policing moral and local matters. Scotland has full census records available from 1841 to 1921. Wills are another great source of information. The records consistently show that Margaret Finlayson's maiden name was Wilkie. In addition, there are Finnish records that are relevant as they provide corroboration.

In Finland, until the year 1917, practically all Finns were members of the Evangelic-Lutheran or orthodox church. The parishes kept official population records until 1999, when the population register centre and the local register offices took over. The church law from 1686 stipulated that every parish in the country must keep communion books and gave exact rules about the content. In the communion books the whole parish was catalogued according to villages and farms. In addition to basic information (name, profession or relation to the master of the farm, birth date and place, death date and place) remarks were made about the ability to read and write, knowledge of religion and taking part in the Holy Communion. In the communion book in Tampere for 1825–1831 and 1832–1838, Margaret is enumerated as Fru (Mrs) Margaretta Wilki, with her husband James Finlayson in the cotton factory in Tampere. The record is in Swedish (see Figures 7 and 8).

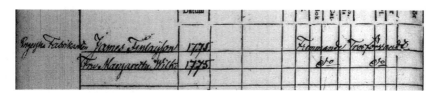

Figure 7: Finland Communion book 1825–1831

Source: Rippikirjat (Communion Book) 1825–1831 James Finlayson and Margaretta Wilki. Tampere church archives (The National Archives of Finland, Hämeenlinna)

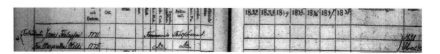

Figure 8: Finland Communion book 1832–1838

Source: Rippikirjat (Communion Book) 1832–1838 James Finlayson and Margaretta Wilki. Tampere church archives (The National Archives of Finland, Hämeenlinna)

ScotlandsPeople records 256 marriages of a Margaret Wilkie and only one of them is with a James Finlayson in any variation of spelling recorded in the Church of Scotland, Old Parish Registers. However, this is not conclusive as at the time there were irregular marriages that were not always recorded in the Old Parish Registers. There were no instances in the other church registers or Roman Catholic Church registers. Paisley was a likely location based on the cotton industry for James to work.

Figure 9 shows the marriage proclamation record of James Finlayson and Margaret Wilkie in Abbey, Paisley on 1 December 1792.

According to Chris Paton, when the term 'of this parish' is used for the bride or groom it usually denotes the place of origin.[1] Therefore, the record, 'James Findlayson of Pacily & Margaret Wilkie of this parish were booked in order to marriage 1 Dec' suggests that James originated in Paisley and Margaret was born in Abbey parish. However, this was not always the case and it is possible that Margaret's family moved to Abbey parish. James did not originate from Paisley, as the previous chapter shows.

In addition, Margaret's death certificate for 15 February 1855 names her as Margaret Wilkie or Finlayson married to James Finlayson. The burial record in 1855 in Newington Cemetery also states that Margaret Wilkie is the widow of James Finlayson (see Figures 10 and 11).

The next search was to look for information on Margaret Wilkie's baptism. A baptism in 1776 was found in Abbey, Paisley where Margaret's parents were named as Petter Wilkie and Elizabeth Jamieson (Figure 12).

On the face of it, this aligns with the information on the marriage registration above. Ten children were registered with the same couple, as listed in Table 5.

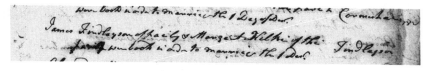

Figure 9: Marriage record James Findlayson & Margaret Wilkie 1792. **Transcript**: James Findlayson of Pasily & Margaret Wilkie of this parish were bookd in order to marriage the 1 Dec.

Source: Abbey (Paisley) Parish. 'Marriages (Old Parish Registers) 01/12/1792 Findlayson, James and Wilkie, Margaret', 1792. 559/ 40 412. ScotlandsPeople. ©Crown copyright, National Records of Scotland, [archival reference]

Figure 10: Death certificate for Margaret Wilkie page 1

Source: 'Deaths (Statutory Registers Deaths) Finlayson, Margaret', 15 February 1855. 685/3 124. ScotlandsPeople. ©Crown copyright, National Records of Scotland, [archival reference]

Figure 11: Death certificate for Margaret Wilkie page 2

Source: 'Deaths (Statutory Registers Deaths) Finlayson, Margaret', 15 February 1855. 685/3 124. ScotlandsPeople. ©Crown copyright, National Records of Scotland, [archival reference]

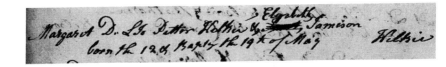

Figure 12: Baptism of Margaret Wilkie in 1776, Abbey, Paisley. **Transcript**: Margaret Dr [daughter] L [legitimate] to Petter Wilkie & Elizabeth Jamison born the 12th & baptized the 19th May

Source: Abbey (Paisley) Parish. 'Births (Old Parish Registers) 19/05/1776 Wilkie, Margaret Abbey)', n.d. 559/ 20 492. ScotlandsPeople. Accessed 24 March 2020. ©Crown copyright, National Records of Scotland, [archival reference]

Table 5: Baptisms of children of Peter Wilkie and Elizabeth Jamison 1767–1787

Name	Parents	Gender	Birth	Parish	Ref No.
Wilkie, William	Peter Wilkie & Elizabeth Jamison	M	8/05/1767	573/3 Paisley Burgh or Low	20/32
Wilkie, Elizabeth	Peter Wilkie, weaver & Elizabeth Jamison	F	05/09/1769	573/3 Paisley Burgh or Low	20/51
Wilkie, John	Petter Wilkie & Elizabeth Jemison	M	17/05/1773	559 Abbey	20/454
Wilkie, John	Petter Wilkie & Elizabeth Jamison	M	18/05/1774	559 Abbey	20/467
Wilkie, Margaret	Peter Wilkie & Elizabeth Jamison	F	12/05/1776	559 Abbey	20/492
Wilkie, James	Peter Wilkie & Elizabeth Jamison	M	11/06/1778	559 Abbey	20/518
Wilkie, Agnes	Peter Wilkie & Elizabeth Jamison	F	10/12/1780	559 Abbey	20/550
Willie, Petter	Peter Wilkie & Elizabeth Jamison	M	20/03/1783	559 Abbey	20/597
Wilkie, Lillias	Peter Wilkie & Elizabeth Jamison	F	17/04/1785	559 Abbey	30/11
Wilkie, Janet	Peter Wilkie & Elizabeth Jamison	F	23/07/1787	559 Abbey	30/71

Source: Abbey (Paisley) Parish. 'Births (Old Parish Registers) ScotlandsPeople. © Crown copyright, National Records of Scotland, [archival reference].

In 1769, Peter Wilkie's occupation was described as a weaver. However, in the first Glasgow directory by John Tait of 1783, Peter Wilkie, grocer, was included in the list of merchants of the town of Paisley at Smith Hills.

Paisley in the Eighteenth Century

Margaret resided in Abbey parish and James was living in Paisley at the time of their marriage in 1792. The Hammermen of Paisley provide the following history on their website:

> In 1760 Paisley was a small market town of around 7000 inhabitants. Over the next 60 years the population grew to almost 60,000 mainly by immigration from Renfrewshire and Ayrshire. Most industries were in their infancy with the majority of metal and mechanical equipment made by hand by smiths, wrights and clockmakers.

> In 1726 the first mechanised flax mill was built in Paisley and in 1759 the production of silk gauze started. The manufacture of shawls was begun in Paisley at the height of the muslin trade, in the 1770s, and shawls became the product for which the town was most famous. In 1779, a new town was built on the east bank of the River Cart. The new streets were given names to reflect the town's industry, for example, Cotton Street, Silk Street, Gauze Street and Lawn Street. With this new extension to the town, the population had reached 24,000 and Paisley was ranked third in size in Scotland after Glasgow and Edinburgh. By the 1790s cotton production was beginning to replace flax production.

The first machine-making workshop was started in 1793 at Stoney Brae by Hunter & Walkinshaw, a firm of timber merchants, making equipment for the cotton mills which were developing in the North of the town. At the end of the eighteenth century and into the early part of the nineteenth century many small enterprises were springing up in the town which required the services of qualified Hammermen. Small iron foundries were established making parts and gadgets for the burgeoning weaving trade. There were loom makers in Causeyside and brass founders and coppersmiths in Smithhills and the High Street.

The weaving of shawls grew massively, especially after a swirling pattern based on Kashmiri designs, later named 'Paisley pattern', was introduced to the town in 1805.'[2]

It is possible that James worked for Hunter & Walkinshaw. He would have been twenty-three at the time it started. In the next chapter on James Finlayson in Glasgow, we explain that James was affiliated with Hammermen, that is, with smith work. Although, Hunter & Wilkinshaw essentially were related to timber machine making and as such more related to the occupation of a Wright, they also employed iron-turners — craftsmen and apprentices.[3]

Whereabouts and Weather

Paisley in Renfrewshire sits primarily on an expanse of low ground around 12 metres (40 ft) above sea level surrounding the White Cart Water, which runs through the town. The civil parish of Abbey historically included all of Paisley and John-stone to the WNW and surrounding hamlets until 1736, when three small parishes were formed in Paisley Burgh, termed High, Middle and Low, with a small part of Abbey parish remaining within the Burgh. Paisley town centre (latitude 55°49'54'N, longitude 4°25'57'W) is 7 miles (11.5km) west of Glasgow Cross and 4 miles (6.5km) south of the River Clyde, the White Cart Water joining the Black Cart to flow into the River Clyde by Clydebank, Dunbartonshire.

The following are extracts from the Old Statistical Accounts for Scotland for Paisley and Abbey.

Town of Paisley:

... one of the most considerable manufacturing towns in Scotland ... Its situation upon the banks of the River Cart is equally pleasant and commodious.[4]

The trade and manufactures of Paisley, which have always chiefly been in the weaving branch, are the main articles which render it of importance in a history of this nature ... About the year 1760, the making of silk gauze was first attempted at Paisley, in imitation of that of Spittalfields in London. The success was beyond the most sanguine expectations of those engaged in it ... It appears, from the best calculations that could be made, that, in the year 1784 the manufactures of Paisley, in silk gauze, lawn and linen gauze, and white sewing thread, amounted to the value of 579,185l. 16s. 6d. and that no fewer than 26,484 persons were employed in carrying them on. It is difficult to give an exact account of the state of its manufactures at present. The silk branch has evidently declined, but the muslin has so far come into its room, and the thread manufacture is considerably increased ...

Population of Paisley (1695–1792)
In 1695   2,200 individuals
In 1755   4,290 individuals
In 1782   11,100 individuals
In 1792   13,800 individuals

These numbers do not include the suburbs, which are to be referred to in Abbey parish ... There are two large dissenting populations in the town, those of the Antiburgher persuasion and the Relief. The first of these has existed there for upwards of 30 years; the other is of late date; and they are both supplied with Ministers ... There is likewise a small congregation of Cameronians.[5]

Parish of the Abbey of Paisley:

The parish is described as:

> ... in length, from east to west, about 9 miles, varying in breadth from about half a mile to three ... The air is moist, a necessary consequence of the prevailing south-west winds, which coming loaded with vapour from the Atlantic, produce frequent and heavy rains. The effects of this moist atmosphere appear in rheumatisms, quinseys, pneumonic ailments, and all the tribe of inflammatory disorders. Upon the whole, however, and even the neighbouring town, cannot be said to be unhealthy.[6]

The spinning of cotton was introduced into this parish in 1783. The principal seat of that manufacture is at Johnstoun, a neat and regularly built village about three miles west of Paisley, upon the estate of Mr Houston of Johnstoun. The feuing of that village was begun in 1782, and it contained at Whitsunday

last 293 families, or 1434 souls. There are five
companies established in it for cotton spinning. Two
of these carry on their principal operations by water
machinery. In the two mills employed in them, there
are going at present 11,672 spindles; but, when the
whole machinery in both shall be compleated, there
will be 22,572. The number of persons, young and
old, at present employed in both mills is 660. There
are besides about 120 spinning Jeenies employed
throughout the parish, but the number is daily
increasing, and, when the machinery is compleated
which the buildings already erected are calculated to
contain, there will be about 150 Jeenies, exclusive of
those in the two great mills. The number of persons
employed in this branch at present is, in all, about
1020.

It is painful to think, that a manufacture which gives
employment to so many hands, and which may be a
source of great wealth to individuals, may be produc-
tive of very unhappy effects upon both the health and
morals of the children employed in it.

The bleaching business in this parish is carried on
to a very considerable extent. There are 10 fields for
whitening muslin and lawns, and about as many for
thread, almost wholly employed by the manufacturers
in Paisley ... The starch manufacture is but lately
established.[7]

The following extracts from the New Statistical Account
mainly relate to the years after about 1800 when the Finlaysons' links with Paisley ended. It contains much detail on
Paisley and the wider Abbey parish.

On the parishes of the Town of Paisley and the Abbey
of Paisley:

...it will be convenient to consider the whole as
forming one parish, especially as the town of
Paisley occupies but a small extent of surface, and is
completely surrounded, by what is now, by way of
distinction, called the Abbey parish.[8]

In consequence of a short canal being cut to avoid
the shallows at Inchinnan bridge, and other improvements on the river, made about fifty years ago, the
Cart is navigable up to the town of Paisley, for vessels
of from sixty to eighty tons burden.[9]

Rebellions 1715 and 1745. On both of these occasions the inhabitants of Paisley were distinguished for
their loyalty.[10]

Johnston, which is still included in the parish, quoad
civilia, exhibits a most striking illustration of the
effects of manufactures, in originating and increasing
towns. About fifty years ago, near that bridge across
the Black Cart, which, till lately, gave to the place
the popular name of 'Brig of Johnston', merely a
few cottages were to be seen, where now is a town
consisting of two large squares, many considerable
streets, and numerous public works ... The rapid
increase of this place is not exceeded, if equalled, in
the annals of Scottish history. It began to be feued in
the year 1781, when it contained only ten persons.
Towards the end of October 1782, nine houses of the
New Town of Johnston were built, two others were
being erected, and ground on which forty-two more
were to be built was feued. In 1792 the inhabitants
amounted to 1,434 in number; in 1811, to 3,647; in
1818, to about 5,000; and 1831, to 5617.

As the introduction of the manufacture of cotton yarn by mill machinery led to the founding of Johnston, so has the extension of the same manufacture contributed to its rapid increase and its present prosperity. Within the boundary of this place are situated not less than eleven cotton mills.[11]

In place of the linen thread formerly made in this town, there has sprung up a pretty extensive cotton-thread trade. There are eight or nine factories employed in making this thread. They are propelled by steam, the whole power being about 200 horse, and the value of the thread made being above L100,000 Sterling ... It is a matter of regret, that the expense incurred in procuring patents for inventions and discoveries, should be so great as we are convinced that many ingenious men of the operative classes, both in Paisley and elsewhere, have from this cause alone been prevented from enlarging, as they might have done, the manufacturing genius and industry of their country. In a letter which we have just received from an ingenious mechanic there is the following statement, 'As there is no protection in this country, an inventor is obliged to decline putting his improvements into practice, as the moment they make their appearance they will be pirated thereby leaving him nothing, perhaps not even the merit of invention, for his trouble and expense.'[12]

The first cotton-mill in Renfrewshire, and the second in Scotland, was erected on the borders of this parish, at Dovecothall, near Barhead, in the parish of Neilston; but the first extensive establishment of the kind in the county was erected at Johnston, in 1782 ... Cotton spinning commenced in the town of Paisley, soon after steam power began to be applied to machinery for that department of manufacture.

The locality, however, has not been found favourable
to the increase of this great branch of our national
trade; chiefly owing to the high price of fuel, and the
expense of conveying the raw material from, and the
manufactured article to, Glasgow.[13]

Paisley climate – General Description

Winters in Paisley are usually mild for Scotland, with January
daily temperatures of about 6.8°C and nights cooling off to
1.6°C in the coldest month. Summers are very warm, with
daytime temperatures in July typically reaching 19.7°C and
nights dipping to 11.9°C (Table 6).

Inconsistencies about Margaret being born in Paisley in 1766

There are inconsistencies about the birthplace and birth date
of Margaret Finlayson. Also, the later life data does not fit
comfortably with this baptism for the following reasons:

- Margaret had technical as well as commercial skills organ-
  ising the making of knitted stockings and a chemical 'dry
  cleaning' enterprise in Finland. Would she have learned
  these as a daughter to Petter Wilkie, a weaver/grocer in
  Abbey?
- Evidence of behaving as an 'elite' woman in her corre-
  spondence and friendships with educated women such as
  Jean Paterson, the wife of the missionary Reverend John
  Paterson; Sarah Wheeler daughter of British Quaker
  minister, teacher and missionary in Russia and the South
  Pacific, Daniel Wheeler; William Swan, missionary in
  Siberia; and Augusta Lundahl (1811–1892), who was

referred to as 'learned' and a woman of 'genius' because she was so widely read.[14] If she married at 16, what would her education have been?

- Evidence in letters written to her of being evangelical. Would James have married a traditional Church of Scotland woman, having been brought up as an antiburgher?

- Evidence in 1841 and 1851 censuses of Margaret's birthplace being in county of Lanarkshire and Glasgow respectively.

Between 1770 and 1780, there were 21 instances of a Margaret Wilkie being baptised in the Old Parish Registers. In addition, one was recorded in the Other Church Registers. None of them were in Lanarkshire or Glasgow. There were no Roman Catholic baptisms. It is possible, especially if the baptism was from a dissenting parish, that the baptism was not in records released by ScotlandsPeople. James' family practised as Antiburgher Seceders and this was a relatively closed sect. It is quite possible that Margaret came from a similar background. In later life her correspondence demonstrated evangelical tendencies.

There are three churches that may have held the information: Glasgow, Shuttle Street Secession Congregation (Burgher congregation); Havannah Street, later Duke Street Cathedral Square Church (Duke Street) Glasgow (Antiburgher congregation): and Bellshill Relief Church (Bellshill Relief Church originated with a substantial withdrawal from Bothwell parish over a patronage issue in 1763)

James and Margaret moved to Shuttle Street and then 32, Havannah Street by 19 June 1800 and 1804 respectively and the churches may have been the reason for settling there.

Table 6: 30-year climate averages 1991–2020 for Paisley

Month	Max. temp. (°C)	Min. temp. (°C)	Days of air frost (days)	Sun-shine (hours)	Rainfall (mm)	Days of rainfall ≥1 mm (days)	Monthly mean wind speed at 10 m (knots)
January	7.15	2.08	8.02	38.62	146.37	17.71	6.14
February	7.81	2.17	6.77	67.29	115.24	14.74	6.65
March	9.83	3.19	4.20	104.34	97.41	13.75	6.02
April	12.98	5.07	1.01	141.44	66.13	12.34	5.70
May	16.14	7.44	0.22	186.77	68.78	12.11	5.53
June	18.35	10.30	0.00	155.56	67.83	12.14	5.27
July	19.75	12.09	0.00	151.53	82.85	13.25	4.96
August	19.26	11.86	0.00	145.53	94.82	13.94	6.42
September	16.69	9.90	0.00	114.63	98.40	13.92	5.30
October	12.99	6.82	0.80	86.34	131.82	16.24	5.48
November	9.59	4.20	3.66	53.90	131.82	17.26	5.85
December	7.37	2.11	8.25	33.67	161.36	16.94	5.44
Annual	13.19	6.46	32.93	1279.62	1262.83	174.34	5.73

Source: UK Meteorological Office data. Note: Location – Met. Stn. Paisley (55°50′50′N, 4°26′20′W, 16m asl) & also for Glasgow. Contains public sector information licensed under the Open Government Licence v3.0

Shuttle Street Secession Congregation (Burgher congregation) – Greyfriars baptismal register and proclamations

There are three WILKIE families in the Shuttle Street congregation:[15]

(a) James WILKIE (weaver) and Jean DUNLOP children baptised

> 6 September 1761 Agnes WILKIE (born 3 Sep 1761)
> 15 March 1764 Margaret WILKIE (born 12 Mar 1764)
> 12 April 1767 Marion WILKIE (born 12 Apr 1767)

15 July 1773 Mary WILKIE (born 12 Apr 1767)
30 June 1776 James WILKIE (born 5 Jun 1776)

(b) Andrew WILKIE (weaver) and Ann MCINTIRE
baptised
20 May 1770 Patrick WILKIE (born 16 May 1770)
22 Dec 1771 Katherine WILKIE (born 20 Dec 1771)
23 Jan 1773 Andrew & Ann WILKIE (born 17 Jan
1773)

(c) William WILKIE (Cloather in Cathcart) and Margaret
GILMORE proclamation of marriage 20 Jun 1755. No
linked baptisms

(d) David WILKIE, wright and Elizabeth MAXWELL
proclamation of marriage 27 Nov 1756. No linked
baptisms.

(e) Andrew WILKIE, linen manufacturer and Jean
Lumsden proclamation of marriage 4 Dec 1773 married
20 Dec 1773. No linked baptisms unless Andrew remar-
ried Ann MCINTIRE.

No mention of Wilkie names was made in the Shuttle Street
Secession Congregation session records held in the National
Records of Scotland of the years 1763–1769 (CH3/469/280)
and 1770–1774 (CH3/469/281).

Havannah Street, later Duke Street Cathedral Square
Church (Duke Street) Glasgow (Antiburgher congregation)

Unfortunately, there are no records for 1760–1780 in the
National Records of Scotland catalogue.

In the 1841 census in Govan (see Figure 13), Margaret's age is given as 66 (this means that her birth was between 7 June 1774 and 6 June 1775) and the place of birth given as Lanarkshire.[16] This could be an enumerator error or maybe the wrong information was given.

In the 1851 census (see Figure 14) her age is given as 77 (means birth was between 31 March 1773 and 30 March 1774) and her place of birth was enumerated as Glasgow.[17] Again, this could be an enumerator error or maybe the wrong information was given. However, the censuses are consistent with each other. In both cases the enumerators were in Scotland, rather than elsewhere in the United Kingdom, and it does seem unlikely that either Paisley or Renfrewshire would be confused with Glasgow and Lanarkshire.

With conflicting evidence about the birthplace and birth date of Margaret Wilkie, the following additional sources were searched:

- Passport application (found but no details of birth date or place)
- Finlayson-Forssa histories (translated but no evidence)
- Margaret Finlayson's correspondence (some found but no evidence)

In the communion books in Finland for 1825–1831 and 1832–1838 mentioned above, Margaret's date of birth is given as 1775. At the same time, James' birth year is given as 1771 and this is incorrect but only by one year. The record is in Swedish.

The marriage

If Margaret was born on 15 May 1776, her marriage on 1 Dec 1792 means that she was 16 years, 6 months, and 19 days old at the time. This was a legal age to marry in Scotland without parental consent. However, it would appear that she was an educated woman, based on her life and correspondence in Russia and Finland, and it might be more likely that she was older than this.

Margaret's death certificate and burial

The death certificate on 15 February 1855 states that Margaret Wilkie's age was 82 (that means she was born between 16 February 1772 and 15 February 1773). No date of birth or location was known by the Registrar. The burial record in 1855 in Newington Cemetery repeats the death certificate information. Both death and burial records can be unreliable

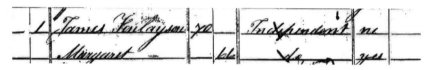

Figure 13: Govan 1841 census record for James and Margaret Finlayson

Source: 'Census Records, Scotland. Govan, Lanark. Finlayson, Margaret', 6 June 1841. 646/ 2/ 43. ScotlandsPeople. www.scotlandspeople.gov.uk. ©Crown copyright, National Records of Scotland, [archival reference].

Figure 14: Edinburgh 1851 census record for James and Margaret Finlayson

Source: Census Records, Scotland. St Cuthbert's, Midlothian. Finlayson, James and Margaret, 30 March 1851. 685/2 193/ ScotlandsPeople. www.scotlandspeople.gov.uk. ©Crown copyright, National Records of Scotland, [archival reference].

as there was no next of kin and an undertaker made the arrangements. However, it seems that, the Scottish records were more diligent about the age at death.

> From the imperfect manner in which the old Registers were kept, it is often impossible to procure satisfactory evidence of the ages of those who die at extreme old ages. It is, however, one of the peculiarities of the Scottish race, that they use every effort to ascertain the exact age of the deceased, so that, as a general rule, the age at death may be relied on as being correct.[18]

Margaret Wilkie's will

No evidence of a will for Margaret Wilkie or Finlayson or James Finlayson has been found on ScotlandsPeople.

Table 7 reveals the conflicting information concerning Margaret's date and place of birth.

The calculated birth years are consistent within one year but the birth places are different. This could be an enumerator error or maybe the wrong information was given. In addition, the circumstances of her adult life do not fit with her birth being in Paisley. All documents provide conflicting information and do not support the hypothesis that she was born in 1776. In fact, it is more likely she was born about 1774, possibly in Abbey, Paisley. However, a conclusive statement cannot be made without further evidence.

All we can say definitively is that Margaret Wilkie married James Finlayson in Paisley. How, when or why Margaret arrived in Paisley is unknown. However, it is not surprising that James moved there from Penicuik. Paisley is a large town situated 7 miles (11 km) West of Glasgow, and 53 miles (85 km) West of Edinburgh and is the largest town in Renfrewshire.

Table 7: Conflicting evidence of Margaret Wilkie's birth

		Document name			
	Baptism	Finland communion books	1841 census	1851 census	Death & burial
Year document created	1776	1825–1831 and 1832–1838	1841	1851	1855
Age	Not given	Not given	66	77	82
Actual or calculated birth date	12 May 1776	1775	Bet. 7 Jun 1774 and 6 Jun 1775	Bet. 31 Mar 1773 and 30 Mar 1774	Bet. 16 Feb 1772 and 15 Feb 1773
Place of birth	Abbey, Paisley, Renfrews-hire	Not given	County of Lanark	Glasgow	Not given

We have found one piece of information about Margaret's family. On 27 September 1828, Margaret received a letter from the Reverend William Swan when she was living in Tampere.

> Speaking of dreams let me tell you I was much pleased with the waking dreams which you say still warm your heart respecting a certain lady and your poor brother. I thought she had long ago been the wife of another – for a gentleman in Glasgow wrote to me I think before I left Petersburg that he was almost to be married to her – I suppose he gave me this information that if I had any claim upon her I might enter it – I answered his letter wishing him all joy in his intended connection. But if it was you say that she is still single, and as there may be a possibility that the cause of her remaining so, is what you hint at I should

like to ascertain it. I shd be very sorry to think of her cherishing any secret wish which may to her seem almost hopeless – and perhaps the best way of settling it may be for me to write her in such a way as to learn her mind without saying any more at present. If the providence of God shd so order it, I shd look upon it as a great blessing to have such a companion here, and I may say I have the same affection for her still that I had the day I gave her the opportunity of becoming a missionarys wife for no other object has since usurped her place in my heart – she wished me to write her 'as a friend' and nothing more – but for prudential reasons I thought it better not to do so – but perhaps I may now send her one letter 'as a friend' – and that will discover whether it may be possible I shd ever be to her any thing more. The difficulty is how to convey a letter for I know not how to address it – Perhaps you can accomplish this and if I continued in my present mind I may inclose one which you thought your friends who came from her place may be able to forward it. I wrote you on this subject as on all others with perfect freedom, and in all simplicity of mind – If it is of the Lord it will come to pass – if not – it will not and should not ... My [torn] upon second thoughts I have considered it better to write through another con[vey]ance – not if you can learn any further particulars from your friends concerning that matter you will not – communicate [torn] – Her mother was the obstacle at the former period – and she may be so still.[19]

William Swan (1791–1866) was a regular correspondent to Margaret. He was a missionary and worked in Siberia. On a visit to Scotland, he married Hannah Cullen in 1832.[20] It does not mean that Hannah was the woman he was writing about to Margaret.

Who was this 'poor brother' that Swan writes about? There was a John Wilkie who was a hosier/stocking/glover manufacturer in Glasgow at a number of addresses: in the Post Office directories in Glasgow, he was at the following places:

1801–1804 – 459, Gallowgate

1805–1811 – 66, Glassford Street

1812–1820 – 58, Trongate

1825–1836 – 117, Trongate House & in last year also 126, Norfolk Street

There were no entries for him after 1835–1836 in the Glasgow Post Office Directories.[21] John Cullen was Hannah Cullen's father and was baptised on 19 April 1767 in Kilmadock, Perthshire and married Marion Downie on 20 Feb 1795 in Kilmadock, Perthshire. John Cullen was a manufacturer in Glasgow and was in the Post Office directories in Glasgow at the following place:

1812 – 66, Glassford Street

There is a possible link to John Wilkie as he was the previous tenant in the 1811 directory where he was listed as a stocking-manufacturer at 66, Glassford Street. This seems to be a different man from John Wilkie, hosier at 58, Trongate.

John Cullen's son George Downie Cullen was married to Jane Carstairs on 7 Jun 1831 South Leith. He was a Congregational Minister and was called to Leith. This might explain the reason for Hannah and her father being in Leith. George Downie Cullen, an English Congregational minister, was born at Doune, in October 1799. Receiving his education at Glasgow College and Theological Academy, in 1822 he accepted a call to Leith, which church he served until his retirement in 1869. He served as secretary of the Widows' Fund of the Scottish Churches, and chairman of the fund until his death. He also carried on the Yardheads Mission and Leith Sailors' School in connection with his pastorate, and was one of the founders of the Edinburgh Medical Missionary Society, and of the National Bible Society of Scotland, and was also connected with several other societies of like character. He died 1 October 1891.

It is a possibility that William Swan had connections with the Cullen family prior to his marriage, which supports the notion that John Wilkie was Margaret's brother. Randall wrote about William Nicolson and the British and Foreign Society in Russia, 1869–1897 and mentions William Swan. Nicolson, Cullen and Swan attended the Congregational Church on Constitution Street, Leith in Edinburgh.

> Cullen had close links with the Bible Society of Scotland, and so Nicolson was introduced to aspects of Bible Society endeavours. Another minister in the church was William Swan, who from 1818 to 1841 had served with the London Missionary Society in Russia. Swan was one of the translators of the Bible into the Mongolian language. In this period, therefore, Nicolson, then in his early twenties, was hearing about life in Russia. [22]

It is also possible that this John Wilkie was a member (cousin) of the Wilkie of Knowehead family[23]. John Wilkie (c1740 – 1813) was a stocking manufacturer in Glasgow. He entered a number of partnerships including Hunter & Wilkie from 1809 operating from 180 Saltmarket, Glasgow. After his

first sequestration by 1809, James Finlayson partnered with
John Napier and became a hosier and woollen manufacturer.[24]
This could be a coincidence that both were in the same line of
business. However, it might also explain Margaret's knowledge
of stocking manufacture and chemical treatments. In addition,
some of the Wilkie's of Uddingston moved from Bothwell
Parish church in October 1763 to the newly established
dissenting church in Bellshill. Two James Wilkies the bond
pledging payment for the new church. The following baptisms
were found:

Bellshill Relief Church

Baptisms 1764–1780[25]

(a) James WILKIE & Margaret HAMILTON baptised
   30 December 1764 Robert WILKIE (born same day
   in Uddingston)
   9 July 1769 Mary WILKIE (born 18 Jun 1769 in
   Uddingston)
   15 August 1771 Mary WILKIE (born 26 Jul 1771 in
   Uddingston)
   |7 March 1777 Daniel WILKIE (born same day in
   Uddingston)

(b) John WILKIE & Jean HAMILTON baptized
   21 Sep 1766 Jean WILKIE (born 18 Sep 1766 in
   Uddingston)

(c) John WILKIE & Agnes? [difficult to read and might be
   Jean] HAMILTON baptized
   13 January 1771 Janet WILKIE (born 6 Jan 1771 in
   Uddingston)

Summary of argument concerning Margaret's birth

As shown above, the only baptism found is not proven by corroborating evidence. Just because one baptism for Margaret Wilkie exists, it does not mean that it is correct. To take the assumption that is proven could be making the same mistake that was originally made about James Finlayson's birth. There are many reasons that baptisms were not recorded and there are a number of dissenting baptisms for Wilkie children in and around Glasgow. Several records do not point to the same date, and contradict other documentation. We, therefore, have reason to doubt the accuracy of the 1776 baptism in Abbey. The balance of evidence suggests that Margaret Wilkie was born some time in 1774 in Glasgow, although we cannot yet establish an exact date or parish for her birth.

NOTES

1 Paton, C. (2016) Discover Scottish church records. 2nd edn. Ridgehaven Australia: Unlock the Past. p. 30.

2 Paisley Hammermen Society, History of Paisley, https://paisleyhammermen.org/ : accessed 15 March 2023. Used with permission.

3 Clark, S. (1984) A survey of early Paisley engineers. Scottish Industrial history, 6.2.

4 Sinclair, S. J. (1999) The Statistical Account of Scotland, Paisley, Renfrew, Vol. 7. p. 62. The Statistical Accounts of Scotland online service: Edinburgh: William Creech; University of Edinburgh; University of Glasgow. http:www.stataccscot.edina.ac.uk:443/link/osa-vol7-p62-parish-renfrew-paisley.

5 Sinclair, S.J. (1999) pp. 63–68.

6 Sinclair, S.J. (1999) pp. 74–75

7 Sinclair, S.J. (1999) pp. 88–89.

8 Gordon, J. ed. (1845) The New Statistical Account of Scotland / by the ministers of the respective parishes, under the superintendence of a committee of the Society for the Benefit of the Sons and Daughters of the Clergy. Paisley, Renfrew, Vol. 7, Edinburgh: Blackwoods and Sons, p. 135. University of Edinburgh, University of Glasgow. (1999) The Statistical Accounts of Scotland online service: https://stataccscot.edina.ac.uk:443/link/nsa-vol7-p135-parish-renfrew-paisley.

9 Gordon, J. ed. (1845) p. 146.

10 Gordon, J. ed. (1845) p. 179.

11 Gordon, J. ed. (1845) pp. 201–202.

12 Gordon, J. ed. (1845) pp. 267–268.

13 Gordon, J. ed. (1845) p. 273.

14 Huhtala, L. (2012) The bittersweet pleasure of self-sacrifice [online], The History of Nordic Women's Literature. https://nordicwomensliterature.net/2012/02/17/the-bittersweet-pleasure-of-self-sacrifice/ : accessed: 13 March 2023).

15 Greyfriars baptismal register and proclamations (1729-1779). Scotland. Glasgow, Shuttle Street Secession Congregation. CH3/469/39. ©Crown copyright, National Records of Scotland, [archival reference].

16 Census records. Scotland. Govan, Lanark. 06 June 1841, FINLAYSON, Margaret. 646/ 2/ 43. http://www.scotlandspeople.gov.uk : accessed 19 March 2020.

17 Census records. Scotland. St. Cuthbert's, Midlothian. 30 March 1851. FINLAYSON, Margaret 685/2 193/2. http://www.scotlandspeople.gov.uk : accessed 24 March 2020.

18 Stark, J. (1874) Sixteenth detailed annual report of Registrar General of Births, Deaths and Marriages in Scotland BPP XIV [C.897] xli. General Register Office for Scotland. htNtp://www.histpop.org : accessed: 15 August 2023.

19 Swan, W. (1828) Letter to Margaret Finlayson, 27 September. The Margareta Finlayson Archive/Central Archives for Finnish Business Records (ELKA). ELKA-00427-000001-009-DOC. Used with permission.

20 Marriages (OPR) Scotland, Leith South. 25 April 1832. SWAN, William and CULLEN, Hannah. 692/ 2. http://www.scotlandspeople.gov.uk : accessed 26 January 2024.

21 Directories. Scotland. Scottish Post Office Directory of Glasgow (1835–1836). https://digital.nls.uk/directories/ : accessed 8 May 2020.

22 Randall, I. M. (2018) "That the progress of the Word be not hindered": William Nicolson and the British and Foreign Bible Society in Russia, 1869-1897. Baptistic Theologies, 10(2). p. 23.

23 Findlay, A. M. (2022) The Wilkies of Knowehead. Uddingston: Rectory Press (The Wilkies of Uddingston).

24 Trial papers of Thomas Stewart, journeyman wright in Glasgow, and Robert Wright, journeyman weaver in Glasgow, both presently prisoners in the tolbooth of Glasgow, for the crimes of housebreaking and theft. (1809). High Court of Justiciary. West Circuit, Glasgow. ©Crown copyright. National Records of Scotland JC26/1809/35.

25 Baptisms 1764–1833, Burials 1797–1809 and 1816–33. Scotland. Bellshill Relief Church, North Lanarkshire. CH3/1037/9. ©Crown copyright, National Records of Scotland, [archival reference].

– CHAPTER FOUR –

Together in Glasgow

I t is perhaps not surprising that James and Margaret moved to Glasgow. Like Paisley, Glasgow became renowned for its textile industry with '*cotton mills, bleachfields and printfields [have been] installed on almost all the streams in the neighbourhood*'.[1] Glasgow, in contrast to Edinburgh, was a city of international trade and industry. The varied branches of manufacture in Glasgow caused 'a very great increase in the wages of all kinds of manufacturers, mechanics and labourers'.[2] New industries were based on the traditions of engineering and machine making within the city and the regional exploitation of coal and iron. Although the city was relatively compact during the early years of the nineteenth century, the rapid growth in population strained the capacity to provide housing. Glasgow's population rose from 30,000 in 1750 to 85,000 in 1800 and nearly 200,000 in 1830.[3] The average population density in 1801 has been estimated at 15 persons per acre.[4]

We do not know when James and Margaret moved to Glasgow after their marriage in 1792, as we could find no definitive records in either Paisley or Glasgow before 1800. There is one record in the Visitors Book for New Lanark Mills dated 21 August 1795 (see Figure 15). This states that Mr and

Figure 15: New Lanark Mills Visitors book 1795

Source: Visitor's Book Titled Cotton Mills, New Lanark, 1795-1799. Records of Gourock Ropeworks Co Ltd, Rope Makers and Textile Manufacturers, Port Glasgow, Inverclyde, Scotland, n.d. in University of Glasgow Archive Services

Mrs Finlayson from Glasgow visited the mills. No first names are given and this could be our James and Margaret and that would mean they were residing in Glasgow by 21 August 1795. However, the next visitors in the book were Reverend James Finlayson and his wife, Mary, from Carstairs. It might be a coincidence or it could be that the couples were related. There is no evidence that this was the case for James and Margaret.

Another piece of evidence that suggests that James and Margaret were not residing in Glasgow at that time is contained in the Consolidated Assessed Tax Records. They are reasonably accurate as they were based on real property, the most important elements being the Inhabited House and Window Tax. However, not all heads of household were captured in the tax. Nenadic pointed out that the Glasgow tax schedules listed about 5,230 inhabited houses whereas the 1801 census enumerated 20,276 separate household units. She observed that the tax schedule's interpretation of 'inhabited houses' differed from the census' and the former reflected property ownership and occupancy rather than heads of household.[5]

James and Margaret lived at least 13 years in the City of Glasgow. It was an exciting time for the city as it expanded in wealth and population.

Whereabouts and weather

This section provides a context for the Finlaysons when they lived in Glasgow. At this time Glasgow was expanding in population and in industrial growth.

The influence of America

By the 1770s Glasgow had become 'the premier tobacco port of the UK.[6] The American War of Independence (1774–1783) changed much, including the pattern of trade between the former North American settlements and the UK. The Old Statistical Account (OSA) notes:

> By the American Colonies shaking off their
> dependence on this country, the intercourse between
> Glasgow and America was nearly put a stop to; and as
> the greatest part of the fortunes of the merchants in
> Glasgow was embarked in that trade, and very large
> sums owing them, which they were prevented from
> recovering, it proved the ruin of many; and would
> have been fatal to more, had it not been the great
> rise on the price of tobacco, which then fortunately

took place, which enabled those who had a large
quantity of that commodity, to stand the shock which
their credit at that time received, and to make up in
part for the immense losses sustained by them, in
their American debts.' Those tobacco merchants of
Glasgow who survived then prospered and diversified
into land, property, shipping and industry, notably
textiles, with linen production long having been
important, but then cotton production took over
increasing Glasgow's overseas trading importance.[7]

Growing pains

From the start of the nineteenth century steam-power fuelled
by locally mined coal drove the industrialisation and rapid
urban expansion of Glasgow. The Old Statistical Account
(OSA) states its population in 1755 as 23,546 and in 1791–2 as
61,945.[8] Gorbals, on the south side of the Clyde, was created
a separate parish in 1771 out of Govan parish, and stated to
have an additional population of 5,000 in 1791–2. The New
Statistical Account (NSA) records the 1801 census total for
Glasgow as 77,385, but if the connected suburbs are added of
6,384, the total for Glasgow becomes 83,769.[9] On the same
page of the NSA, the 1811 census data for Glasgow is stated as
100,749, with a similar part of connected suburbs to be added
of 9,711, bringing the 1811 total for Glasgow to 110,460.

The OSA describes the great variety of industry and manufacturing then carried on in Glasgow, noting:

> ... a very great increase in the wages of all kinds
> of manufacturers, mechanics and labourers; and
> notwithstanding the great increase of the inhabitants,
> and the many late inventions for abridging the labour,
> there is still a difficulty to procure a sufficient number
> of hands to perform the work ... The weekly wages

of journeymen tradesmen in Glasgow at present,
are nearly as follows: shoemakers from 9s. to 12s.;
women employed in binding shoes, from 5s. to 7s;
ordinary wrights, or carpenters, from 8s. to 12s.and
some of the best workmen so high as from 12s. to 18s
... stocking weavers, from 5s. to 10s. and some of the
best workmen, from 10s. to 16s.; women at seaming
stockings, from 3s. to 5s. a-week.[10]

The NSA describes in great detail the many industrial,
chemical and manufacturing processes undertaken in Glasgow
at that time, including improvements to textile spinning and
weaving; in many cases, however, rather outside the dates and
scope of this narrative.[11]

The OSA observes,

> Riches in Glasgow were formerly the portion of a few
> merchants. These, from the influence of the manufac-
> tures, are diffusing themselves widely among a great
> number of manufacturers, mechanics and artisans.
> This has made an alteration in the houses, dress,
> furniture, education and amusements of the people
> of Glasgow within a few years, which is astonishing
> to the older inhabitants; and has been followed by
> a proportional alteration in the manners, customs,
> and style of living of the inhabitants. And so many
> of the merchants have of late years been engaged in
> manufactures and trade, the distance in point of rank
> and consequence, between merchants and tradesmen,
> has now become less conspicuous, than it was before
> the American war...
>
> The strict severity and apparent sanctity of manners,
> formerly remarkable here, have yielded to the
> opposite extreme. There is now a great deal more
> industry on six days of the week, and a great deal
> more dissipation and licentiousness on the seventh.[12]

City limits

The map of Glasgow given in Plate 2 is reduced from six sheets of the City of Glasgow and suburbs published by Peter Fleming 20 April 1808.[13] This also shows development in the separate parish of Gorbals on the south side of the Clyde. On the north side the urban area is shown extending north just beyond George Street towards the fields of Cowcaddens, with Port Dundas a short distance north. To the west the built-up area extends to the then weaving village of Anderston (now straddled by the M8 north of Kingston Bridge), to include Blythswood (shown as New Building Land). To the east it extends to the High Street/ Duke Street junction, Camlachie Burn and beyond towards Bridewell (Duke Street) Prison, demolished in 1958 to make way for the Ladywell housing scheme. To the southeast the built-up area is shown extending to Camlachie, then a weaving village.

The Map References list 30 Churches & Religious Meeting Houses, including:

> Albion Street Chapel, Albion St.
> Antiburgher Meeting House,
> > Cheapside St. Anderston
> > Duke Street
> Baptist Meeting House, George St.
> Burgher Meeting House,
> > Campbell St.
> > Inkle, Factory Lane
> Cameronian Meeting House, High St. Calton
> English Chapel, South St Andrews Lane
> Methodist Meeting House, John Street.
> Releif (sic) Meeting House,
> > Campbell St.

Broad St. Hutcheson

Cochrane Street

Great Dove Hill

High St. Anderston

John St. Bridgeton

Roman Catholic Church, Marshall St,

Tabernacle, Jamaica St.

The Map References also list 33 Public Works, including:

Cotton Work, Geo. Yule & Co., Duke, St.

Dye Work, Murdoch Buchannan & Co., Burnside

Machine Factory, W. Dan, Rottenrow Lane

Machine Factory & Cotton Work, J. Cook, Narrow St, Gorbals

Cotton Work, A. McKerlie, Narrow St, Gorbals

Machine Factory, J. Smith, Narrow St, Gorbals

Cotton Work, Crum & Carnegie, High St, Anderston

Cotton Work, Holdsworth & Co.,

   Cheapside St, Anderston

   Clyde St., Anderston

Dye Work, Holdsworth & Co., Clyde St., Anderston

Cotton Work, Wm. Ferguson,

   McKechnie St., Calton

   Grahames St.

Cotton Work, Wm. Henry & Son, Barrowfield St., Calton

Cotton Work, Alexander Norris, Barrowfield St., Calton

Cotton Work, Joseph Bartholomew, Barrowfield St., Calton

Cotton Work, J. Pattison & Co,

   Mill St., Calton

   Sommer St., Mile End

Cotton Work, Joseph Dunlop & Co. Dalmarnock St., Bridgeton

Cotton Work, W. Houldsworth & Hussey, Howard St., Bridgeton

Dye Work, Andrew Campbell & Co., Trafalgar Bank

Glasgow's climate

In Greater Glasgow, the summers are usually cool; the winters can be long, cold, wet and windy, dependent on elevation and location; it is mostly cloudy year-round, temperatures typically varying from 34°F (1°C) to 66°F (19°C) and rarely below 22°F (-5.5°C) or above 74°F (23°C). The Meteorological Station recording the thirty-year 1991–2020 average temperatures for Glasgow is at Bishopton, about 2 miles (3km) south of the Clyde at an elevation of 59m. above sea level. It is considered, therefore, that this location would not be really representative of the weather in the older part of the city centre under consideration here and the figures for Paisley may be more relevant.

Machine maker in Glasgow

At the time James set up his business, a new tax was introduced that could affect the income he received. In December 1798 the Prime Minister, William Pitt the Younger, set the new Income Tax such that it began at two old pence in the pound on incomes over £60, and increased up to a maximum of 2 shillings in the pound on incomes of over £200. It was collected through self-assessment as everybody stated the amount of tax they proposed to pay.[14] According to Hobsbawm, around 1800 (less than 15% of British families) had an income of more than £50 per year and there had been about 100,000 tax-payers earning above £150 a year in Britain.[15] We do not know what James' income was at this time, and whether he was liable for the tax but it seems more than likely that income tax was unpopular in his social circle in Glasgow.

The first evidence of the Glasgow residence occurs in the 19 June 1800 edition of The Caledonian Mercury.

JAMES FINLAYSON,
MACHINE MAKER & TURNER,

Still continues to carry on these Branches, at his General Bobbin Manufactory, Shuttle Street, Glasgow, and takes this opportunity of acknowledging with gratitude, the liberal support he has ever received from Flax and Cotton Spinning Companies in various part of the country. From the experience J. F. has had in Spinning Machinery in general, he is convinced of the necessity for particular accuracy in all such work which he is determined to observe – Bobbins to any pattern and size, done on the shortest notice.

☞ Wants an Apprentice or two.
Glasgow, June 16, 1800

[Transcript of *Caledonian Mercury* (Edinburgh, Scotland) 19 Jun 1800, p. 1.]

It is interesting that the phrase 'still continues ...' is used. It suggests that he was in business prior to this date but gives no indication of whether he was self-employed or the location of the employment. The address given for his bobbin manufactory is Shuttle Street, Glasgow and we assume he lived on the premises. Peter Fleming's map of the City of Glasgow and Suburbs (1807), in Plate 2, shows Shuttle Street. Havannah Street and the Molendinar Burn. Shuttle Street was built on the lands of Shuttlefield. It was previously known as Greyfriars Wynd due to its proximity to the Franciscan Monastery on College Street. The Monastery was destroyed in the Reformation. [16] In 1768, at the corner of Shuttle Street and the Greyfriars Wynd, a meeting place was erected for the

Old Scotch Independents, a dissenting sect. David Dale, the founder of New Lanark Mills was a lay preacher and elder in this church and some called the sect Daleites.[17] Dale's church gained the nickname Caun'le Kirk, because its erection was financed by a candlemaker friend of his. Dale was a well-known philanthropist and was involved in the Glasgow Chamber of Commerce. It is likely that James will have known him or heard of him through business links. We do not know which congregation housed James and Margaret and it is possible they joined the Old Scotch Independents. There were 139 members in 1804.[18] Although there is a list of members, it is incomplete. The archivist in Glasgow City Archives checked for Margaret and James and could not find them.[19]

As stated above, we do not know when James and Margaret moved to Shuttle Street. Perhaps they were living there when a temporary prison was created for French Prisoners.

FRENCH PRISONERS IN GLASGOW

Very few of this generation are aware of the fact, that among the many stirring events in our city towards the close of the last century, was that of the arrival of a numerous party of French prisoners of war, who had been captured on the Irish coast. They were landed at Greenock, and marched in one column to Glasgow, *en route* to the depot for prisoners of war. About the close of the year 1796–7 a large military force went forth from this city to escort these unfortunates; for both the volunteer corps and regular troops conducted them into town. An immense multitude witnessed their entrance and procession through the city – both windows and housetops being occupied throughout the line of march to see them pass to their lodgings in the Old Correction House (the officers were lodged in the Tontine at the Cross) the grand entrance to

which was on the east side of Shuttle Street by an
antique archway, secured by an enormous gate, which
was immediately to the north where College Street is
now built.[20]

The next advertisement that James inserted was dated 3
August 1801. This one and the next few advertisements show
that James now focused on Linen Mangles.

TO THE NOBILITY AND GENTRY.

JAMES FINLAYSON, Machine Maker, Glasgow,
Makes LINEN MANGLES on an entire new
construction, which give an admirable gloss, and are
remarkably easy drove. Orders addressed to him, or
the following Agents, will be punctually attended to:
Mess. W. Anderson & Sons, Ironmongers, West Bow,
Mr March, Shoe Warehouse, Terrace, and Mr Gilchrist,
Glover, Cross, Edinburgh; Mr J. Rattray, Merchant,
Perth; Mr A. Gilroy, Montrose; and Mr J. Philip,
Wright, Cupar Fife.

A draught of the Machine will be shown by John
Finlayson, at Mr Carfrae's, Canongate.

[Transcript of *Caledonian Mercury*, Monday, 3 August 1801, page 1.]

Another advertisement appeared in the 3 October 1801
edition.

LINEN MANGLE

THE removal of all unnecessary Friction in
Machinery, where Human Force is applied, is
certainly of great importance.—This is so completely
done in the new improven Patent LINEN MANGLE,

that a child of 7 or 8 years of age will work it with ease, and produce the effect in little more than half the time of common ones. It is not subject to go soon out of repair; but the maker has no objections to keep it in repair for the first two years gratis.

Orders addressed to J. Finlayson, Machine-maker, Shuttle Street, Glasgow, will be carefully attended to. Reduced price is Eighteen Pounds only, ready money.

[Transcript of *Caledonian Mercury*, 3 Oct 1801, page 1]

James continued to advertise on 30 January 1802.

GREAT SAVING TO PRIVATE FAMILIES.

JAMES FINLAYSON, Machine Maker, Shuttle Street, Glasgow, informs the Public, that owing to a fall in the price of wood and iron, &c. he is happy in reducing also the price of his improven and much esteemed elegant LINEN MANGLES, which from the small space they occupy, and neatness of construction, are particularly a great saving to private families, from the remarkable ease with which they are wrought and most beautiful gloss they give the linens. Instead of requiring a man's power to drive, and a maid to manage J. F. engages that a child of eight years of age shall do it with great ease. They are packed in such a manner as may be sent to any distance by sea or land; and delivered in Edinburgh, or Leith, carriage free. Ladies or Gentlemen by applying at Mr J. Carfrae's Office, Canongate, Edinburgh, will see one of them, who takes orders for J. F. also Mr March, Shoe Warehouse, Terrace, and Mr F. Brown, No. 3, St Ann's Street, Edinburgh.

N. B — Gentlemen having Carpenters of their own,
may have the machinery separately, carefully packed,
with a draught for the wood work.

[Transcript of *Caledonian Mercury*, Saturday, 30 January 1802, page 1]

From the advertisements, it seems as though James was
the owner of the patent. However, we were not able to find a
patent registered to him. It is probable that James was making
and selling the patented mangle by Edward Beetham of
London. This ingenious product was first advertised in 1793.
There were other men advertising patented mangles, such as
Hugh Oxenham, Thomas Hayes and Richard Baker.

INFORMATION to the PUBLIC.– THOMAS
OXENHAM, MANGLE-MAKER to their MAJES-
TIES and ROYAL FAMILY, No 354, Oxford-Street,
near the Pantheon, and No. 39, Bishopsgate-Street,
thinks it a duty incumbent on him, from the many
favours received, thus publicly to inform the Public,
that on a trial of Cause, Beetham against Oxenham, in
the Court of Common Pleas, before a Special Jury, in
Michaelmas Term, it was proved that Hayes invention
for an improvement on Mangles sold by Beetham and
Baker was known and in use prior to the grant of the
Patent, and as the Public have paid much for such improvement, T. Oxenham thus publicly informs them,
that he manufactures Mangles on every principle now
in use, and the public may be supplied from 10 to 20
per cent. cheaper, at his warehouses, the pretended
monopoly being now at an end. – N.B. The trial will
shortly be published, due notice of which will be given
in all the Papers.

[Transcript *The Times* (London), Tue, 11 Mar 1800, p. 1]

Patents were important as they provided a monopoly for the inventor. Usually this was for 14 years. However, there were separate systems in England and Wales, Ireland and Scotland. English patents were applicable to England, Wales and Berwick upon Tweed. When Richard Arkwright sued David Dale for breaching the patent in the New Lanark Mills, the court decided that the patent did not apply in Scotland. The Baker patent mangle was embossed with Royal Insignia and 'Baker, 65 Fore Street, London'. It is interesting that James did not claim a name for the patent and there is no mention of a Royal Insignia. Figure 16 shows an example of a box mangle made by Baker that is in the National Trust property at Erddig, Wrexham, North Wales.

James aimed his advertisements for his mangles at the gentry and the middle class. Probably this was a growing market, as middleclass families were consuming more clothing and had the space to house these horizontal machines. We do not know whether he made a success of mangle-making. However, in 1802 he reverted to cotton and flax machinery, as shown by the following advertisement:

COTTON AND FLAX MACHINERY

JAMES FINLAYSON, Shuttle Street, Glasgow, takes this opportunity of acquainting the Public. That he has now begun to Make all sorts of COTTON and FLAX MACHINERY, &c in a new commodious Work Shop. Orders answered on shortest notice for Thorle Jeanies [21], Rollers of all kinds, Spindles and Flies. Bobbins, &c. warranted

[Transcript of *Caledonian Mercury* (Edinburgh, Scotland), 16 Oct 1802 p 3]

Figure 16: Baker's Box Mangle

Source: Gronnow, Susanne. Baker's Box Mangle. n.d. Erddig, Wrexham, National Trust.Used with permission.

In 1806 James placed an advertisement in Belfast targeting the market of flax spinning machinery. Within it he mentions that he has done some work there fitting his machinery.

Whether James was successful in winning business, we do not know.

Belfast Dec 30 1806
FLAX SPINNING

JAMES FINLAYSON, MACHINE MAKER respectfully acquaints the Manufacturers of Ireland, that having applied much of his attention in the making of machinery for Spinning Flax, he has now brought it to such a state of improvement, as enables him to promise complete satisfaction to such Gentlemen as may honour him with their employment.
Having already been engaged in making and fitting up of Cotton Machinery for some of the first Manufacturers in the North of Ireland, he hopes these specimens of his workmanship will recommend him to future employment
Orders addressed to him, at his Manufactory, Glasgow, or at the News-Letter Office, Belfast, will be punctually attended to.

[Transcript *Belfast Newsletter*, 30 Dec 1806]

James and Margaret, middling sort of people in Glasgow

For a time, British society was classified in bipolar terms – the landed elite and the poor. It encompassed a conventional ranking on the basis of status: 'The classic social hierarchy – noblemen; gentlemen; yeomen; citizens and burgesses; husbandmen; artisans; labourers'.[22] However, in Tudor times, a third rank developed between the two. 'Middling sort' is a term that commentators use to socially categorise British society from Tudor to Victorian times in imprecise and variable terms. The middling sort had to work for their livelihood and were usually self-employed. They derived their identity from their occupations.[23] They were caught in the trap of being compelled to work in order to support their middling sort of lifestyle.[24]

We have chosen to use 'middling sort' to describe James and Margaret. The middling sort is the social ranking between the labouring working class and the gentry and nobility class. Servant-keeping is a commonly used index of middling sort membership and so is consumerism of luxury goods, such as chinaware, where the acquisition is the product of the consumers' perceptions of the fashionable status of the objects they acquire.[25] In addition, social networks of trade organisations and voluntary groups also delineated the middle class from the working class. Another differentiating attribute is 'epistolary literacy', or letter writing. Whyman advocates its inclusion as a criterion for inclusion in the middling sort.[26] Whyman was writing about England and it is important to note that levels of literacy across society Scotland were slightly different. Although the myth has been challenged by Houston:

> The story of Scottish education and literacy has reached the status of a legend. In view of Scotland's palpably superior attainment of basic literacy in the mid-nineteenth century compared to England, and because of Scotland's long history of national legislation on educational provision, it has been claimed that Scotland became a highly literate country at an early date. Like eighteenth-century Sweden, Scotland has become a reference standard for early modern societies. [27]

Margaret was in correspondence over a number of years with Sarah Tanner, née Wheeler, and William Swan when she resided in St Petersburg and Tampere. The records we have discovered are unfortunately one-sided and are almost completely letters written to Margaret.

Although we do not have contemporaneous accounts of their time in Glasgow, as indicated in the next chapter, Margaret left Glasgow in 1814 with one servant and tableware and teaware. James also was identified in the Glasgow trade directories and obtained a burgess ticket through his application to the Incorporation of Hammermen of Glasgow. In Glasgow, the two main organisations for the business community and the control of trade, professions and crafts were the Merchants House and the Trades House.

The trade guilds or Trades House consists of 14 incorporations, one of which was the Hammermen. From the sixteenth century the Incorporation of Hammermen of Glasgow originally comprised craftsmen associated with metalworking – traditionally 'men who wielded the hammer', namely blacksmiths, goldsmiths, lorimers, cutlers, armourers, sword-makers, clockmakers, locksmiths, pewterers, tinsmiths etc. The Incorporation of Hammermen's crest is a hammer surmounted by a crown, and its motto 'By Hammer in the Hand, All Arts do Stand'.

In the history of the Hammermen of Glasgow, there are three entries that are of interest: John Napier, William Dunn and James Finlayson.[28] There are two men named James Finlayson who joined the Hammermen. The second one, who entered on 18 August 1807, was a jeweller. He had a number of apprentices and this confused us for a time as the apprenticeships occurred when James was in Russia.

Table 8: The Hammermen of Glasgow entries

No.	Date of entry	Name	Occupation	Class	Date of burgess ticket
606	Aug 29 1800	John Napier	Iron founder	S (Son)	Aug 29 1800
Essay: A screw & nut					
Note: John Napier was the Dues Collector in 1807 and Deacon in 1809.					
619	Aug 28 1801	William Dunn	Machine Maker	Str (stranger)	Aug 28 1801
Essay: A screw & nut					
Note: William Dunn was the Dues Collector in 1806					
651.2	Aug 26 1803	James Finlayson	Machine Maker	Str (stranger)	Aug 26 1803
Essay: A fire chisel					

Source: Lumsden, H., and P. H. Aitken. History of the Hammermen of Glasgow: A Study Typical of Scottish Craft Life and Organisation. Paisley: Alexander Gardner, 1912.

The requisites for membership were the same for all entrants:

(a) Enrolment as a burgess;

(b) Ability to turn out good work;

(c) Residence in the burgh

(d) Payment of the entry money and other charges, which varied in amount according to whether the entrant was

a stranger;

a son or son-in-law of a member; or

a booked apprentice of a member.

(e) Taking the 'oath de fideli' or 'making faith':

On 25 March, 1757, the oath as recorded was as follows : ' I [insert name] do hereby solemnly swear that I shall be a true and faithful member of the

Hammermen trade in Glasgow, into which I am now
about to be admitted a freeman, shall obey, imple-
ment and fulfil the haill rules, acts and regulations
made or about to be made for the good and benefit of
the said trade, or maintenance and sustenance of the
poor thereof, shall not pack or peel with non-freemen
thereof nor any way directly or indirectly be
concerned with as a partner in any branch of the said
trade with any person whom-soever until first he be
entered freeman with the said trade, and so often as I
shall violate this my oath or any part thereof, I agree
to forfeit and pay a new upset for the use of the poor
of the said Trade So help me God.

Till 1757 the oath was spoken. The new members
in later years could be required to subscribe the oath
written out in full in the Minute Book.[29]

The accounts of the Hammermen record the payments
James made to become a member:

(1) Dr William Lang Junr in account of intro-
     mission with the funds of the Hammermen
     Incorporation as their collector from 20
     September 1801 to 24 September 1802.
     Appendix to collector Lang's Account. No 1.
     Freedom Fines.
     #17 James Finlayson a stranger first half £6 6s

(2) William Mitchell in account of intromission
     with the funds of the Hammermen Incorpo-
     ration as their collector from September 1802
     to September 1803. Appendix to collector
     Mitchell's Account, No 1. Freedom Fines
     #14 James Finlayson last half of entry wt 2nd
     accnt £6 6s.[30]

However, the Incorporations were more than controllers of trade. They were also social organisations. They often resembled gentleman's clubs.[31]

The trade directories of the time did not include all individuals (or heads of household) resident within a town – and the inclusion of specific individuals was generally not based upon objective criteria. The Glasgow Directory claimed to be a list of the 'Merchants, traders, manufacturers and principal inhabitants' of the city. The first Glasgow Directory was published in 1787. The Directory of 1800 has 1,870 entries (2.5% of the local population).[32] The fact that James was included in the following directories is one indication that through his occupation he identified as middle class.

We argue that the plot of James' trajectory could be seen as a tragic drama that follows the path of Freytag's Pyramid (see Figure 17). [42]

Gustav Freytag was a nineteenth century playright and novelist who based his analysis on Aristotle's theory of tragedy, but Freytag used five stages. In applying his pyramid to James' life up to this point, we have introduced James and Margaret and their settings *(exposition)* and the Finlaysons were apparently doing well in Glasgow *(rising action)*. There are signs of the character flaw of ambition that leads to a reversal of fortune *(climax)*. We have called these 'twists in the yarn' in the following chapter. Everything afterwards in James' life heads towards tragedy *(falling action)*. This ends in the final scene of James' death *(catastrophe)* in impoverished circumstances.

Table 9: James Finlayson entries in Glasgow Post Office Directories 1799–1813

1799	No entry
1800	No edition
1801[33]	Finlayson, James, machinery maker, Shuttle Street
1802	No edition
1803	No entry
1804[34]	Finlayson, James, machine-maker, 32, Havannah-Str.
1805[35]	Finlayson, James, machine-maker, 32, Havannah-Str.
1806[36]	Finlayson, James, machine-maker, 32, Havannah-Str.
1807[37]	Finlayson, James, machine-maker, 32, Havannah-Str.
1808	No directory
1809[38]	Finlayson, Js. machine-maker, 32, Havannah-Str.
1810[39]	Finlayson, Js. machine-maker, 32, Havannah-Str
1811[40]	Finlayson, Js. machine-maker, 32, Havannah-Str
1812[41]	Finlayson, Js. wool-spinner, 32, Havannah-Str
1813	No entry

Source: Scottish Post Office Directories (1799–1828). Glasgow: Walter McFeat. National Library of Scotland

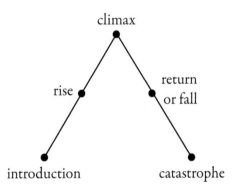

Figure 17: Freytag's Pyramid

Source: SinjoroFoster, 2019, Representation of the pyramid of Gustav Freytag, with English labels Creative Commons CC0 1.0 Universal Public Domain Dedication

NOTES

1 Sinclair, S. J. (1999) The Statistical Account of Scotland, Glasgow, Lanark. The Statistical Accounts of Scotland online service: Edinburgh: William Creech; University of Edinburgh; University of Glasgow. http://www.stataccscot.edina.ac.uk:443/link/osa-vol5-p502-parish-lanark-glasgow.

2 Sinclair, S. J. (1999) p. 505.

3 Devine, T. M. (1988) Urbanisation. In: T. M. Devine and R. Mitchison (eds) People and Society in Scotland, 1760-1830. pp. 27–52.

4 Nenadic, S. S. (1986) The structures, values and influence of the Scottish urban middle class, Glasgow 1800 to 1870. PhD thesis. University of Glasgow.

5 Nenadic, S. S. (1986) The structures, values and influence of the Scottish urban middle class, Glasgow 1800 to 1870. p. 410

6 Maver, Irene (2011) 18th century Glasgow. BBC History. https://www.bbc.co.uk/history/british/civil_war_revolution/scotland_glasgow_01.shtml : accessed 1 September 2023.

7 Sinclair, S. J. (1999) pp. 499–500.

8 Sinclair, S. J. (1999).

9 Gordon, J. (ed.) (1845) The New Statistical Account of Scotland by the ministers of the respective parishes, under the superintendence of a committee of the Society for the Benefit of the Sons and Daughters of the Clergy. Glasgow, Lanark. (1999). Edinburgh: Blackwoods and Sons. Vol. 6. p. 130.

10 Sinclair, S. J. (1999) pp. 505–506.

11 Sinclair, S. J. (1999) pp. 501–506.

12 Sinclair, S. J. (1999) pp. 534–535.

13 Fleming, P. (1808) Map of the City of Glasgow and suburbs. Reduced from the same in 6 sheets from actual survey.Glasgow, 1808. https://maps.nls.uk/view/216443187 : accessed 9 January 2023.

14 O'Brien, P. K. (2016) The triumph and denouement of the British fiscal state: taxation for the wars against revolutionary and Napoleonic France, 1793–1815. In: The fiscal-military state in eighteenth-century Europe. Routledge.

15 Hobsbawm, E. (1962) Age of revolution: 1789-1848 [Kindle]. London: Phoenix Press.

16 Foreman, C. (2007) Glasgow street names. 2nd edn. Edinburgh: Birlinn.

17 McLaren, D. J. (2015) David Dale: A Life. Stenlake Publishing

18 McLaren, D. J. (2015) David Dale: Life. Stenlake Publishing.

19 Tunnicliffe, N. (2023) Email to Angela Harris, 01 August. Topic: Search for James and Margaret in Old Scots Independent Church, Oswald Street, Glasgow records'. Glasgow City Archives.

20 Pagan, J. (ed.) (1851) Glasgow, past and present: Illustrated in Dean of Guild Court reports, and in the reminiscences and communications of Senex, Aliquis, J. B., &c. Glasgow: James Macnab. p. 211.

21 THORL, n. Also thorle. Sc. forms and usages of Eng.whorl:1. As in Eng.; a small fly-wheel on the spindle of a spinning wheel to maintain or regulate the speed JEANIE,n. Also jeannie. Sc. forms of Eng. jenny, a spinning machine Dictionary of the Scots Language. 2004. Scottish Language Dictionaries Ltd. Accessed 2 May 2023 <http://www.dsl.ac.uk/entry/snd/thorl>

22 Wrightson, K. (1994) "Sorts of people" in Tudor and Stuart England, In: The middling sort of people: Culture, society and politics in England, 1550–1800. Basingstoke: Macmillan. p. 28.

23 Whyman, S. E. (2009) The pen and the people: English letter writers 1660-1800. Oxford: Oxford University Press. p. 114.

24 Nenadic, S. S. (1986).

25 Nenadic, S. (1994) Middle-rank consumers and domestic culture in Edinburgh and Glasgow 1720–1840. Past and Present, 145(1).

26 Whyman, S. E. (2007) Letter Writing and the Rise of the Novel: The Epistolary Literacy of Jane Johnson and Samuel Richardson. Huntington Library Quarterly, 70(4). p. 579.

27 Houston, R. (1982) The literacy myth? Illiteracy in Scotland 1630–
    1760. Past and Present. 96(1), pp. 81–102. p. 81. By permission of
    Oxford University Press.

28 Lumsden, H. and Aitken, P. H. (1912) History of the Hammermen of
    Glasgow: A study typical of Scottish craft life and organisation. Paisley:
    Alexander Gardner, p. 300

29 Lumsden, H. and Aitken, P. H. (1912) p. 17.

30 Incorporation of Hammermen in Glasgow (no date).. Register for Their
    Collectors Accounts Begun in the Year 1766 and Ending in the Year
    1816. Register of the Incorporation of Hammermen in Glasgow for
    their Collectors Accounts begun in the year 1766 and ending in the year
    1816. Glasgow City Archives. GB243/T-TH2.

31 Nenadic, S. S. (1986).

32 Nenadic, S. S. (1986).

33 Directories. Scotland. (1801) Scottish Post Office Directory of Glasgow.
    p. 33. https://digital.nls.uk/directories/ : accessed 27 April 2023.

34 Directories. Scotland. (1804) Scottish Post Office Directory of Glasgow.
    p. 36. https://digital.nls.uk/directories/ : accessed 27 April 2023.

35 Directories. Scotland. (1805) Scottish Post Office Directory of Glasgow.
    p. 37. https://digital.nls.uk/directories/ : accessed 27 April 2023

36 Directories. Scotland. (1806) Scottish Post Office Directory of Glasgow.
    p. 37. https://digital.nls.uk/directories/ : accessed 27 April 2023.

37 Directories. Scotland. (1807) Scottish Post Office Directory of Glasgow.
    p. 36. https://digital.nls.uk/directories/ : accessed 27 April 2023.

38 Directories. Scotland. (1809) Scottish Post Office Directory of Glasgow.
    p. 39. https://digital.nls.uk/directories/ : accessed 27 April 2023.

39 Directories. Scotland. (1810) Scottish Post Office Directory of Glasgow.
    p. 45. https://digital.nls.uk/directories/ : accessed 27 April 2023.

40 Directories. Scotland.(1811) Scottish Post Office Directory of Glasgow.
    p. 49. https://digital.nls.uk/directories/ : accessed 27 April 2023.

41 Directories. Scotland. (1812) Scottish Post Office Directory of Glasgow. p. 52. https://digital.nls.uk/directories/ : accessed 27 April 2023.

42 Freytag, G. (1895) Technique of the drama: An exposition of dramatic composition and art. S. Griggs.

– CHAPTER FIVE –

Twists in the yarn in Glasgow

James and Margaret must have started their lives in Glasgow with ambition and hopes. For a number of years, they seemed to have done well. As shown in the directories they moved from Shuttle Street to larger premises in Havannah Street and James was admitted to the Incorporation of Hammermen of Glasgow, joining respected industrialists such as John Napier and William Dunn. However, in 1805, difficulties arose.

Disputes with the Wrights

Incorporations in Glasgow or trade guilds were territorial and, where the trades overlapped, there were demarcation disputes. This affected James and on 7 June 1805, James McRuer, Collector of the Incorporation of Wrights in Glasgow petitioned the Magistrates of Glasgow as follows:

> That by the exclusive privilege of said corporation no person is entitled to exercise the business of a wright within the City until first he become a member of the Corporation or be otherways privileged. That notwithstanding of such privilege, James Finlayson

Jennie Maker in Glasgow without being a member of
the Petitioners corporation or otherways privileged,
carries on and exercises within the City the business
of a wright, to the hurt and prejudice of the liberties
of the petitioners Corpn as aforesaid.

May it therefore please your Honours to grant
warrant to Officers of Court to apprehend and bring
before you the said James Finlayson for examination
on the facts before stated, and upon his admitting the
same, or the petitioners proving them, to prohibit and
discharge him from exercising the business of a wright
within the City until he first become a member of
the petitioners Corpn; To fine and amerciate him for
behalf of the poor of said Corpn and also find him
liable in the expense of the present application and
subsequent procedures. ... Justice George Crawley'

James appeared and made the following defence:

Appeared the defender James Finlayson who being
examined declared that he is not a freeman of the
incorporation of Wrights in Glasgow nor otherways
privileged to carry on the business, but that in the city
(or at least on the Burnside Lane ... part of Havannah
Street) makes mules for spinning cotton on, and
that he keeps journeymen who make any wooden or
wright work of which it may be composed, altho he
could make those machines without any wright or
wooden work at all, Declares that he is a freeman of
the Incorporation of Hammermen in Glasgow, and
this he declares to be truth.
James Finlayson.[1]

The court based their decision on a prior case of William
Dunn v Incorporation of Wrights 1804–1809.[2] William

Dunn mentions an earlier case in 1792 of Robert McKay, who called himself 'Jenny maker in Glasgow', against the Incorporation of Wrights of Glasgow. The advocation at the instance of Robert McKay came before Lord Eskgrove, who appears to have considered it with the most deliberate attention. The argument made by the Incorporation of Wrights was that a spinning jenny was a form of square wright work and therefore came within their purview. The court agreed with the wrights and instructed the three men to abstain from making jennies until they became members of the Wrights. William Dunn appealed this decision in a very detailed manner compared to James' defence. William Dunn's one habit that was 'an excessive liking for law pleas, and so he was constantly in the Court of Session'. He made the rather sensible remark on this score, that if a man wanted to be successful in his law plea, even though it should run down his opponent, it was best to keep the wheels of the agent 'well-greased' for the work.'[3]

William Dunn won his appeal in 1809:

> The Maker of cotton machines called mule-jennies,
> is not obliged to enter with the incorporation of
> wrights, nor to employ them to make the wooden
> work of these machines. – No. 73, Wrights of
> Glasgow contra William Dunn, February 24, 1809.[4]

It is not clear whether waiting for the appeal decision restricted James in his business. It would be understandable that he would be affected by the stress and work involved in fighting his case before the Court of Session. This might have played a part in the failure of his business in 1807. We first see this in an advertisement in 8 May 1806, when James puts some of his machinery up for sale.

COTTON MACHINERY
FOR SALE

To be sold, by auction on Wednesday the 14h curt.
at one o'clock P.M. if not previously disposed of by
private bargain, in the Cotton Work let by
Mr. Finlayson, about the middle of Havannah
Street, Glasgow,

COTTON MACHINERY, consisting of 2 CARD-
ING ENGINES, with Drawing and Roving, &c. 1
STRETCHING FRAME, 5 MULE JEANIES. The
above Machinery is nearly new, and may be seen by
applying to John Grier, at the work.

[Transcript 8 May 1806 p. 3 *Glasgow Courier* No..2299]

Bankruptcy

In Scotland, there are a number of statutes regulating the
treatment of bankruptcy cases. The statute that is relevant
in James' story is the Act of Parliament passed in 1793 titled
*An Act for rendering the payment of creditors more equal and
expeditious in that part of Great Britain called Scotland.*[5] The
purpose of the statute is to provide a process for the orderly
collection of a debtor's assets and a fair distribution of those
assets.[6] It overcame the possibility that the first creditors
receive everything at the expense of the other creditors. An
insolvent person could apply for sequestration or their creditors. This is a mercantile sequestration and only merchants
were covered.

Process of Sequestration in the Statute dated 1793: An Act for rendering the payment of creditors more equal and expeditious in that part of Great Britain called Scotland.[7]

(1) The individual does not have enough assets to meet all debts, or is unable to pay debts as and when they are due and is insolvent and as a result enters the process of sequestration [Scotland] or bankruptcy.

(2) An application for sequestration through a petition to the Court of Session is made either by the bankrupt or the one or more of the creditors or a combination.

(3) Provided that the following criteria are met, the sequestration is awarded

　　(a) The bankrupt is a trader, merchant, manufacturer, artificer or mechanic

　　(b) The bankrupt resides or does business in Scotland

　　(c) The bankrupt owes more than £100 to one creditor (or £150 to two creditors or £200 to three or more).

(4) By the judgment awarding sequestration, the Court sequestrates the whole estate and effects, heritable and moveable, real and personal, of the bankrupt. Under the law, creditors are formed into a community and the Court appoints the creditors to meet on a certain day, and at a certain place and hour, to choose an interim factor on the sequestrated estate; and appoints them to meet a second time, at the same place, at a certain day and hour, for the purpose of naming a trustee or trustees on the sequestrated estate. and ordains the petitioners

instantly to advertise the sequestration in the *Edinburgh Gazette* with time and place of meetings.

(5) The creditors provide evidence of the debts and swear an oath of verity and are enrolled in the book of sederunt and are qualified to vote at the meeting or to mandate agents to act on their behalf.

(6) An interim factor is elected at the first meeting of creditors. This meeting is held not more than three weeks after the award of sequestration. The duty of the interim factor is to manage the estate until a trustee is elected and is entitled to take possession of the bankrupt's whole estate and effects. The interim factor receives all the books and papers of the estate and works with the bankrupt in preparing inventories of the affairs.

(7) A trustee is elected by the creditors at the second meeting. The trustee is the assignee for the estate and funds and manages them for the creditors and disposes of them with the advice of the committee of creditors and distributes the funds when the interests of all creditors are settled. The trustee provides security. At this meeting, the bankrupt is ordered to exhibit the state of affairs of the estate to the trustee.

(8) The trustee applies to the Court of session to be confirmed in the role.

(9) The bankrupt attends examination meetings where the trustee interrogates the bankrupt and other relevant parties, such as spouse and family and people connected

with the business, on the evidence. The purpose is to provide full disclosure on the estate and effects.

(10) A third meeting of creditors is held after the examinations are finished to review the whole materials. A committee of creditors is elected for the purpose of giving directions about the recovery and disposal of the estate and receiving an offer of composition, if made. This meeting is to be advertised in the *Edinburgh Gazette.*

(11) A 'preses' is elected for each meeting to chair the meeting and minutes are taken.

(12) If authorised by four fifths of the creditors at a general meeting, the commissioners have discretionary powers to give an allowance limited to three guineas to the bankrupt for helping the process.

(13) The offer of composition should be advertised twice in the *London* and the *Edinburgh Gazettes.*

(14) At an adjourned meeting, the offer is considered and must be agreed by nine tenths of the creditors in terms of number and value.

(15) The Court of Session is petitioned to confirm the settlement.

(16) The funds, if any, are distributed through two or more dividends. The first is at twelve months and the second at eighteen months from the first deliverance of the petition for sequestration and from then on every

six months until the whole division is finished. If the funds exceed the debts, a settlement is made with the bankrupt.

(17) After eighteen months from the sequestration the bankrupt may apply for discharge if authorised by four fifths of the creditors. It was once questioned, whether a discharge could be granted to a debtor while abroad but it was held that absence was no bar to discharge.

(18) If the bankrupt is discharged, this is announced in the *Edinburgh Gazette*, on the walls of the Court (inner and outer) and in the minute book.

Bankruptcy could be seen as a public humiliation:

> Bankrupts were not only punished, but their situation was also published to warn creditors to be cautious when dealing with the debtor. Bankruptcy proceedings have been recorded in the *Gazette* since the eighteenth century in order to place notices in the public domain. By 1712, insolvent debtors and meetings of creditors were detailed, and by 1750, dissolutions of business partnerships[8]

Insolvency notices placed in the *London, Edinburgh* or *Belfast Gazettes* allowed transparency for the public, the credit industry such as bankers and concerned individuals to quantify risk, and also to inform creditors:

- at what stage of the insolvency process individuals had progressed to
- details of any forthcoming meetings
- the person in charge of the sequestration process.

Table 10: Economic fluctuations of the Scottish cotton industry

1707	The Treaty of Union of England and Scotland opened up London and colonial markets for Scottish goods. Up until then Scotland's main trading partners were France, Holland and the Scandinavian states.
1720–1774	Glasgow and the Clyde ports of Port Glasgow and Port Greenock had overtaken Edinburgh and the ports of the Forth valley due to the tobacco and cotton Atlantic trade.
1775–1783	American war of independence. The tobacco industry collapsed and merchants moved to linen trade with other countries, e.g. Canada, Nova Scotia, other European countries and Florida
1775–1790	Forth-Clyde canal completed and link between banking in Edinburgh and Clyde industry as well as coalfields. Cotton industry concentrated within a 25-mile radius of Glasgow.
1783	Peace of Paris. Raw cotton imported from West Indies but innovation and efficiency required to make use of it.
1792	Spectacular fluctuations
1792–1802	French revolution
1793–1794	Crisis when output fell to half followed by period of stagnation following outbreak of the French wars and series of Scottish banks failed.
1798–1802	Boom in output
1803	Slump
1805–1806	Napoleon blockade
1807–1809	American Embargo
1808	Major slump following Napoleon blockade
1810	Recovery
1811–1814	Slump
1818	Peak
1819–1821	Slump
1822–1823	Output rallied
1824–1827	Stagnated

Source: Data drawn from: Robertson, A. J. 'The Growth of the Cotton Industry and Scottish Economic Development, 1780–1835'. M.A Thesis, University of Glasgow, 1963; and Cooke, Anthony. The Rise and Fall of the Scottish Cotton Industry, 1778–1914: 'The Secret Spring'. Manchester: Manchester University Press, 2010.[12]

For a middling sort of man, the 'right to privacy was a hard-won prize for the middle-class'.[9] However, the notices only gave the above information and did not publish the reasons for the insolvency. At this time, the public were beginning to recognise that 'businessmen generally fail not because they are bad people but rather because they are bad at business'.[10] Although there was an element that the bankrupts had betrayed the trust of their creditors, the reasons for this might be out of their control. For example, there were many fluctuations in trading conditions in the cotton industry, as shown in Table 10.[11] These were different in Scotland from England, because Scotland specialized in fine muslins whereas England tended to mass-produce lower quality material. Also, Scottish banking was supportive. Fluctuations of the period 1793–1815 were ascribed to uncertainty for the market of cotton goods in times of wartime made worse by the scarcity of American cotton during the War of Independence. Also, there was increased competition – for example, from France.

First Sequestration

A major setback for James was his first sequestration, the Scottish term for bankruptcy, in 1807. As part of the documentation, there is a petition that provides a summary of the sequestration case for James.

> Petition of 11th July 1807 James Finlayson Machine Maker in Glasgow
>
> That the Petitioner the said James Finlayson is tacksman of the following subjects lying within the burgh of Glasgow viz all and haill[13] that piece of ground consisting of 318 yards or thereby, lying

within the burgh of Glasgow on the north side of the
Havannah Street thereof by the said Havannah Street
on the South, the lands of William Watson on the
West, the lands of the heirs of Gavin Pettigrew and of
James Coutts respective on the north, and the malt
barn and stable of John Aitken maltman and brewer
in Glasgow on the east part being part of the land
purchased from and disponed to the said John Aitken
by John Hamilton of Barns, William Cochran and
the deceased Thomas Johnston merchant in Glasgow,
and William Chrystee dyer in Stirling together with
the large brick house built by Grant Wood ... carpet
manufacturers in Glasgow upon the said piece of
ground with the free ish & entry[14] thereto whole
parts & pertinents[15] thereof which subjects were let
to the said James Finlayson his heirs subtenants or
assignees by Tack[16] dated the 9th and 20th days of
July 1803 entered into betwixt James Murdoch Junior
merchant in Glasgow heritable proprietor of the
same on the one part, and the said James Finlayson
as principal and William Kelly merchant in Glasgow
as cautioner[17] for him on the other part that for the
space of 19 years from & after the term of 10 July
1803 for which the said James Finlayson became
bound to pay to the said James Murdoch Senr his
heirs .... the sum of £60 ... yearly rent & that at two
times in the year .... by equal portions with penalty
and interest as mentioned in the said Tack. That the
said James Finlayson is likewise sub tacksman of a
piece of ground consisting of about thirty falls[18] lying
on the fourth side of the Molendinar burn and within
the royalty of the burgh of Glasgow, which ground
he possesses in virtue of a missive of subtack from
the said James Murdoch above designed who holds
it in Tack from the College of Glasgow. That the
Petitioner having found security to the Creditors for
his faithful management he now humbly reports the
minutes of the Creditors and his Bond of Caution,

and he hopes your Lordship will confirm his nomination as Trustee, in the usual manner and at same
time appoint the Bankrupt to execute a disposition in
the petitioners favour in terms of the foresaid act of
Parliament. May it therefore please your Lordship to
confirm the nomination of the Petitioner.

We can learn from this petition that James was a tacksman
of the Havannah Street property from July 1803: that means
he leased it.

The creditors agreed to provide James Finlayson with an
allowance.

In Scotland, the allowance is regulated differently;
proceeding on another principle altogether. 1. Instead
of a settled proportional allowance, the creditors have
the sole right of granting or refusing the allowance;
by which means there is always a fair adaptation of
the allowance to the circumstances and conduct
of the bankrupt. 2. It is not as a stock for future
subsistence that the allowance is given; for every man
is supposed capable of supporting himself when he is
free to exert his industry for that purpose: but it is as
subsistence-money while the creditors require his aid,
or have him entirely at their call, so as to prevent his
turning his exertions to his own benefit. 3. This subsistence-money is limited so as in no case to exceed 5
per cent., or two guineas per week: it is given to the
bankrupt at a time when it is most necessary for him
to receive it. 4. The allowance is refused altogether
when the bankrupt has not kept such books as may
enable his creditors to obtain a clear knowledge of
his affairs. The allowance stops at the period assigned
for the payment of the second dividend; that is to say,
at the end of eighteen months from the date of the
first deliverance, when the bankrupt, if entitled by
his conduct, may apply for his discharge, and turn his
industry to his own subsistence. [19]

Table 11: List of Claims ranked on James Finlayson's Estate in 1807

James and John Brown, Glasgow (Colourmen)	£36.19.5
John Arneil, Calton (Wright)	£24.10.9
John Motherwell, Paisley (Merchant)	£157.7.4
James Sword and Company, Glasgow (Iron mongers)	£66.17.3
Morehead, Lowden and Company, Glasgow (Merchants)	£14.17.3
John Cameron for Glasgow Currier Society	£35.3.6
William Fleming, Sawmillfield, (Timber merchants)	£13.19.11
William Alexander, Glasgow (Tobacconist)	£120.0.0
W. and J. Craig and Company, Glasgow (Timber merchants)	£82.4.8 ¼
John Napier, Glasgow (Iron founder)	£51.2.7
James Sword, Junior, Glasgow (Iron monger)	£152.16.1
David Hill, Glasgow (Leather merchant)	£80.0.0
Mrs Jean Muir, residing in Glasgow	£39.0.0
James McLaclan, Gorbals (Iron founder)	£33.5.5
William Leechman, Glasgow (Iron monger)	£414.16.2
Leechman and McVicar, Glasgow (Tin smiths)	£114.18.5
George Young, Glasgow (Smith)	£17.15.0
John Kirkwood, Calton (Wright)	£94.0.0
James and Robert Watson, Glasgow (Bankers)	£30.0.0
James McLeran, Glasgow (Iron monger)	£204.0.0
Andrew McGeorge, Glasgow (Writer)	£20.18.3
Joseph Cauvin, Writer to the Signet, Edinburgh	£17.7.5
Grove and March, Birmingham (Factors)	£91.11.4
William and John Craig and Co. 2d claim, Glasgow (Timber merchants)	£130.0.0
James Dawson, Glasgow (Brass founder)	£150.0.0

John Napier, 2d claim, Glasgow (Iron founder)	£89.17.0
John and James Dawson, Glasgow (Brass founder)	£140.5.10
Total	£2,423.18.6 ¼

Source: James Finlayson, Glasgow, 1807, Court of Session: Unextracted Processes, 1st Arrangement, Innes-Durie Office 1669–1837. National Records of Scotland, Edinburgh. ©Crown copyright. National Records of Scotland, CS234/SEQNS/F/1/22.

In this case, the unanimous decision was to pay one guinea per week.

> The meeting unanimously resolved that the bankrupt shall be allowed a guinea per week out of the proceeds of the estate for the maintenance of himself and family commencing as on the date of the sequestration and continue during the pleasure of the creditors and the trustee was authorized to pay him that allowance accordingly.[20]

James Sword, Junior, iron monger, John Napier, iron founder, and Peter Cumming, shoe maker, offered themselves as cautioners (guarantors) for the offer of composition.[21]

It is not simple to calculate the current day worth of **£2,423**. The table from http://www.measuringworth.com[22] provides the present worth of a past monetary value.[23] Current data is only available up to 2021. In 2021, the relative worth of **£2,423 18s 6d** from 1807 is:

- £205,000.00 using the retail price index
- £203,000.00 using the GDP deflator
- Current data is only available till 2021. In 2021, the relative *wage or income* worth of £2,423 18s 6d from 1807 is: £2,470,000.00 using the average earnings
- £2,670,000.00 using the per capita GDP

- Current data is only available till 2021. In 2021, the relative *output* worth of £2423 18s 6d from 1807 is: £14,200,000.00 using the GDP

The variation between calculations of current worth between £203,000 to £14,200,000 is large but even at the lower end is a significant amount.

The sequestration was resolved by the subscribers agreeing with James to a settlement at the rate of ten shillings per pound, payable at six, twelve and eighteen months from 8 June 1807.

The petition gives further details about James' residence in Glasgow. It would seem that he moved from Shuttle Street to Havannah Street near the Molendinar Burn on 10 July 1803, when he entered a lease and became bound to pay to James Murdoch Senr the sum of £60 yearly rent, payable biannually by equal portions with penalty and interest. This explains why he was not listed in the 1803 Glasgow Directory.

In the minutes of James' creditors of 24 March 1807, we learn that he employed a number of workmen in his business:

> The meeting also authorized the trustee to pay to the bankrupt's workmen the arrears of wages due to them prior to his election as factor amounting to twenty pounds three shillings and three pence in addition to the wages paid to the work men who are not yet discharged.
>
> Mr Leechman & Mr Napier appointed a committee to assist in finishing or not finishing & disposing of machinery on hand.[24]

As a result of this sequestration, a public roup was held.[25]

Sale Postponed
COTTON MACHINERY & TOOLS
FOR SALE

To be sold, by public roup within the Works of
JAMES
FINLAYSON, Machine Maker in Havannah Street
of Glasgow on Wednesday the 26th of August (in
place of Wednesday the 29th of July as formerly
advertised) at twelve o'clock, if not previously sold by
private bargain.

13 CARDING ENGINES, of various breadths,
with Cast iron Framing;
1 DRAWING FRAME, four Heads, with Doublers;
1 ROVING FRAME, with eight Cans;
8 MULES, of 192 Spindles, adapted for coarse
numbers;
1 STRETCHING FRAME of 96 Spindles.

All the above articles are new and in good order, and
made on the most approved plan.

Also, a variety of SMITHS' TOOLS, such as Bellows,
Anvils, Board-tools, Vices, Turning-laths, Spindles,
and Flyers; also, a variety of WRIGHTS' TOOLS,
such as Benches, Cramps, &c. with considerable
quantities of Roller-iron, and of well-seasoned Wood
of various lengths, and for covering Card-cylinders.

Application may be made to James Finlayson, at the
works.

[Transcript Vol XVI Saturday 25 July 1807, p. 3 *Glasgow Courier* No..2489]

After the sequestration

After the sequestration, James Finlayson changed direction and entered a partnership with John Napier, the iron founder, as hosiers and wool manufacturers. It is probable that Napier was the senior partner as he had the money and the business was called John Napier & Co. John Napier (1752–1813) belonged to a well-known family of engineers and ship-builders. His business as an iron founder prospered. He became a burgess of Glasgow in 1775 and was elected to the Glasgow Town Council in 1790. As stated above, in 1800 he became a member of the Incorporation of Hammermen in Glasgow and was appointed collector and deacon. He was one of the founders and directors of the Philosophical Society of Glasgow.[26]

In 1809, Thomas Stewart (Journeyman Wright) and Robert Wright (Journeyman Weaver) were accused of entering the premises of Messrs Allan, Tennant and company, stocking manufacturers and stealing amongst other items: Two stocking pantaloon pieces with a quantity of lamb wool worsted yarns property of John Napier & Co. At the trial on 28 September 1809, *James Finlayson, Acting Partner of Messrs John Napier & Company woolen manufacturer in Glasgow* appeared. The verdict was 'not proven' and the case was dismissed.[27]

In 1810, these notices were printed:

GLASGOW LAMB WOOL MANUFACTORY

JOHN NAPIER & CO return their grateful acknowledgments to their Friends and the Public, for the liberal encouragement afforded to their Manufacture, which has lately been farther honoured by the BOARD of TRUSTEES, in their annual distribution of PREMIUMS. They now beg leave to intimate,

that, from arrangements recently made, they will
always have on hand, ready for sale, a more abundant
supply of the various articles they manufacture, and
which they pledge themselves will be found moderate
in price, and of the best quality.

Lambs Wool Yarn, of all sizes for Hosiers. Knitting
Yarn, fine and coarse, from 2s. 4d. to 7s. per lib. Fine
soft Lambs Wool for Ladies Mantles, Winter and
Travelling Shawls, and Underdresses.

Drawers, Pantaloons and Breeches Pieces, double
and single milled, &c. in great variety, wholesale and
retail. *** Hosiers and Merchants supplied on the
shortest notice. Nos. 32 and 36, Havannah Street,
Glasgow.

[Transcript *The Caledonian Mercury* (Edinburgh, Edinburgh, Scotland)
Sat, Feb 10, 1810]

The Honourable Board of Trustees at Edinburgh,
have been pleased to grant a premium of L.100
sterling, to John Napier and Co of Glasgow, for
their extensive and improved establishment as lamb
wool-spinners and hosiers.

[Transcript *Aberdeen Journal*, and *General Advertiser for the North of Scotland*
(Aberdeen, Aberdeen, Scotland) · Wed, Aug 15, 1810]

In 1727 the Scottish Privy Council formed the Board of
Trustees for Fisheries, Manufactures & Improvements in
Scotland. Its duty was to improve the Scottish economy by
allocating £6,000 per annum to the development of linen,
wool and the fisheries.[28]

On 14 May 1810, John Napier and James Finlayson, wool
spinners and hosiers in Glasgow, purchased land, equally

between them, from Glasgow College in the University of Glasgow under a 'contract of ground annual'.[29] In Scotland, and prior to 1974, this was a form of pecuniary real burden to the title. A 'contract of ground annual' was the sale of land to be paid for by annual payments in perpetuity.[30]

> ... that Lot of ground situated within the Burgh of Glasgow on the East side of the Molendinar Burn containing one thousand four hundred and seventy eight square yards or thereby at present possessed by the said James Finlayson & John Napier in which measurement both parties acquiesce be the same more or less And which lot of ground is bounded on the west by the road or Street passing along the Eastside of the Molendinar Burn which shall be an open and common road which time coming and extending eighty feet or thereby along the said Road, and on the South by the Lot of Ground desponed by the said first parties to James Monach Cotton Spinner in Glasgow and extending over one hundred seventy nine feet which a crooked line along the said south boundary and bounded on the East by other Ground belonging to the said Principal and Professors, and extending seventy eight feet or thereby along the said East boundary and bounded on the North by a lane leading from the Bridge at the foot of Havannah Street to the grounds belonging to the said Principal and Professors and which lane separates the ground hereby desponed from the lands belonging to Simon Pellance & his partners

and to _ _ _ _ _ _ _ _ _ _ Nessmith and _ _ _
_ _ _ _ _ _ _ Macorne, and the said piece of
ground hereby desponed extends one hundred
and eighty four feet or thereby along the North
boundary'.[31]

As well as annual ground rent, as part of the purchase, James renounced the lease to the property that he had gained in 1810. They also agreed to erect houses on the site by May 1813.

At the same time, James Finlayson entered an arrangement with James Watts, who appeared to have taken over the machine tools side of the business, as shown by this advertisement.

JAMES WATTS & CO.
Machine Makers,
No. 36, Havannah Street, Glasgow,

Beg leave to acquaint the Public, that they will be
ready, by the 11th curt. To execute orders, to any
extent, of all kinds of MACHINERY, on the most
approved plans, and on the shortest notice.
They also wish to intimate to Flax Spinners, &c. a
new and singular Improvement, by which any
Manager, in the course of two minutes, may alter
the velocity of the machinery, from one to eighty
revolutions, without the least intricacy, and at same
time beyond the reach of any one of the work people,
without his consent.
The vast importance of this, whether in Flax or
Cotton Spinning by water frame, must be evident to
all who have had any experience of the loss and in-
convenience attending the usual, and but too limited
mode of changing the motion hitherto adopted.
June 4

[Transcript *The Caledonian Mercury* 18 June 1810 p.1 from Newspapers.com]

However, James Finlayson disassociated himself from James Watts in a notice in the *Edinburgh Gazette*, backdated to June 1810.

NOTICE

The Subscriber hereby gives notice, that since the month of June last, he has had no concern with the Machine-Making business carried on here under the firm of JAMES WATTS & Co

JAMES FINLAYSON Havannah Street Glasgow, January 25, 1811

On 29 January 1811, John Napier made over to James his share of the title to the ground apart from the brick building fronting the Molendinar Burn on Burnside Lane and the said piece of ground immediately behind the building containing three hundred and fifty-nine square yards. James Finlayson's interest in this last area of land was conveyed at the same date to John Napier[32]

On 7 February 1811, James acknowledged a debt of £1,000 to John Napier which was due 1 March 1814 for an annual rent of £50. The security James provided was the whole property.[33]

On 1 February 1811, there was a notice in the *Edinburgh Gazette*, that the business carried out under John Napier & Company was dissolved on 21 January 1811, with James Finlayson taking on the debts and the business.

NOTICE.

The Wool-Spinning and Hosiery business carried on here under the firm of JOHN NAIPER & COMPANY, was DISSOLVED, on 21st January current, by mutual consent. The debts due to, and

owing by the company, will be discharged by the
Subscriber, James Finlayson, by whom the business is
in future to be carried on.

JOHN NAIPER.
JAMES FINLAYSON.
NATH. STEVENSON, *Witness.*
ALEX. MORRISON, *Witness.*
Glasgow, January 29, 1811.

[Transcript *Edinburgh Gazette*, No. 1836, from FRIDAY,
FEBRUARY 1st to TUESDAY, 5 FEBRUARY 1811, p.36]

John's last name was given as 'Naiper' which is a common
variation.[34] No reason for the dissolution is given and we do
not know if the two men were on difficult terms, whether the
business was struggling or whether Napier's health was failing.
David Napier took over the John's iron-founder business in
Camlachie in 1810 due to his father's ill health.[35]

The withdrawal of John Napier might have been the cause
for James Finlayson's second sequestration in 1813.[36] No reason
for this is published, but it might well have been due to a
problem with cash flow and insufficient cash reserves. John
Napier died on 29 July 1813. In the inventory for his will, there
is no mention of James Finlayson as creditor or debtor and this
suggests that any financial debts had been resolved by then.

Second Sequestration

James Finlayson signed a Promissory note for £239 18s to John
Napier dated 24 July 1812, payable three months after that
date. This was not paid and Thomas Edington & Nathaniel
Stevenson started poinding[37] proceedings against James on 18

December 1812. On 1 February 1813 they initiated sequestration to avoid some of the creditors poinding the property to the disadvantage of other creditors. James also authorised this through a mandate. The Court of Session granted sequestration on 5 February 1813.

This debt is less than the debt of his first sequestration. It is noticeable that there are no bankers as creditors and this suggests that John Napier was the source of funding. Having been sequestered in 1807, it is probable that bankers would not offer any credit to James. Perhaps Napier's guidance meant that the business had less financial exposure.

The creditors held meetings on 13 February and 12 March 1813 at the Black Bull Inn in Glasgow. The meetings were advertised in the Caledonian Mercury on 6 February 1813.On 17 March, the Court of Session ordained James to deliver to Nathaniel Stevenson, the trustee of the sequestered estate, all his account books and deeds. On 6 and 20 April 1813, James was examined at the Sheriff Court House in Glasgow as advertised in the Caledonian Mercury and Glasgow Courier.

Table 12: List of Claims ranked on James Finlayson's Estate in 1813

Richard Branleston, wooller of Glasgow	£58. 0s. 0d.
John Napier, founder of Glasgow	£1,557 2s. 1d.
Robertson & Hastie, hosiers of Glasgow	£52 17s. 4d.
Cumming & Kirk, shoemakers of Glasgow	£10 0s. 0d.
Total:	£1,667 19s 5d.

Source: James Finlayson, hosier and woollen draper, 1813, Glasgow Court of Session: Unextracted Processes, 1st Arrangement, Inglis Office 1657–1863. National Records of Scotland, Edinburgh. ©Crown copyright. National Records of Scotland, CS233/SEQNS/F/1/19

SEQUESTRATION
EXAMINATIONS, DIVIDENDS, &c.

James Finlayson, hosier and woollen-manufacturer in
Glasgow, to be examined in the Sheriff Court-house,
there, 6th and 20th April at eleven o'clock. Creditors
to meet in the office of Nathaniel Stevenson, writer,
there, the trustee, 21st April, at two o'clock, to choose
Commissioners. Claims to be lodged before 5th
December.

[Transcript 6 April 1813 *Glasgow Courier*]

James Finlayson conveyed to Nathaniel Stevenson, trustee
for his creditors, the title to his property by the Molendinar
Burn on 14 May 1813. James' lease and manufacturing utensils
were advertised to be auctioned.

TO BE SOLD

By public roup, within the house of James Curl,
vintner, west end of the Exchange on Thursday the 3d
of June, at two o'clock afternoon,

THE BENEFIT of a LEASE, whereof nine years are
yet to run after Whitsunday 1813 of the PREMISES
at the FOOT of HAVANNAH STREET, occupied
by James Finlayson as Woollen Spinning Factory, with
Steam Engine of six horse power, with all its Shafts
and Appurtenances; six Woollen Carding Machines;
eleven Spinning Jeanies; two Roving Billies; two
Twining Mills, and two Wauk Mills. The Spinning
House contains three flats, all heated with Steam, 23
feet by 68 feet within. The Lease and the Engine will
be sold with or without the Machinery. The premises
are well adapted for Woollen or Cotton Spinning, or
Weaving by Power. Immediate possession may be had.

Also,
That LOT of GROUND at the FOOT of
HAVANNAH STREET, on the south side of the
Carpet Factory containing 1119 square yards or
thereby, with range of Buildings thereon, either in
one or separate lots. Apply to Nathaniel Stevenson,
writer in Glasgow, in whose hands may be seen the
articles of roup and title deeds. The premises will be
shewn by James Finlayson

[Transcript 1 June 1813 *Glasgow Courier* p.4 No. 4005]

SALE POSTPONED FOR ONE DAY.
TO BE SOLD,

By public roup, within the house of James Curl,
vintner, west end of the Exchange on Thursday the 3d
of June, at two o'clock afternoon,

THE BENEFIT of a LEASE, whereof nine years are
yet to run after Whitsunday 1813 of the PREMISES
at the FOOT of HAVANNAH STREET, occupied
by James Finlayson as Woollen Spinning Factory, with
Steam Engine of six horse power, with all its Shafts
and Appurtenances; six Woollen Carding Machines;
eleven Spinning Jeanies; two Roving Billies; two
Twining Mills, and two Wauk Mills. The Spinning
House contains three flats, all heated with Steam, 23
feet by 68 feet within. The Lease and the Engine will
be sold with or without the Machinery. The premises
are well adapted for Woollen or Cotton Spinning, or
Weaving by Power.

The Works will be kept going till the 8th July, and
till that time will be shown by James Finlayson, after

which the key of the premises will be found with the
Trustee on Mr. Finlayson's Estate. Possession may be
had immediately after the Sale.

Apply to Nathaniel Stevenson, writer in Glasgow,
trustee on the Sequestered Estate of James Finlayson
in whose hands may be seen the articles of roup and
title deeds.

[Transcript *Glasgow Courier*, 13 July 1813]

It is interesting that James was not going to be available
after 8 July 1813 and this corresponds with his arrival date in
the port of Kronstadt, as covered in the next chapter on James
and Margaret's time in St Petersburg, Russia.

MANUFACTURING UTENSILS,
FOR SALE.

To be sold, by public roup on Thursday the 26th inst.
At the Works, Havannah-street, lately possessed by
Mr. James Finlayson, Woollen Manufacturer, and
belonging to his Sequestered Estate.

A great Variety of VALUABLE UTENSILS, suitable
for carrying on a WOOLLEN MANUFACTORY,
great part of which may be useful for various other
Manufacturing purposes.

They consist of a Skutching Machine, four Stocking
Frames, one 28 inches, one 20 inches, one 16 inches,
and one 9; Steam and Lead Pipes, Beams, Scales and
Weights, various sizes; a lot of Cast and Malleable
Iron and Lead; Tubs for water; Wool Sheets, Dressing
Frames, and Poles; Cast Iron Block Tackle and Beam;
a Fir Table with 7 drawers for holding Stockings; a

Mahogany Table; a Packing Press; several dozen of
Legboards, Framing Stenters and Rafters for drying
goods; a two wheeled Hurley; Turning Tools, Chisels,
and various articles of Tools and Materials useful
about a Steam Engine; Fuller's Earth; a Stove and
Pipe; a Writing Desk; a Roving Frame, Head and
Cans; a Set of Billy Geering; an Oil Cistern that
would answer for a Blue Dyer's Vat; 60 Mill Bobbins,
a doz hand-wheels or whisks, a Dross Wheel Barrow
and two Field Barrows, a Watch Dog, &c.

Sale to begin at half past 11 o'clock forenoon.
R. & D. MALCOLM, Vendue Masters.

[Transcript *Glasgow Courier* 21 Aug 1813]

This advertisement shows the type of equipment James
used in his business. If his household goods were auctioned,
they were not identified as belonging to him and might have
been included in a general auction.

After James' emigration, the last notice appeared on 6
January 1814 and announced a meeting for creditors on 9 Feb-
ruary 1814. with Nathaniel Stevenson at John Napier's offices.
Possibly, this meeting was to wind up the sequestration.

NOTICE
TO THE CREDITORS OF
JAMES FINLAYSON,
Woollen Manufacturer in Glasgow.

NATHANIEL STEVENSON, writer in Glasgow,
Trustee upon the Estate of the said James Finlayson,
hereby intimates, that a state of the affairs of the
bankrupt has been made up and doqueted by the
Commissioner and lies at his office for the inspection
of the Creditors. No dividend.

The Trustee requests a meeting of the Creditors in his office on the 9th day of February next, at two o'clock afternoon, to choose a Commissioner in room of the deceased Mr John Napier.

NATH STEVENSON, Trustee

Glasgow, December 31, 1813

[Transcript *The Caledonian Mercury* (Edinburgh, Edinburgh, Scotland) · Thu, Jan 6, 1814 · Page 1 from Newspapers.com]

It is interesting that John Napier died either on 24 July 1814 as announced in the *Caledonian Mercury*, or 29 July as stated in his will (see Figures 18 and 19).[38]

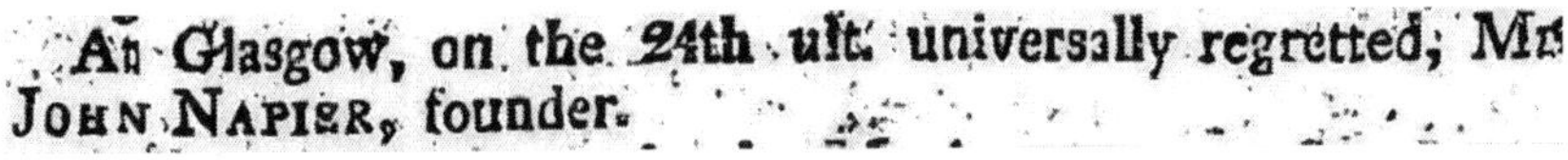
At Glasgow, on the 24th ult. universally regretted; Mr JOHN NAPIER, founder.

Figure 18: Death announcement of John Napier. **Transcript**: At Glasgow, on the 24th ult. Universally regretted, Mr JOHN NAPIER, founder

Source: Caledonian Mercury. 'Died John Napier, Glasgow'. 5 August 1813

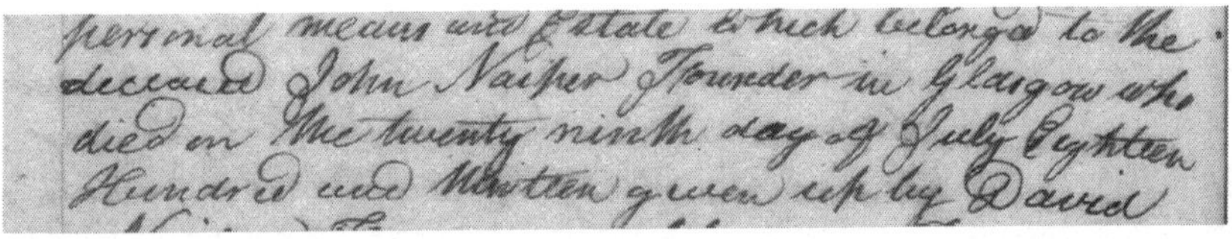
personal means and Estate which belonged to the
deceased John Naiper Founder in Glasgow who
died on the twenty ninth day of July Eighteen
Hundred and thirteen given up by David

Figure 19: Extract from John Naiper's inventory. **Transcript**: ... personal means and estate which belonged to the deceased John Naiper [sic] Founder in Glasgow who died on the twenty ninth day of July Eighteen Hundred and thirteen ...

Source: 'Naiper [Sic], John (Wills and Testaments, Glasgow Sheriff Court Inventories) Image 571 Last Image 583.', 1814. National Records of Scotland.

There is no evidence that James' emigration and John Napier's death are directly linked. The final papers of the sequestration are missing from the archives and we do not know how it ended. There is no record of an offer of composition to the creditors advertised in the *Edinburgh Gazette*. We therefore assume that all James' property and assets were seized from him apart from necessary apparel and bedding for the Finlaysons and James' work tools. He took tools and models with him to Russia. We speculate that the sequestration was resolved in such a way as to allow James to leave the country.

NOTES

1 Court of Session records. James Finlayson v Incorporation of Wrights of Glasgow' (1805). Court of Session: Bill Chamber Processes, Old Series (1670-1852). ©Crown copyright. National Records of Scotland, CS271/59373, with permission from National Records of Scotland.

2 Court of Session: Unextracted processes, 1st arrangement, Potts office (1669-1862). CS237/G/7/35. ©Crown copyright. National Records of Scotland, with permission from National Records of Scotland.

3 Watson, T. (1894) Kirkintilloch: Town and parish. Glasgow: John Smith and Sons. pp. 333-334.

4 Halkerston, P. (1819) A compendium or general abridgement, of the faculty collection of decisions of the Lords of Council and Session, from February 4, 1752 to the session of 1817. p. 84.

5 Statutes, Great Britain (1794) The Statutes at Large: Part 1, From 32nd to 33rd Year of the Reign of King George III. Edited by D. Pickering. J. Bentham (The Statutes at Large: From the Magna Charta, to the End of the Eleventh Parliament of Great Britain, Anno 1761 [continued to 1807]).

6 The Gazette (no date). Gazette Firsts: The history of The Gazette and insolvency notices. http://www.thegazette.co.uk/insolvency/content/103906 : accessed: 4 June 2023).

7 Bell, G. J. (1810) Commentaries on the laws of Scotland, and on the principles of mercantile jurisprudence, considered in relation to bankruptcy; competitions of creditors; and imprisonment for debt ... 2nd edn. Edinburgh: Archibald Constable & Company. pp. 309–91.

8 Wood, A. (no date). The historical treatment and perception of bankrupts. The Gazette. http://www.thegazette.co.uk/all-notices/content/100723 : accessed: 24 May 2023.

9 Vause, E. (2014) The business of reputations: Secrecy, shame, and social standing in nineteenth-century French debtors' and creditors' newspapers. Journal of Social History, 48(1). pp. 47–71. p. 48.

10 Crawford, K. (2013) The law and economics of orderly and effective insolvency. PhD thesis. University of Nottingham. pp. 184–85.

11 Robertson, A. J. (1963) The growth of the cotton industry and Scottish economic development, 1780-1835. M.A Thesis. University of Glasgow.

12 Robertson, A. J. (1963); Cooke, A. (2010) The rise and fall of the Scottish Cotton industry, 1778-1914: 'The secret spring'. Manchester: Manchester University Press.

13 Scots phrase meaning all and whole.

14 Scots phrase right or facility of exit or egress.

15 Appurtenances.

16 A term corresponding to the English 'lease'.

17 In Scottish law. A surety; a bondsman.

18 Scottish measure: 1 fall = 6.1766 yards.

19 Bell, G. J. (1810).

20 Court of Session records. Scotland. (1807) James Finlayson, Glasgow. Unextracted processes, 1st arrangement, Innes-Durie office 1669-1837. CS234/SEQNS/F/1/22, with permission of National Records of Scotland. ©Crown copyright. National Records of Scotland.

21 Court of Session records. Scotland. (1807).

22 MeasuringWorth (2024) 'Five Ways to Compute the Relative Value of a UK Pound Amount, 1270 to Present'. http://www.measuringworth. com/ukcompare/ : accessed: 2 May 2023.

23 MeasuringWorth (2024).

24 Court of Session records. Scotland. (1807) 'James Finlayson, Glasgow'. Court of Session records. Scotland. (1807).

25 A 'roup' is the Scottish term for a sale by auction.

26 Napier, D. D. (1912) David Napier, engineer, 1790-1869: [and] an autobiographical sketch, with notes. Glasgow: J. Maclehose.

27 High Court of Justiciary records. Scotland. (1809). Trial Papers of Thomas Stewart, Journeyman Wright in Glasgow, and Robert Wright, Journeyman Weaver in Glasgow, Both Presently Prisoners in the Tolbooth of Glasgow, for the Crimes of Housebreaking and Theft. West Circuit, Glasgow. National Records of Scotland. Used with permission of National Records of Scotland. ©Crown copyright. National Records of Scotland.

28 Devine, T. M. (2005) The modern economy: Scotland and the Act of Union. In: The transformation of Scotland: The economy since 1700. Edinburgh: Edinburgh University Press. pp. 13–33.

29 Sasines. Scotland. Second Extract June 1810 Supp 18636. Second Extract, Regtd Contract of Ground & Annual between the Principal & Professors of Glasgow College and James Finlayson & John Napier. Original volume held in Glasgow City Archives. With permission from Glasgow City Archives.

30 Stewart, W. J, (2001) 'Ground Annual.' In: Collins Dictionary of Law. 2nd edition. London: PerfectBound. p. 186 Available at: legal-dictionary.thefreedictionary.com/ground+annual : accessed: 20 June 2023).

31 Sasines. Scotland. 14 May 1810. Glasgow College to Finlayson, James. Register of Sasines within Burgh Book 7, Second extract B10/4/7, Folio CLXV (165). Original volume held in Glasgow City Archives, Mitchell Library, with permission from Glasgow City Archives.

32 Sasines. Scotland. 7 February 1811. Finlayson, James and Napier, John. Register of Sasines within Burgh Book 7 ' B10/4/7. Folio CLXIV. Original volume held in Glasgow City Archives, Mitchell Library, with permission from Glasgow City Archives.

33 Sasines. Scotland. 7 February 1811. Finlayson, James to Napier, John. Register of Sasines within Burgh Book 7 ' B10/4/7. Folio CLXX. Original volume held in Glasgow City Archives, Mitchell Library, with permission from Glasgow City Archives.

34 Napier, D. D. (1912) David Napier, engineer, 1790-1869.

35 Watson, N. (no date) Maritime science and technology: Changing our world. Lloyd's Register Foundation.

36 Court of Session records. Scotland. (1813) James Finlayson, hosier and woollen draper, Glasgow. Unextracted Processes, 1st Arrangement, Inglis Office 1657-1863. CS234/SEQNS/F/1/22, with permission of National Records of Scotland. ©Crown copyright. National Records of Scotland.

37 Poinding means seizing

38 Testamentary records. Scotland. 3 May 1814. NAIPER [Sic], John. Inventory and settlement, Glasgow Sheriff Court Inventories. SC36/48/8. http://www.scotlandspeople.gov.uk : accessed 20 June 2023, with permission of National Records of Scotland. ©Crown copyright. National Records of Scotland.

– CHAPTER SIX –

From the Clyde to the Neva

Linking East and West – the Forth and Clyde Canal

James Finlayson left Glasgow in 1813 for St Petersburg in Russia to take up a job, to be followed a year later by Margaret. The start of their separate journeys might have been greatly eased by the Forth and Clyde Canal, which opened in 1790. Its entrance on the Clyde is about 3 miles (5km) downstream from Clydebank at Bowling. By linking the Clyde to the Firth of Forth at Grangemouth, this canal transformed the movement of goods and people across Scotland and beyond to Europe and America. It provided a safe and direct passage for seagoing vessels of the time between the Clyde and the Forth where the Lowlands of Scotland are at their narrowest. The 35-mile (56km) route of the canal roughly follows that of the Roman Antonine Wall and is connected to the Forth by a short stretch of the River Carron near Grangemouth, Stirlingshire. Before this canal was built bulky cargoes had to go by the long and hazardous sea route between the east and west coasts of Scotland; from the Clyde around the Mull of Kintyre out into the Atlantic and then north through the Minches, past the Hebrides, to round Cape Wrath and into the Pentland Firth between the mainland and the Orkney Islands, then southerly to the east coast ports. This long sea route was through treacherous waters and delays by contrary winds were common, with a risk of being blown onshore and wrecked. The Forth and Clyde Canal therefore provided much greater certainty for shippers, and also offered a direct link to the City of Glasgow by a branch at Maryhill, terminating in a basin at Port Dundas by Cowcaddens on the north side of the city just over a mile (1.8km) north of Glasgow Cross (55°51'24'N, 4°14'38'W) where the High Street crosses between Trongate and Gallowgate. This branch of the Canal facilitated the transport of food and farm produce into the rapidly growing city and adjacent parts of Lanarkshire, ensuring that Glasgow's industries, commerce and prosperity grew apace, as did its population. The business of James Finlayson and John Napier in Havannah Street was about 1.25m (2km) to the South East of this Glasgow terminus of the canal at Port Dundas. Plate 3 shows the route map of the canal.

We have not discovered which ship James took to St Petersburg. However, we found that he left Glasgow in July 1813, as there is a window from his unavailability at his premises (9 July 1813) and his arrival at Kronstadt (21 August 1813. The most likely ship that James left Scotland on is the ship *Fame* with Master Munn, starting off from Glasgow, possibly Port Dundas or Greenock. She sailed from Grangemouth on 12 July 1813, carrying cotton yarn.

In the Roads.

SAILINGS.
... July 12. Lilly Campbell, Greenock, do. Sugar, –
Fame, Munn, Glasgow, St. Petersburg, cotton yarn.
Wind Southerly.   ALEX. LAIRD

[Transcript excerpt *Glasgow Courier*, Thursday 15 July 2013]

It is likely the ship joined a convoy at Leith Roads but there is no mention of it in the *Caledonian Mercury* or *Glasgow Courier*. However, there is mention of a convoy for Gottenburgh guided by the gun-brig, *Furious*, sailing from Leith Roads on 15 July.

> The *Griffin* sloop of war arrived in Leith Roads, on Thursday, from the Downs; likewise the *Kangaroo* sloop of war, from the southward. – Same day, the *Furious* gun-brig sailed from the Roads, with a convoy for Gottenburgh; likewise the *Maria* tender, with a convoy to the southward.
>
> [Transcript *Caledonian Mercury* – Saturday 17 July 1813 p. 3 of 4 from britishnewspapersarchive]

As a result of the Napoleonic War, British merchant ships were herded together and given the protection of naval frigates and brigs to their destinations.[1] The Baltic trade sailed from Britain from four ports: the Nore (Yarmouth, Norfolk), the Humber, Leith and Long Hope Sound (the *rendevous* in the Orkneys for Baltic traders from the north-west ports).[2]

> The depth of water in the harbour of Leith is stated at only sixteen feet at spring-tides, and ten feet at neap-tides; so that very large vessels cannot enter the port; but at a mile from the mouth of the harbour there is excellent anchorage in what is called Leith Roads.[3]

His bankruptcies were, no doubt, what drove James to seek work outside UK and these are explored further in this narrative. It was a critical time for skilled artisans to try to leave the UK, as well as there being bans on the export of the machinery their skills produced. Permission for a skilled artisan to emigrate had to be obtained from the Board of Trade, with policing of the ports and coasts being in the hands of the Commissioners of Customs, although there were many other agencies involved as well, resulting in confusion and opportunities for evasion. The prolonged war with France (1793–1815) made critical the loss of skilled workers due to emigration from the UK. From the early 1800s, there seems to have been attempts at industrial espionage, such as when Charles Baird, acting for Charles Gascoigne in Russia, sought to obtain information and machinery from Manchester and Glasgow. Maybe the further away from the major English ports, such as London, Liverpool and Bristol, the easier it was to slip away unnoticed. Although James must have known of the emigration restrictions, these may have been the least of his worries.[4]

We were unable to discover where Margaret was staying during the year following James' departure until she left. Perhaps it was with her brother in Glasgow. She travelled with a servant on the ship *Favourite* whose master was Strong. *Favourite* was escorted by the gun-brig *Ernest* from Leith Roads on 21 June 1814.

EDINBURGH NEWS CONTINUED.

The *Ernest* gun-brig sailed from Leith Roads on Tuesday evening, With the following vessels under convoy to Elsineur viz. —
Providence, Marshal; Favourite, Strong; Cestes, Codling; Lovely Ann, Crombie; Olive, Ogilvy, Jenny, Hunter, and Harmony, McDonald for St Petersburg. — Alariner, Elsdon, Stockholm; Venus Skinner for Gothenburg; Briton, Hog,

and Mary, Greenson for Copenhagen.
Another convoy will sail for the same place,
on the 5th of July.

[Transcript *Caledonian Mercury* – Saturday 25 June 1814
p 4 of 4 from Newspapers.com]

It is likely that Margaret travelled from Glasgow to Leith Roads using the Forth Clyde Canal. She might have made use of the passenger service that had added an additional boat on 21 June 1813 as shown in the advertisement in the *Glasgow Courier*.

THE GREAT CANAL PASSAGE BOAT

On and after Monday the 21st of June current
an ADDITIONAL BOAT will DEPART from
PORT-DUNDAS, and one from Lock 16,
near Falkirk, and continue every lawful day
till notice be given.

The Hours of Starting will then be,

From Port-Dundas, at 8 o'clock morning, 11 o'clock forenoon, 4 o'clock afternoon } Each Beat will perform the passage in five hours and a half

From Lock No. 16 at 5 o'clock morning,
10 o'clock forenoon,
2 o'clock afternoon

As the Falkirk Clocks are generally behind Glasgow,
the Boats will start from No. 16 one quarter of an
hour earlier, by the Falkirk Clock.

The Fares are as usual Four Shillings in the best
Cabin, and Two Shillings in the Steerage, for the
whole distance of twenty-five miles intermediates as
in the Way Bills. No charge for children under a year
old, from one to ten pay Half Fare. The Masters have
a discretionary power to make allowance to large
families, and particularly to poor persons.

The COACH from STIRLING continues to run to
Castlecarry, as usual; the Boat that takes the Passengers for that Coach will leave Port-Dundas
at eleven o'clock.

As the above arrangement of time is particularly
favourable for Coaches from Edinburgh to the Boats
at Lock No. 16, any respectable persons wishing to
be concerned by such an undertaking, will meet with
liberal encouragement from the Canal Company.

H. BAIRD.
Kelvinhead, by Kilsyth, June 15, 1813

[Transcript 17 June 1813 *Glasgow Courier*]

Alternatively, she might have boarded the *Favourite* at
Greenock or Port Dundas and travelled sea-to-sea through
the canal. We found a tantalising notice in the newspapers
about the re-opening of the canal following a short closure
of the sea-to-sea route, 15 June to circa 28 July 1814, as two
locks were damaged. However, there was no announcement
of the nature of the damage, or the closure or actual date of
opening. This would have occurred around the time Margaret left Glasgow.

We are glad to understand from authority that the rebuilding of the two Locks on the Forth and Clyde Navigation is nearly completed, and that the navigation will be again opened in a few days, for vessels to pass sea to sea. Much credit is due to the canal overseers and workmen, for the great dispatch used by them in the execution of the work, the navigation having only been stopped since 15th curt.[5]

[Transcript, *Glasgow Courier* Tuesday 28 June 1814]

An advertisement for the *Phoebe* was printed on 12 July 1814 in the *Glasgow Courier* She sailed on 20 July 1814. Some of Margaret's goods travelled unaccompanied on *Phoebe*, Captain Blair, including two places of tea ware with the rest of the porcelain and faience utensils and household utensils.

For St. Petersburgh.

THE Sloop *PHOEBE*, Capt. BLAIR, is loading at *Port Dundas,* and having three-fourths of her cargo engaged, she will sail in time to join the Convoy from Leith on the 20th inst. This vessel has good accommodation for passengers.

For freight or passage, apply to the Master, on board; or to JOHN MACDOUGALL & CO. Glasgow, 12th July 1814

Transcript *Glasgow Courier* 12 July 1814

The *Cheerly* gun brig sailed on Wednesday, with the
following vessels under convoy, for Elsineur, viz. —
Tees, Williams; Hope, Canning.; Hero, Dunn;
Phoebe, Blair; British Tar, —; John Easdale,
Phillips; Venus. Ferrier; Happy Return, Elder; Aid,
Caithness; Alert, Ure: and Nancy, Steven, for St
Petersburgh.— Amity, Crozier, for Bubeck. Riga
Merchant, Marrington, and Mariner, Stronach, for
Gottenburgh.—Providence, Meland, for Riga. –
Betsey, Hutchinson, for Stockholm,
and Margaret, Johns, for the Baltic.

[Transcript *The Caledonian Mercury*, Sat, Jul 23, 1814 ·
Page 4 from Newspapers.com]

How long did it take to sail across the Northern seas to the Baltic?

The Caird library at the Royal Museums of Greenwich advise
that the length of the journey from Leith to St Petersburg
would vary according to the vagaries of the weather; the
size of the ship; the size and number of sails the ship had;
the time of year it sailed; its hull shape, and whether the ship
was in heavy cargo, light cargo or a warship. Sailing times
would also depend on techniques and methods of navigation,
instruments and personal knowledge of ship captains. The
map from George III's collection of Northern Europe (Plate
4), dated 1800, shows the scale of the journey the Finlaysons
made. At the time Luffman drew the map, Finland was part of
Sweden, and remained so until the Finnish War of 1809, after
which Finland became an autonomous part of the Russian
Empire as the Grand Duchy of Finland.

According to Dmitry Fedosov,[6] the links between Scots
and Russians go back to the Middle-Ages and continue to

the present. James was not the first Scot to emigrate to Russia and we do not know what links he had with Scots in Russia. We wonder what James was thinking as he boarded the ship taking him from Glasgow to St Petersburg. Was he angry, ashamed, or frightened to venture into the unknown leaving behind a history of business failure? There is a missing piece of information linked to how he was recruited and funded in this venture. The price of the tickets varied between £10.12.15 to £30 according to Alex Rogerson in his letter to his brother, written on his arrival at St Petersburg dated 17 July 1813.

> I arrived here on the 14th July (new Style), after a
> tedious passage of six weeks from Leith we not having
> a fair wind during the Passage but for three days. We
> paid a most extravagant passage money out here viz
> £30 each being the highest out here this year and ever
> known to be paid. £10.12.15 are commonly paid 15
> is thought to be very high and we living upon Salt
> Beef all the passage only two days we had fresh meat
> but all that is of no consequence now, we having got
> safe here, as we could do no better in the meantime;
> or else have remained in Edinburgh ill the next
> Convoy which would have detained us to [sic] long.
> And we not knowing the usual passage money to St
> Petersburgh[7]

We can calculate that Margaret's journey from Leith Roads was shorter than Rogerson's and took two weeks and six days. Rayford Ramble claimed his passage from the Thames to Kronstadt in 1819 in a trading sailing vessel took twelve days including a stop at Elsineur to view Shakespeare's setting for Hamlet.[8] Sir Alexander Wilson was the manager for the Tsarist administration of manufactories at Alexandrovsk and Kolpino that James joined. Did he fund Finlayson's passage? Another alternative is that a family member or friend paid. James would not have been left sufficient money after the sequestration unless he was left with a residue having settled his debts.

However it was arranged, 1813 was a dangerous time to travel to the Baltic. Quite apart from the dangers of sea travel, it was during the time of the Napoleonic war. The Gunboat War (1807–1814) was a naval conflict between Denmark and Norway against the British fleets during the Napoleonic wars. Between 1803 and 1815, Britain was at war with ten countries. In order to maintain its hegemony of the seas, Britain relied on convoys that were protected by warships.[9]

The Baltic Sea is one of the enclosed seas that surround Europe on three sides. Three narrow Danish Straits run through the Danish Islands: the Sound between Sjaelland and the Swedish mainland of Skåne; the Great Belt between Sjaelland and Fyn; and the Little Belt between Fyn and the Jutland peninsula.[10] The route from Leith Roads to Kronstadt was under convoy in 1813 and 1814.[11] The merchantmen rendezvoused in Vinga Sound, near Gothenburg where they met up with the Baltic fleet which took over the guard. From there, they had a choice of one or other of the two narrow entrances to the Baltic Sea – the Sound or the Great Belt. The Great Belt is 37 miles (60km) long and 10–20 miles (16–32km) wide. Figure 20 shows the approaches to the Southern Baltic

This was the most hazardous part of the voyage as British merchantmen were harried by Danish gunboats.

> The navigation was intricate, the ships having to pick their way amongst shoals from which the buoys and markers were removed by the Danes. The difficulties were increased in the Belt by currents, strong enough to make a ship unmanageable. Apart from these natural risks the conditions favoured the Danish raiders.[12]

Figure 20: The southern Baltic and its approaches (showing modern coastline)

Source: Barney, John. North Sea and Baltic Convoy 1793–1814: As Experienced by Merchant Masters Employed by Michael Henley & Son. The Mariner's Mirror 95, no. 4 (2009) p.431. © Thom Richardson, courtesy of the Society for Nautical Research. By permission of Oxford University Press.

In this strait, a dedicated shuttle service provided cover for the merchant ships.

> The Baltic, despite the best efforts of the Danes, actually proved between 1808 and 1813 to be the largest open breach in Napoleon's Continental System. The preferred route for British convoys became the Belt, which took five to six days to traverse, but it offered fewer opportunities for Danish gunboats to ambush convoys and was also deep enough throughout to allow the British to utilize their far more powerful line of battle ships to protect the convoys.[13]

Arrival

When James Finlayson reached St Petersburg in the summer of 1813, like all travellers arriving by way of the Baltic Sea and the Gulf of Finland, he first had the obligatory stopover at Kronstadt on the Island of Kotlin, an immigration centre and customs post of its time. Kotlin Island, in the Gulf of Finland, is 19 miles (30km) from St Petersburg. The fortress of Kronstadt was established in 1703/4 by Peter the Great after wresting the island from Sweden. Especially during the reign of Catherine the Great, a fortified Kronstadt became a centre of commerce, as well as St. Petersburg, attracting Dutch, German and British merchants. Many of the latter were Scots, who became agents or 'factors'.

Once passengers and cargo were cleared for St. Petersburg, ships had to use a navigable channel from Kronstadt to the city through shallow waters to one of the many outlets of the River Neva. Twentieth century (1978–2011) infrastructure changed all this, notably the Saint Petersburg Flood Prevention Facility, which by a 25.4km (15.8miles) series of embankments, bridges and floodgates, protects St. Petersburg from storm surges of up to 5m (16ft.), separating the Gulf of Finland from the Neva bay and delta. Shipping can use two sea-gates, closeable when a surge threatens, which between Kotlin Island and the south shore incorporate a 1.2km underwater road tunnel linked to a six-lane highway on top of the embankments, forming part of the Saint Petersburg Ring Road. The map illustrated in Plate 5 was published circa 1900, well after the Finlaysons had left Russia. However, it clearly shows the relative positions of Kronstadt, St. Petersburg, Okta (where the Wheelers lived) and Alexandrovsk (Alexandrovs kaia).

On 31 December 1810, Tsar Alexander I opened Russian ports to neutral vessels. This would have eased the immigration through Kronstadt into St Petersburg in 1813 and 1814.

In the autumn of 1812, Napoleon's 600,000-strong Grande Armée entered Russia in a disastrous campaign that led ultimately to Napoleon's defeat. When James emigrated to Russia in the summer of 1813, the aftershocks of Alexander's campaign of retreat from Moscow and the decimation of Napoleon's army would have been felt in St Petersburg. It is estimated that Napoleon lost approximately 41,000 troops to combat and approximately 200,000 to disease.[14] To understand the vicarious trauma experienced by Russians, consider the findings of the Siaures Miestelis excavation in Vilnius, Lithuania, where archaeologists discovered more than 1,000 skeletons of Napoleon's soldiers in a mass grave:

> At first, the people of Vilnius cremated the thousands of bodies piling up all over the city, but eventually the smoke and smell of burning flesh became overwhelming, and they began burying them in mass graves dug by Napoleon's surviving soldiers. Most of those in the grave just excavated were between 15 and 20 years old ...[15]

Saint Petersburg

Saint Petersburg is now a federal city, the second most populous in Russia, after Moscow. Administratively it is divided into 18 districts (rayony), which are in turn divided into municipal towns or settlements (okruga). Kronstadt has already been referred to and is within Kronshtadtsky district. Outside the central area of the city, at least two districts are also connected with this narrative, Kolpinsky, which includes the town of Kolpino, and Pushkinsky, which includes the settlement of Alexandrovskaya (Alexandrovsk).

British Artisans in St Petersburg and the transfer of British technology

St Petersburg became a major industrial centre, starting when Peter the Great gathered artisans from all parts of Russia and also from overseas with many blacksmiths, gun and cannon yards, an arms factory and other metal-working enterprises. During the second half of the eighteenth and the first half of the nineteenth century, St Petersburg was the most important centre of mechanical engineering in Russia and the largest region of the textile industry. Machine production was first introduced in paper spinning on imported cotton in the St. Petersburg region. The migration of artisans from Britain to St Petersburg was encouraged in order to catch up on industrialisation and overcome backwardness in economic development.[16] One example of this transference of British technology through employment was William Cockerill, who made jennies in Lancashire. He went to St Petersburg in 1794 to work for Catherine the Great.[17] Charles Gascoigne was another artisan to migrate to Russia. In his earlier career, he had become in 1765 the principal partner in the Carron

Company (1759–1982), an ironworks on the River Carron, near Falkirk. Gascoigne is credited with overcoming the Ironwork's quality and reliability problems and also producing the 'Carronade', a short-barrelled cannon for the British Royal Navy. In the process, however, Gascoigne became bankrupt and in 1786 he went to Russia to undertake ironworks there, gathering around him a number of the Carron Company's former workers and the Wilsons (James and Alexander). Gascoigne remained in Russia, being awarded many honours, and died in Kolpino in July 1806.

Engineer-General Alexander Wilson – director at Kolpino and Alexandrovsk

Alexander Wilson's reputation as an engineer is considerable. He was the eldest son of James Wilson and was born on 27 February 1776 in Edinburgh, subsequently attending the High School in the Canongate. However, in 1784 his education was interrupted as the family emigrated to Russia, where his father had taken up employment supervising ironwork installation in the Palace of Tsarskoye Selo. Alexander's education resumed during family relocations to other places in Tsarist Russia where his father was employed as a supervising smith.

As well as having a broadly based education, Alexander also tackled technical subjects including draughtsmanship and in 1800 was engaged as interpreter and secretary to Charles Gascoigne, who was then head of many imperial mechanical works. In 1803, James Wilson and family relocated to Kolpino, which became the Wilson family home. In 1806, on the death of Charles Gascoigne, Alexander Wilson succeeded him as director of the works at Alexandrovsk and Kolpino, having been his assistant from 1803.

Alexander Wilson during his long working life also gained many awards and honours, including that of Engineer-General, having progressed through the lower grades of the Corps of Mines and transferring to the Engineering and Building Department of the Tsarist Admiralty. He became a Member of the Institution of Civil Engineers (ICE), corresponding with many notable engineers of the time, visiting the UK ten times to keep abreast of new developments. He advised on many other projects throughout Russia. Alexander Wilson never married, but took a keen interest in his many nephews and nieces and their offspring who remained in Russia.

Kolpino

Kolpino is on the river Izhora, a major tributary of the Neva, about 26km (16 miles) southeast of Saint Petersburg itself. Founded around 1722, by the 1760s Kolpino had become a centre for the production of chains and other ironwork for the Russian Navy and by the 1780s British expertise in iron smelting and casting was being employed there.[18] The ICE obituary sets out Alexander Wilson's achievements at Kolpino, notably the reconstruction of existing sluices and water-wheels and new installations, the introduction of steam power as an auxiliary to water-power, the building of steamships, the town planning of Kolpino, including schools, hospital and workers housing and the expansion of industrial facilities. In correspondence and papers the latter are often referred to as the 'Izhora' plants or factories.[19]

By the time Wilson died, Kolpino had grown to a small town of about 8,000 inhabitants, its population in 1897 being stated as 8,076, growing to 81,000 by 1972 and 138,000 by 2022/23. During the 1941–44 siege of Leningrad in WW2, Kolpino was in the front line and suffered much damage and destruction from bombardment and fighting. As a consequence by January 1945 the population had dropped to around 7,000, below the nineteenth century figure. However, it rapidly recovered, with a large postwar programme of reconstruction. Due to WW2 and its aftermath, the Wilson family home and his grave in Kolpino were lost.

Alexandrovsk Zavod (Manufactory)[20]

Even before the arrival of James Finlayson at Alexandrovsk, a cloth manufactory there had for some time been in the forefront of the mechanization of cotton textile production in Russia. Under Wilson's direction, Alexandrovsk grew from a small village to a small town. British technicians were invited to work at the Alexandrovsk Manufactory and to transfer their skills. When in August 1813 James Finlayson arrived at Kronstadt, it was at a very active period in its development.

The first cotton factory in Russia was the Alexander State Treasury Manufactory near St. Petersburg on the Shlisselburg tract.

In 1797, with the assistance of the government, the Polish abbot Mikhail Ossovsky founded a mechanical paper spinning near St. Petersburg, which was turned two years later (after Ossovsky's death) into the state-owned Alexandrovsky manufactory, which was at the St. Petersburg orphanage under the direct supervision of Paul I's wife, Maria Fedorovna. As far as we know, this is the earliest and, moreover, practically-tangible result of the influence of the industrial revolution in England on the technical basis of Russian industry at that time, which allows us to consider the boundary – the end of the eighteenth – the beginning of the nineteenth century. – the starting date in the history of the Russian machine industry.[21]

The Alexandrovsk Manufactory attracted visitors from overseas, who marvelled at and published descriptions of the factory, including: John Quincy Adams on 7 April 1810;[22] a Gentleman from Perth, Scotland on 21 September 1815;[23] William Allen on 9 January 1819;[24] Capt. George Matthew Jones on 21 October 1822;[25] and Augustus Bozzi Granville on 28 October–12 December 1827.[26] It is Wilson who escorted eminent visitors around the Alexandrovsk manufactory.

The *Perthshire Courier* of Thursday 19 December 1816 has a report of a visit on 21 September 1815 of a party from Perth to 'the Cotton and Linen Spinning manufactories at Alexandreoffsky, about 12 versts *(13km, 8 miles)* from St Petersburgh, on the banks of the River Neva'. This report refers to the machinery as being driven by four steam engines from Murray and Fenton of Leeds (Fenton Murray and Co 1795–1844). It also refers to the cotton spinning department and notes that a new mill is being erected for spinning flax. It describes in some detail how labour is mostly provided by boys and girls from the adjacent orphanage, supervised by its patroness Empress Maria Feodorovna (1759–1828), the second wife of Emperor Paul I. The orphanage at Alexandrovsk was intended to be a place where children from the Imperial Foundling Hospital of Saint Petersburg could live and be educated and employed. It and other charities came under the control of the Office of the Institutions of Empress Maria, founded by her in 1796. It is interesting that no mention is made in the article of James Finlayson, a fellow Scot. In 1816, James would have been working at Alexandrovsk.

It seems most likely that the drive to mechanise thread spinning and allied activities, as well as weaving, arose earlier in the eighteenth century from the demand for linen sailcloth for ships' sails from the Admiralty for the Russian Imperial Navy. A 1934 paper by K. A. Zeitlin refers to a mechanical cotton mill being founded in 1797 and taken over in 1799 as the State Alexandrovsk Manufactory, associated with the Foundling Hospital in Saint Petersburg.[27] The same paper compares the productivity of mechanising carding and spinning with earlier manual operations at Alexandrovsk and also refers to the installation of water-power in 1801 at the Manufactory.

The UK Institution of Civil Engineers' obituary of Alexander Wilson describes his activities at Alexandrovsk, including building an orphanage:

> ... an immense institution for 800 boys and girls, provided with a library, schools, washhouses etc at that time novelties in Russia ... constructed extensive mills, containing all the improvements known at that time. The large flax mill at Alexandrovsk supplied sailcloth for all the Russian navy ... Cotton mills, plain and figured weaving looms and a manufactory for playing cards.[28]

James' employment at Alexandrovsk

Amazingly, correspondence from Alexander Wilson and Imperial officials has survived in the Russian State Historic Archive (RGIA) despite the battles of World War 2. When in August 1813 James Finlayson arrived at Kronstadt, Alexander Wilson managed James' entry through immigration and customs. Wilson requested a passport for James and he intended for James to work at Alexandrovsk, noting that he had his own establishment in Glasgow for the preparation of hosiery woollen yarn by means of machines, and was a man who knew everything that relates to the arrangement of spinning machines. This meant that he could be useful for the manufactory. An added advantage was that he brought some models with him and the tools necessary for his work.[29] It is not clear whether Wilson arranged and funded the passage. From the letter, we can see that James brought tools, models and clothes and so it would seem that he was able to retain his tools and models following the sequestration, as well as clothing.

The passport was arranged through a series of letters and Alexander Wilson received it on 30 August 1813. In October 1813, Wilson wrote outlining the contractual terms for James' employment at Alexandrovsk (translated by Anton Pilvinskii for us).

> I have the honour to reply to the honourable letter from Your Excellency about the mechanic Finlayson, which I have received this day, that the salary of five hundred pounds sterling a year will amount to 7,500 rubles at the current rate, and 22,500 rubles in three years. He also requires 2,400 pounds in 3 years. (sterling) or 36,000 rubles – for this amount they can be more or less for our money, depending on how the rate goes down or up. The promised benefit to them for this payment is that he: 1) Will bring cotton-spinning machines to the position in which the best English machines are now. 2) Will make all the machines needed for spinning fine wool, suitable for hosiery and flannel; also undertakes to establish the preparation of rough cloth and carpets. 3) Undertakes to arrange also a stocking and many different hosiery goods made of wool and 4) undertakes to recruit the necessary workers. On the one hand, I find it very useful to have a special master to bring the cotton spinning machines into proper working order: for, although some of the cards have been altered, there are still drawing frames and the stretching of the frames of the new device to be prepared and I must take up the gradual arrangement

of the spinning machines again and the alteration of
various parts old ones – it will be enough for Master
Smith to do the linen part, and if he is distracted
with cotton machines, then the success of his main
occupation will inevitably decrease. Spinning both
fine and coarse wool is not a small benefit: and as
Finlayson owns a factory himself and brought models
of various machine parts, I believe that the success
of his proposals is correct and can soon be proved in
practice. Hosiery and woollen goods will bring true
benefits, and if you start this business in such a way as
to weave woolen goods in the summer at the present
hosiery factory, and cotton and linen goods in winter,
then not a small part of the salary costs of this master
will return to the manufacture in a short time through
an increase in profit. For spinning wool, I would
suppose to start machines in a sufficient number only
for experience, following the example of those made
for flax – and as Finlayson says that for this, six cards
and 12 spinning machines are enough, which can be
driven by a steam engine in 6 horsepower known as
No. 4, which is now idle; then the expense of such
proof and experience will not extend beyond 60 or
70,000 – machines can always be profitably sold if
they are deemed unnecessary for the manufacture.
When Her High Imperial Majesty's permission to
accept Finlayson would follow, I suppose his salary
would be apportioned so that the cotton-spinning is
for one year's consumption, wool spinning experience
for another, and the hosiery factory for the third.
Finally, in reasoning the high salary of a mechanic
that is required, I dare to note that nowadays it is not
possible to get people who truly know from England
for a low fee: and, if you deliberately call people,
then in addition to the danger associated with calling
such people, the costs are high, both for the passage
of these people, and for rewarding the Commission
agent used. On Friday or Saturday this week, I expect

to have a meeting with Finlayson and if then a change
in proposals will follow, I will not hesitate to inform
Your Excellency – now I humbly ask you to bring
the above written to Her High Imperial Majesty's
information.'[30]

Before James, an earlier British expert, who left with his
family for Moscow, was William Sherwood, employed in
Alexandrovsk from 1800 to about 1809. Initially he was
engaged on the mechanical spinning of wool and later cotton,
but quality problems persisted with the latter. Although the
final contract for Finlayson is not in existence, this arrangement seems to follow the contract for the earlier Sherwood
contract, dated 5 July 1800. The contract is written in Russian
and English.

I the undersigned Sherwood a native of great Britain
do make this contract with the Board of Guardians
of the Imperial Founding house, by which I engage
myself to serve at the mechanical Spinning manufactory of Alexandrovsky on the following conditions.
Having had the direction in England of different
manufactures for spinning wool and perfectly
understanding how to arrange machines within
their art, I engage myself most willingly to discover
everything which is known to me on their respect,
and give advice to Mr. Edwards the mechanic, in
order that he may without the little difficulty put in
order all the manufactory machines for spinning wool
as well as all the preparations necessary for it. When
such wool machines are put in order, I engage myself
likewise to inform in the best manner possible how
to spin upon them and prepare wool for spinning,
as many apprentices as the principals will please to
entrust me with, and to show them all the best and
most advantageous methods of spinning upon them

out of Russian and foreign sheep wool the finest as
well as coarse thread for making cloth and if possible
all other worsted stuff. If they will please in time
to trust me also with the direction of the machines
for spinning cotton, I take it willingly upon myself,
promising to use all my capacities and knowledge for
improving and perfecting such machines as already
exit at the manufactory, and to contributing to the
bar spinning of cotton thread upon them I will do
all that lay in my power, and will give advice for
constructing and arranging machines for spinning
flax, similar to those which I have seen at the
manufactory, engage myself to be perfectly obedient
to my commanders, and to conform my conduct and
service to the established order at the manufactory.
I am to receive from the manufactory for my salary
1500 rubles for year, with a lodging consisting of 3
rooms from which will be taken from a kitchen I am
to have a wood and candles 3 pood. As soon as by
my endeavours wool spinning machines are perfectly
arranged, and a necessary number of apprentices are
instructed in spinning upon them, in a word, when
I bring this new art in Russia exactly to the same
perfection, to which it is brought in England and my
success shall be approved of by my commanders, I am
to receive for this my service as a sole recompense five
thousand roubles. What regards my care and trouble
about spinning cotton and flax, I promise to take this
upon myself merely from my zeal to render my service
to the Imperial Foundling house, therefore I do not
demand for it the least addition to my salary, hoping
however that, if am so fortunate, and agreeable my
good intentions I bring spinning of cotton to the best
order, and arrange upon machines the spinning of flax
I shall be rewarded in proportions to my service done
in this respect my reward will be that her Imperial
Majesty may think proper. All the above conditions

I promise to fulfil with all uprightness and Beatitude
– from this time July 1st 1800. I agree to serve for the
term of three years but my salary is due to me apart
from the contract from October 9th 1799 being the
time I made a verbal agreement with Mr. Edwards
in England and of my circumstances shall oblige to
quit service at the manufactory I am free to do it no
otherwise than by giving notice of my intentions
six months before. Wm Sherwood. This contract
was signed precisely by the hand of the Englishman
Sherwood 1800 July 5 days. Honorary Guardian
Prince Vyazemsky.[31]

Margaret's arrival in St Petersburg in 1814

Alexander Wilson informed Villamov that James' wife, Margaret, was travelling from England with a servant and would dock at the port of Kronstadt. She was aboard the *Favourite*, with the skipper James Strong. In ignorance, she brought with her tableware and teaware and Wilson requested a passport and dispensation for the teaware.[32] The registry describes the tableware and teaware as:

> 1 barrel under the sign IFXX1, in which one full table
> set of blue earthenware
> 2 full porcelain tea sets with gold borders
> 1 pair of carved crystal decanters
> 1 pair of the same salt shakers
> 2 porcelain cups for jam
> 1 basket for [wafers][33]

In another letter, mention is made of further tableware that travelled on the ship *Phoebe* under Captain Blair: two pieces of porcelain and faience and household utensils.[34] The letters make it clear that import of porcelain was forbidden. The trading system of Russia in 1801–1825 was closely related to the struggle between England and France and the policy of protectionism. In 1806, a customs law and a strictly protective customs tariff were published. Also, the import of porcelain was banned. This contributed to the emergence of porcelain factories in Russia. The war with France of 1806–1807, which ended with the Tilsit Peace and led to the accession of Russia to the Continental system, seriously affected Russia's customs policy. In 1808 the import of all goods produced in England and its colonies was prohibited. In 1810–1811 new customs tariff and regulation on Neutral Trade were published. All these prohibitive measures were in effect until 1816 and led to difficult economic conditions. Only in 1816 was a new customs tariff published and trade was liberalised.[35] Another question is: where did Margaret obtain such luxury goods? Presumably she acquired them after the sequestration of 1813, because otherwise they would have been seized. It is possible that they were a leaving present from Margaret's family. Nenadic explains the role of objects in providing tangible mementoes of special people and, as such, they were highly valued.[36]

In addition, the ship *Neva* carried a steam engine and parts for James Finlayson for delivery at Alexandrovsk as well as household baggage for Margaret.

The ship movements linked to correspondence about Margaret's arrival were as follows:

Favourite, Captain James Strong (carried Margaret and her servant plus tableware and teaware).

> 21 June 1814 sailed under convoy of *Ernest*, a gun brig for St Petersburg from Leith Roads[37]
>
> 10 July 1814 arrived St Petersburg from Glasgow[38]

Neva, **Captain James Adams** (carried steam engine and Margaret's personal belongings, unaccompanied).

16 June 1814 advertised for cargo and passengers to sail for St Petersburg[39]

4 July 1814 cleared from Hull for St Petersburg[40]

Phoebe, **Captain Blair** (carried tableware and teaware, unaccompanied).

12 July 1814 advertised for cargo at Port Dundas to sail from Leith[41]

20 July 1814 sailed under convoy of *Cheerly*, a gun brig, from Leith[42]

7 August 1814 arrived St Petersburg from Glasgow[43]

Although some previous histories claim that James Finlayson was employed at the Kolpino works rather than at Alexandovsk, for example in the 150th year history of the Finlayson Company in Finland, there is no evidence of any Kolpino employment.

> He was one of those attracted to the Russian Empire for the building up of a textile industry. For more than twenty years, he worked as a master machinist in the Kolpino workshops near what was then St Petersburg. It is said that during his stay in Kolpino he became personally acquainted with Tsar Alexander 1, whose deep religious interest he shared. James Finlayson was a Quaker.[44]

However, at this stage of his life, James was not a Quaker, although he attended silent prayer meetings. His relationship to the Tsar is also probably overplayed as others had closer ties, such as Alexander Wilson, Daniel Wheeler and John Paterson. Sir Alexander Wilson supervised both Kolpino and

Alexandrovsk and that could be how the inaccuracy occurred. Also, there is some evidence that Kolpino fabricated machinery for Alexandrovsk, which Captain Jones mentions in his travel diary when he describes a visit to Kolpenny [sic].

> They were also making a very large spinning-jenny for Alexandofski, and had lately finished that beautiful machine for running the teeth into leather for carding wool, which was invented by an American, and which has been so much admired and of so much utility in England, and indeed, is said to be the ne plus ultra of mechanism for the woollen trade.[45]

Whereabouts and weather

The River Neva

The Neva flows through St Petersburg and upstream towns and villages lie on a southerly curving 74km (46 mile) course from its start at the southern end of Lake Ladoga about 60km east of the city. It is the only river flowing from Lake Ladoga and is navigable throughout, now part of the Volga-Baltic Waterway and White Sea–Baltic Canal. The river has a fall of 4.27m from start to mouth and is usually ice-covered from early December to early April.

A number of tributaries flow into the Neva, including the Ochta and Izhora. In WW2, during the winters of 1941/2 and 1942/3, Lake Ladoga was vital in supplying the besieged city, the 'Road of Life' being a series of vehicle routes across the frozen lake, established and maintained under enemy fire. Neva Bay at the eastern end of the Gulf of Finland, when not affected by storm surges, has a modest tidal range of about 0.23m; this contrasts with Glasgow at Renfrew Tide Gauge on the Clyde about 2km downstream from the city centre, where the usual tidal range is between −0.27m and +5.79m above sea level.

The history of St. Petersburg is also the history of man-made interventions to the River Neva as it flows through the city. The earlier city areas are built on the delta of the Neva, with additional canals being formed for drainage and the excavated material placed on the low swampy ground to raise the level of the city. The low-lying city centre has been subjected to flooding many times throughout its history, triggered by wave surges in the Baltic Sea, amplified by winds and the shallowness of Neva Bay. The most disastrous floods occurred in 1777, 1824, 1924, 1955 and 1975, leading eventually to the flood prevention scheme referred to above.

The city

An earlier fortress at the mouth of the Neva was captured from the Swedes by Peter the Great in 1703 and he then established on Zayarchy (Hare) Island in the delta what became known as Peter and Paul Fortress, the first brick and stone building of the new city. As well as a garrison, from the mid 1700s the Fortress was a prison, mainly for political prisoners, until 1924 when it became a museum.

Peter the Great wished to expand Russia's trade with all of Europe and for that a better seaport was needed than Archangel in the far north on the White Sea, then closed to shipping during winter. Peter and Paul Fortress (59° 57′ 00′N, 30°19′01′E) is well south of this, Hare Island being at a similar latitude to Lerwick, the principal town of Shetland, north of the Scottish mainland and the Orkneys. Both places enjoy long summer twilight when for a time it does not get dark at night; the 'Simmer Dim' of Shetland, the 'White Nights' of St Petersburg.

From 1713 to 1918, except for 1728–30, St Petersburg was the capital of Russia and the Russian Empire. The city played an important part in the Russian Revolution of 1917 and from 1924 until 1991 was known as Leningrad. Within the bastions of Peter and Paul Fortress, Peter the Great established Peter and Paul Cathedral, which was the Russian Orthodox cathedral church of the city until 1859 when St Isaacs took on this role, currently fulfilled by Kazan Cathedral on Nevsky Prospect. Although a museum since 1924, religious services resumed at Peter and Paul Cathedral in 2000.

Across the Neva and slightly downstream is the Hermitage Museum complex of buildings, including the Winter Palace and what is now known as the Small Hermitage, the first stage of which was completed in 1766 as an extension on the east of the Winter Palace to house Catherine the Great's original collection. Established by Peter the Great, the Winter Palace, throughout many transformations and rebuilding, was the seat of Russian Imperial power and the official home of its sovereigns from 1732 until 1917, although some of the Tsars and their families chose not to reside there. During the October Revolution of 1917, the Winter Palace was shelled, stormed and looted and in 1924 was declared part of the Hermitage Museums. It was damaged by enemy action in WW2 and was carefully restored.

Further along the Embankment to the west of the Hermitage is the Admiralty, with on its landward side the Admiralty Gardens. From here three principal streets radiate, Nevsky Prospect, Gorokhovaya Street and Voznesensky Avenue. By the time of the Finlaysons' arrival in the early 1800s, many of the principal buildings and the inner city streetscape we see today had already been built or were nearing completion, together with some magnificent residences for the nobility. During the nineteenth and twentieth centuries the city continued to expand in size and prosperity, but not always continuously.

The city is the second most populous in Russia after Moscow. Population figures for Saint Petersburg for a range of years are shown in Table 13.

When the Finlaysons were in Saint Petersburg, the population at around 340,000 had already more than doubled from the early years of its foundation; by 1915, a century later, it was 2,314,500, almost seven times the 1815 figure. In WW2 the Siege of Leningrad, as the city was then called, reduced the 1940 population of 2,920,000 to 546,000 by 1944. The siege by the Axis Powers and ferocious Russian defence of the city lasted from September 1941 until January 1944, nearly 900 days; an estimated 800.000 of its people died in the city, mostly from starvation and disease during that time, but also from relentless enemy bombardment. Given this devastation, it is remarkable that so much of the Imperial archive is extant. Maybe another one million of its citizens were evacuated before and during the siege and many of these succumbed to bombardment, starvation, disease and the cold during long marches to remote places elsewhere in Russia. The population of the city was building up again by the end of WW2 in 1945 and by 1950 was approaching its pre-war numbers. The estimate of 5.395m in 2020 was slightly down from previous years due to the COVID pandemic.

Table 13: St Petersburg population 1765–1865

Year	1765	1790	1815	1840	1865
Population in thousands	150.3	218.2	340.0	472.8	539.1

Source: Data abstracted from Wikipedia, Demographics of Saint Petersburg.

St Petersburg climate

This is described as a humid continental climate with cool summers due to the moderating influence of Baltic Sea cyclones. Summers are therefore typically cool, humid and quite short, while winters are long and cold, but with relatively milder spells intervening. Historic record low temperatures for the coldest month, January, from 1743 to 2020 average at −5.9 °C and similarly historic record high temperatures for the same period for the hottest month, June, average at 35.9°C, a wide range. Saint Petersburg climate data is shown in Table 14 and Table 15.

St Petersburg is situated on the 60th parallel North along with the Shetland Isles of Scotland, Greenland, Anchorage, Alaska, Magadan, and Oslo, the capital of Norway. These places are famous for their long twilight or White Nights (St Petersburg) / Simmer Dim (Shetland) where it does not get dark at night from the end of May to mid-July. The Finlaysons would have enjoyed this counterbalance to the long dark nights of winter.

Evangelical community in St Petersburg

There was a thriving British community in St Petersburg made up of merchants, doctors, soldiers, clergy and other ranks of society. The richer of these settled along the English Embankment (Angliyskaya Naberezhnaya) or English Quay, a street along the left bank of the Bolshaya Neva River in Central St Petersburg. English and Scottish skilled artisans from the Midlands and Scotland joined the English merchant ranks in the early 1800s.[46]

Fedosov claims that the many Scots located in St Petersburg formed part of the English community. He explained that Scots in Russia were called 'anglichane' and co-existed with the 'English' community in St Petersburg because the minority was too small to be separate. The term English was used to designate Britons from all over the United Kingdom (*anglitsanie, angliiski* or *angliskaya*), 'collapsing distinctions between the Scots, Welsh, Irish, English and naturalized Britons into one all-embracive category.[47] Episcopalians and Presbyterians had to share a church.[48]

The church Fedosov refers to is the Anglican Church (house number, 56, of the English Embankment). It was known as the

Table 14: Air temperature for St Petersburg

Month	Absolute min. ºC	Average min. ºC	Average ºC	Average max. ºC	Absolute max. ºC
January	−35.9 (1883)	−7.2	−4.8	−2.5	8.7 (2007)
February	−35.2 (1956)	−7.6	−5.0	−2.4	10.2 (1989)
March	−29.9 (1883)	−4.0	−1.0	2.3	15.3 (2015)
April	−21.8 (1881)	1.7	5.2	9.5	25.3 (2000)
May	−6.6 (1885)	7.2	11.5	16.3	33 (2014)
June	0.1 (1930)	12.2	16.1	20.5	35.9 (2021)
July	4.9 (1968)	15.3	19.1	23.3	35.3 (2010)
August	1.3 (1966)	13.9	17.4	21.4	37.1 (2010)
September	−3.1 (1976)	9.4	12.4	16.9	30.4 (1992)
October	−12.9 (1920)	4.1	6.2	8.7	21.0 (1889)
November	−22.2 (1890)	−0.9	0.9	2.8	12.3 (1967)
December	−34.4 (1978)	−4.5	−2.5	−0.5	10.9 (2006)
Year	−35.9 (1883)				37.1 (2010)

Figures stated are 30-year long term averages for the years 1991 to 2020 from pogodaiklimat.ru

Table 15: Precipitation and sun hours for St Petersburg

Month	Precipitation (mm)	Max. snow depth (mm)	Days rain	Days snow	Sun hours
January	46	150	9	25	22
February	36	190	7	23	54
March	36	140	10	16	125
April	37	1	13	8	180
May	47	0	16	1	260
June	69	0	18	0.1	276
July	84	0	17	0	267
August	87	0	17	0	213
September	57	0	20	0.1	129
October	64	0	20	5	70
November	56	30	16	16	27
December	51	90	10	23	13
Year	670	190	173	117	1636

Figures stated are 30-year long term averages for the years 1981–2010 from pogodaiklimat.ru

Anglican Church of Jesus Christ (British), Factory Church, Embassy Church or English Church, and later as the English Church of St Mary & All Saints. It was the established church for English residents.

We could find little about the living circumstances for James and Margaret. It is likely that they were provided lodgings, based on the contract for William Sherwood.[49] However, as they were a married couple, the lodgings might have contained more than three rooms and a kitchen. The information in the public domain is to be found in memoirs of individuals in the Evangelical Christian Community of Congregational Missionaries and Quakers.

Tsar Alexander I's visit to England in 1814

From 6 to 27 June 1814 Tsar Alexander I, King of Prussia and Metternich & Blücher visited England.[50] This coincided with Margaret's departure from Glasgow for St Petersburg. Amongst many meetings with dignitaries, Alexander took time to meet with members of the Society of Friends:

> Yet attending a Quaker meeting and becoming acquainted with Quaker members of the British and Foreign Bible Society, in its country of origin, could only have strengthened the Tsar's interest in the Society's work. The Tsar had given his formal approval for the setting up of a branch of the Society in early 1813 in response to a request from his friend A. N. Golitsyn, but had not had any personal contact with its members or its work. Alexander met Allen and Grellet again in St Petersburg in 1819 and they prayed together. It was an emotional occasion; Grellet recorded that the Tsar was 'bathed in tears' and Allen commented that afterwards they were 'all three quite overcome, so that the Emperor hastened into another room'. Alexander gave the Society his full support and generous financial backing; by the end of 1816 the Society had published forty-three editions of the Bible in the Russian Empire in seventeen different languages or dialects ... It was ironic that probably the deepest impression left with Alexander from his visit to England was made not by the Prince Regent or the politicians whom he met, nor by the ladies and society in which he mixed, nor by the displays of naval might and commercial strength which were arranged especially to impress him, but by a group of uninfluential Quakers. It is also an interesting thought that while the diplomatic results of the visit were not decisive and the commercial results of only temporary significance, the work of the British and

Foreign Bible Society had an impact not only on
what a contemporary described as 'the grateful, pious
Alexander', but also on biblical knowledge and studies
in Russia up to the Revolution and beyond.[51]

The impact of Alexander's support of the Quakers and
British and Foreign Bible Society in St Petersburg was to have
a profound effect on the Finlaysons and this carried into their
future residence in Russia, Finland and Britain. Three men
stand out in these accounts: Reverend John Paterson, Reverend
William Swan and Daniel Wheeler.

Reverend John Paterson, Bible Society Pioneer, 1776–1855

Paterson was about the same age as Margaret. He was brought
up in the Burgher Secession tradition. As a student, Paterson
joined the Independent Church, attending Mr Dale's week-
night meetings in Glasgow.[52] We do not know if Margaret and
James were part of the congregation, but at least there would be
a common interest and topic of conversation between them. He
became a Congregational minister and missionary in Northern
Europe promoting the translation of bibles. He moved to St
Petersburg in 1812 and at the end of that year, a Ukase by Tsar
Alexander I approved the formation of the St Petersburg Bible
Society. The Tsar provided a building beside the Catherine
Canal (now Kanala Griboevova) for the Society's use.

Daniel Wheeler, British Quaker, missionary in Russia & the South Pacific 1771–1840

Tsar Alexander I hired a British Quaker agriculturist to help
him reclaim the marshes near St Petersburg. Daniel volunteered
and in June 1817 he made an exploratory visit. He settled first

at Ochta, on the banks of the Neva, and began reclaiming the first 1000 acres. On 22 June 1818 he moved twenty members of his family and others (his wife, six children, two farm workers and their families, a tutor) with some cows, seeds and tools to his farm at Shoosharry, (Shushari).[53] Richenda Scott wrote that James Finlayson joined Daniel Wheeler regularly in his lodgings for silent worship. Daniel Wheeler in a letter said that James was attracted to the Quaker faith through a brief perusal of Barclay's Apology. However, Scott also claimed that James did not appear to have joined the Quakers.[54]

Daniel and his wife Jane's six children were William, Joshua, Sarah, Charles, Daniel Jr., and Jane. Both his wife and his daughter died in Russia. The Wheeler family members were heavily involved in Finlayson's venture in Tampere.[55]

William Swan, Missionary in Siberia 1791–1866

Swan arrived at St Petersburg on 22 July 1818. He spent a part of the years 1818 and 1819 with the family of Dr Paterson, at St. Petersburg, acquiring the Russian and Mongol languages. He then proceeded with his associate, Robert Yuille, to the field of their missionary labours in Selenginsk. With Richard Stallybrass he worked with Buriats and translated the Bible into Mongolian. As well as his missionary work, Swan was also a poet and his poems were published for private circulation in 1866 under the title of 'Heart musings'.[56]

Congregational Church in St Petersburg

The Evangelical Britons wanted a church of their own, apart from the Anglican Church. In a historical sketch of the Church of Christ at St. Petersburg, consisting of 'English,

Scotch, Irish, and Americans', the beginnings of the Congregational Church in St Petersburg are described:

> Dr. John Paterson having come to St. Petersburg as an
> agent of the British and Foreign Bible Society, made
> the acquaintance of a countryman residing in this
> city, who set a high value on the public ordinances
> of religion. Of him he requested permission to
> expound the Scriptures in his house on the Lord's-day
> evening to such persons as might wish to attend,
> which was immediately granted; and in the year
> 1815 he commenced these labours of love, in which
> he afterwards received occasional assistance from his
> colleague, Dr. Ebenezer Henderson.[57]

The church was officially formed in 1817 with permission
from Tsar Alexander I, and an evening service was held at
the Moravian Sarepta Chapel. Later a morning service was
added. The congregation numbered eight worshippers at the
start:[58] Ebenezer Henderson, William Glen, William Swan,
Edward Stallybrass, Robert Pinkerton, and John J. Carruthers
joined Paterson in holding services there. These men along
with Daniel Wheeler formed a community of evangelicals
and James and Margaret were part of their group. It is perhaps
a coincidence that the façade of the British-American Congregational Church on 16 Novo-Isaakievskaya Ulitsa (now 16
Yakubovicha Ulitsa) built in 1840 for Paterson's congregation,
was modelled on that of the Methodist Chapel, Nicolson
Square in Edinburgh. Nicolson Square is on the south side of
Edinburgh and is where James and Margaret died.

William Allen in his memoir writes about James:

> First Day, Eleventh Month 22nd, 1818: we dined
> with Daniel Wheeler, in company with a person

named Finlayson, who, though not a member of our
Society, attends our meetings.[59]

And:

Eleventh Month 28, 1818 – It seems quite out of
the question, from the state of the river, to think of
going over to Daniel Wheeler's. James Finlayson and
Samuel Stansfield came and sat with us in our little
meeting. [60]

In 1819, the next we hear of James was in the memoir of
John Paterson:

As my friend, Mr. James Finlayson, who had been
engaged, under Sir Alexander Wilson, in making
machinery for the works at Alexanderoffsky, had left
that employment, and was rather in infirm health, I
proposed that he should accompany me on my tour
in Finland.[61]

Paterson does not describe the nature of James' infirmity and
based on comments in correspondence, his rather grandiose
behaviour and his longevity, we have tentatively concluded
that James suffered from bipolar disorder rather than purely
physical infirmities.

Paterson describes the journey to Finland in his book,
The Book for every Land and writes this about the visit to
Tampere:

My friend Finlayson was delighted with the place. He
at once perceived that I had not over-rated it in my
description to him, and my friend Lafren afforded
him every information he required. The Emperor

woman who had come to help to nurse her. On this
she smiled to her, bidding her welcome. But she
soon found that this woman was not like-minded
with herself; and often pleaded with her dear Mrs. F.
to send her out of the room, that they might enjoy
undisturbed that conversation about divine things
in which she delighted. She complained bitterly that
this beloved friend was so reserved in speaking to her
of the Saviour, which she was not wont to be, and
said she could not comprehend the cause, 'You used
to speak to me of the Saviour – why not now? – O
feed me, feed me!' A little sago being offered her,
she took it, saying, with one of her expressive looks,
'That is not the food I want.' We well understood her
meaning; but being enjoined to keep her very quiet,
it was necessary to converse as little as possible. Some
drink was then given, and this she received as before,
saying, 'That is not the drink I want. It was thought
proper to tell her, that we would speak more with
her when she was better, but that at present it would
hurt her to talk much. To which she replied, 'Why
all this care about my body? I am sure it is a poor
diseased body.– Why so much more care taken of my
body than of my mind?' On the Sabbath morning she
appeared some what depressed in mind. She wept and
said, 'I am afraid my sins are not forgiven. I do not
doubt,' said she, 'that I shall be saved, but I am afraid
that my sins have provoked God now to withdraw his
face from me.' She then proposed to Mrs F. that they
should join in prayer. 'It is promised,' said she, 'that
if two shall agree on earth, touching any thing that
they shall ask, it shall be done for them;– unite with
me in asking that the light of my heavenly Father's
countenance may be restored unto me.' After they
had accordingly engaged in prayer, Mrs. F. proposed
that Dr.P. who came in, should pray. He did so, and
also said something appropriate, as well as his feelings

would permit him, to the afflicted saint. She spoke of
the exceeding sinfulness of sin– of herself as a great
sinner, and of what her sins deserved. She seemed
at a loss to conceive how a holy God could pardon
so great a sinner as she was. Her husband then said,
'You know what the Redeemer has done for poor
sinners.' 'And can I hope for forgiveness through
him?' She was answered in the affirmative. She then
exclaimed, 'O blessed Redeemer; speak to me about
the Redeemer! O speak to me about the Redeemer'
At the mention of his name, these 'morning clouds'
vanished away.[67]

It need scarcely be added, for it is unnatural to
suppose the contrary, that the discovery of a similarity
of religious views and habits of thinking, attached her
with peculiar force to some individuals, who of course
became her most intimate and valued associates.[68]

We can discern from these excerpts the close relationship
between Margaret and the Paterson family, and this may help
to explain James and Margaret's relocation to Edinburgh on
their retirement. It also suggests that Margaret shared religious
fervour with Jean and that she might have been part of the
independent congregation led by John Paterson.

Although we discovered details about James and Margaret
in Russia, there remain many gaps in our research. We found
little information about Margaret apart from her arrival and
friendship with Jean Paterson. Did she enter into any entre-
preneurial business such as the work she did in Tampere? Did
she contribute to charitable works alongside Jean Paterson?[69]
There is no official record – or none so far brought to light –
of her charitable work in the archives in St Petersburg. We do
not really know the role James played in Alexandrovsk, nor
the reasons for his exiting employment. We gather that he was

33 Wilson, A. (1814). Letter to His Excellency Grigory Ivanovich Villam-
    ov. Topic: Margaret's teaware and tableware. 10 July 1814. The Russian
    State Historical Archive (RGIA). F. 758, Op. 24, d. 446, L. 209-210.

34 Obrezkov, M. A. (1814) Letter to His Excellency Grigory Ivanovich
    Villamov, Topic: Margaret's additional teaware and tableware. 8 August
    1814. The Russian State Historical Archive (RGIA). F. 759 Op. 6, D.
    1318. L. 4.

35 Pilvinskii, A. (2023). Email to Angela Harris. Topic: Restrictions on
    British Porcelain 1801-1825.', 12 July.

36 Nenadic, S. (1994) Middle-rank consumers and domestic culture in
    Edinburgh and Glasgow 1720–1840. Past and Present, 145(1), pp.
    122–156.

37 Ship news. (1814). Caledonian Mercury. 25 June. Ernest gun-brig. p. 4.

38 Lloyd's List (1814) Favorite, Strong arrived from Glasgow in St Peters-
    burg, 16 August. Hathitrust.org : accessed 10 July 2023.

39 Newspaper advertisement: (1814). Hull Packet, 28 June. For Peters-
    burg, The Fine New Copper-Fastened Ship, Neva, James Adams,
    Master. p.2, British Newspaper Archive. https://www.britishnewspa-
    perarchive.co.uk : accessed 10 July 2023.

40 Ship news. Hull Packet (1814) Hull, July 4,1814 Ship News, foreign
    cleared, 5 July, p. 3. British Newspaper Archive. https://www.british-
    newspaperarchive.co.uk : accessed 10 July 2023.

41 Lloyd's List (1814) Phoebe, Blair arrived in St Petersburg from
    Glasgow', 9 September. Hathitrust.org : accessed 10 July 2023.

42 Ship news. Caledonian Mercury (1814) The Cheerly gun brig sailed on
    Wednesday, 23 July. p. 4.

43 Lloyd's List (1814).

44 Fewster, F.A. (1970) Finlayson 1820-1970. Tampere, Finland: Oy Fin-
    layson Ab. p. 6.

45 Jones, G.M. (1827). pp. 353–54.

46 Karttunen, M.-L. (2005) The making of communal worlds: English merchants in Imperial St. Petersburg. Doctoral Thesis. University of Helsinki. p. 3.

47 Karttunen, M.-L. (2005). p. 115.

48 Fedosov, D. (no date) The Caledonian connection: Scotland-Russia ties: middle ages to early twentieth century a concise biographical list. http://www.scalan.co.uk/scotsinrussia.htm : accessed: 30 June 2023.

49 paleog (2017) sherwood_family. https://sherwood-family.livejournal.com/26280.html : accessed: 23 June 2023.

50 Hartley, J. M. (1995) "It is the Festival of the Crown and Sceptres": The diplomatic, commercial and domestic significance of the visit of Alexander I to England in 1814. The Slavonic and East European Review, 73(2). pp. 246–268.

51 Hartley, J. M. (1995). pp. 267–68.

52 Alexander, J. M. (1972) John Paterson, Bible Society pioneer, 1776-1855. I The earlier years – 1776-1813. The Records of the Scottish Church History Society, XVII, pp. 131–153. p. 134.

53 Scott, R. (1964) Quakers in Russia. London: Michael Joseph.

54 Scott, R. (1964).

55 Selleck, R. G. (1962) Quaker pioneers in Finnish economic development: James Finlayson and the Wheeler Family. Quaker History, 51(1). pp. 32–42.

56 Swan, W. (1866) Heart musings: 'To bring to remembrance'. Edinburgh: T. Constable.

57 Evangelical Magazine and Missionary Chronicle (1839) Laying of the foundation stone of the British and American Chapel, St Petersburg, 17. pp. 446–447, p. 446.

58 Evangelical Magazine and Missionary Chronicle (1839).

59 Allen, W. (1847) Life of William Allen: With selections from his correspondence. in two volumes, vol. 1. Philadelphia: H. Longstreth. p. 319.

The three official histories and the fourth (in publication) are:

1) Sigurd Carl Augustus Roos (1861–1918) was a Finnish journalist and writer and at Tampere University there is an unpublished manuscript, written by him just before his death, in Swedish on the history of Finlayson Oy

(2) Gustav V. Lindfors *Finlayson-fabrikerna I Tammerfors Del 1: 1820–1907*, written in Swedish

(3) *Finlayson 1820–1970*. English version by Fred A Fewster in 1970

(4) In publication in two parts:
 a) Part 1
 b) Part 2 Finlayson. II (1918–2020): The Cotton Giant by Koivuniemi Jussi; Pietarinen, Heidi; Peltola, Jarmo; Lähteenmäki, Marja; Lehto, Anne-Mari; and Lind, Mari

In addition, there have been some detailed articles about James and Margaret:

(1) Roberta G. Selleck (1962): 'Quaker Pioneers in Finnish Economic Development: James Finlayson and the Wheeler Family'

(2) Brian Denoon (1991): 'James Finlayson of Penicuik 1772–1852: industrial founder of Finland's second city'

(3) Esa Hakala (2015): 'James Finlayson'

(4) Jarmo Peltola (2019): 'The British contribution to the birth of the Finnish cotton industry (1820–1870)'

(5) Mervi Kaarninen (2022): 'The Trials of Sarah Wheeler (1807–1867): Experiencing Submission'

Sigurd Roos' manuscript is handwritten and can be located at the Werstas Museum in Tampere. Both Gripenberg (1929) and Lindfors (1938) used it as a source for their own work.[3] These accounts provide a full history of the factory and something about James and Margaret. In this chapter, we have provided only a summary of James' and Margaret's lives in Finland gathered from these sources. Readers are invited to explore the works above. Despite the lack of new facts of their time in Tampere, the evidence we found through research into the Finlaysons' earlier lives has led to a re-evaluation of certain sources.

This part of the narrative starts with James' visit to Tampere with John Paterson in August 1819. Tsar Alexander I also visited in September 1819 as part of the Imperial tour and perhaps this made the Tsar receptive to James' business proposal. On May 10 1820, a Senate decision granted James Finlayson a permit to establish the company, as well as an interest-free government loan over 20 years. James hoped to hire British technicians and engineers and received special dispensation for these workers: exemption from military and Church taxes, as well as the right to make affirmation instead of taking judicial oaths. Therefore, 10 May 1820 is considered as the founding date of the Finlayson Company, when letters patent were granted to set it up, but this account is not a history of the Company.

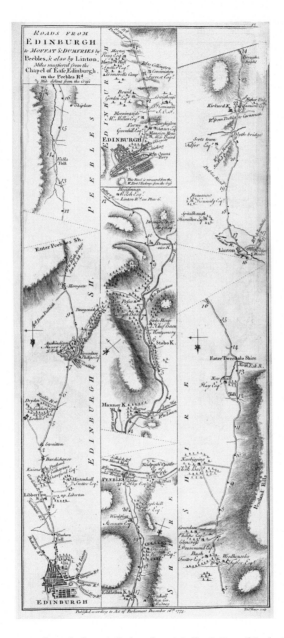

Plate 1: Map of Roads from Edinburgh to Moffat & Dumfries by Peebles & also by Linton. *Credit:* Taylor and Skinner, 1775. National Library of Scotland. Under Creative Commons Attribution (CC-BY) licence.

Plate 2: Map of the City of Glasgow and suburbs. North Centre section.
Credit: Peter Fleming's Map of City of Glasgow and Suburbs (1807), National Library of Scotland. Under Creative Commons Attribution (CC-BY) licence.

Plate 3: Forth and Clyde Navigation and Union Canal route map.
Credit: © waterwayroutes.co.uk, reproduced with permission.

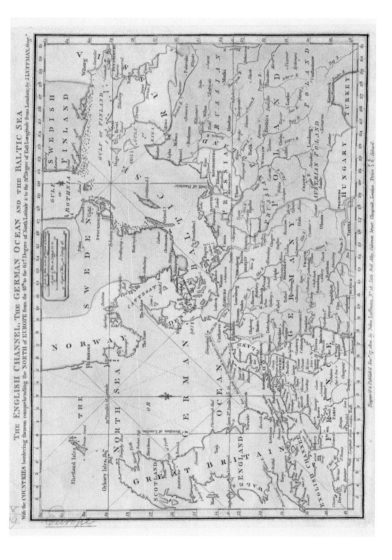

Plate 4: The English Channel, the German Ocean, and the Baltic Sea, with the countries bordering thereon, comprehending the north of Europe. *Credit:* J. Luffman 1800. Former owner: George III, King of Great Britain, 1738-1820, King's Topographical Collection ©The British Library Board.

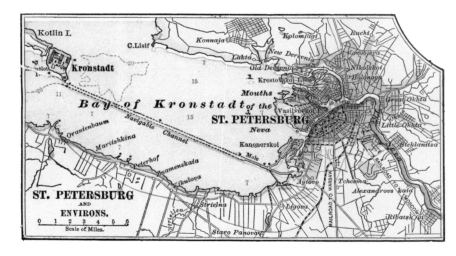

Plate 5: Map of St. Petersburg, circa 1900. *Credit:* The 10th edition of Encyclopaedia Britannica. Universal Images Group North America LLC / Alamy Stock Photo. Reproduced with the permission of Alamy

Plate 6: Skutching machine, manufactured by James Finlayson in 1824. *Credit:* Tampere Museums / Photo: Marika Tamminen

Plate 7: Oil Painting of James Finlayson.
Credit: Tampere Museums / Photo: Saarni Säilynoja

Plate 8: Tammerfors factory drawing. Artist unknown, undated but probably around 1842. *Credit:* Library of the Society of Friends (Quakers) in Britain. LSF MSS 366 Volume 1 Life in Russia Item 136

Plate 9: *View of Tamerfors*, 1820. *Credit:* Artist: Carl Ferdinand von Kügelgen (1772-1832), Germany. The State Hermitage Museum, St. Petersburg. Photograph © The State Hermitage Museum. Photo by Tatyana Gorbokoneva. OR-9887.

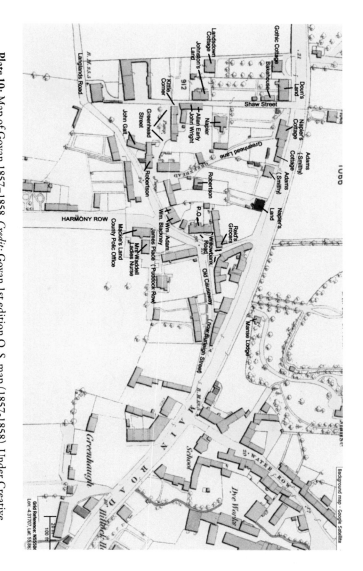

Plate 10: Map of Govan 1857–1858. *Credit:* Govan 1st edition O. S. map (1857–1858). Under Creative Commons Attribution (CC-BY) licence. Permission granted by National Library of Scotland. Annotated by Colin Quigley, used with permission. Probable residence of Finlaysons in blue.

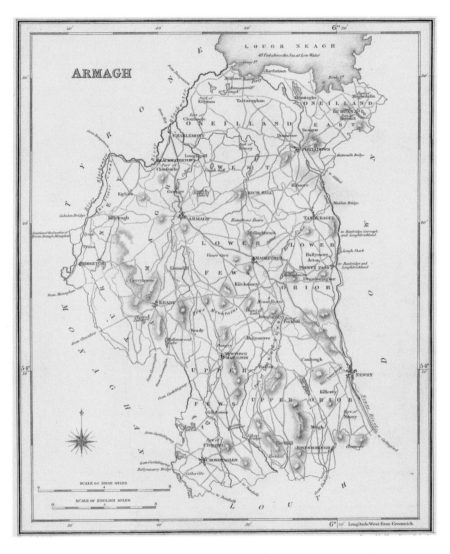

Plate 11: Map of County Armagh 1837. *Credit:* Drawn by R. Creighton, engraved by I. Dower for Samuel Lewis' Topographical Dictionary 1837. Antiqua Print Gallery / Alamy Stock Photo. Used with permission

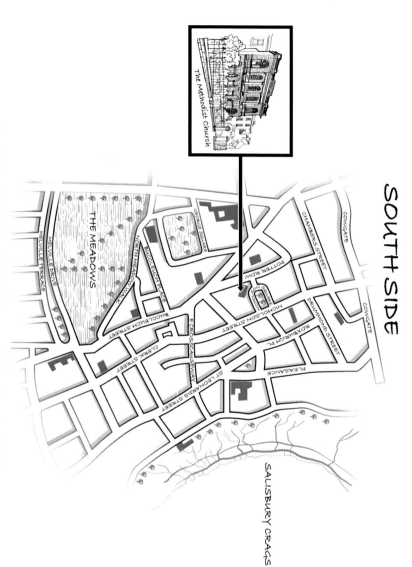

Plate 12: Southside Edinburgh. *Credit:* Illustrator, Richard Bowring (2024).

Plate 13: The Wellington Statue, Edinburgh erected 18th June 1852 by Sir John Steell, sculptor. *Credit:* Lithograph c. 1852 by J. Ramage. Used with permission from City of Edinburgh Council - Edinburgh Libraries www.capitalcollections.org.uk

Plate 14: The monument of William Dunn, Glasgow Necropolis.
Credit: Stephencdickson, 2017. This file is licensed under the Creative
Commons Attribution-Share Alike 4.0 International license.

Plate 15: The headstone of James Finlayson Newington Cemetery.
Credit: Antti Liuttunen, 2023. Vapriikki Photo Archives.

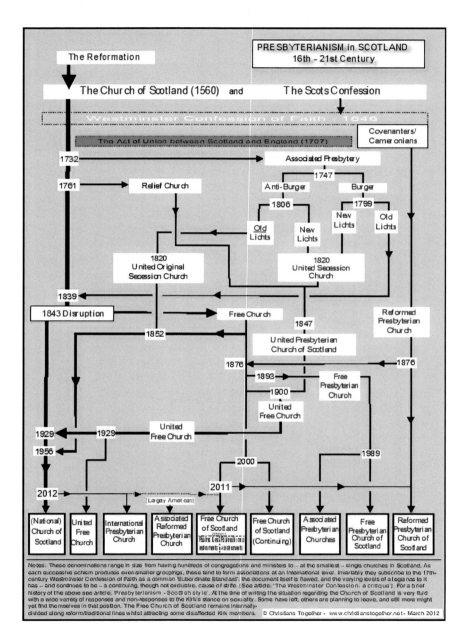

Plate 16: Presbyterianism in Scotland 16th to 21st Century.
Credit: © Christians Together.net. Presbyterianism in Scotland
16th to 21st Century. Reproduced with permission.

Plate 17: Finlayson factory sign in Tampere. *Credit:* Odyssey-Images / Alamy Stock Photo

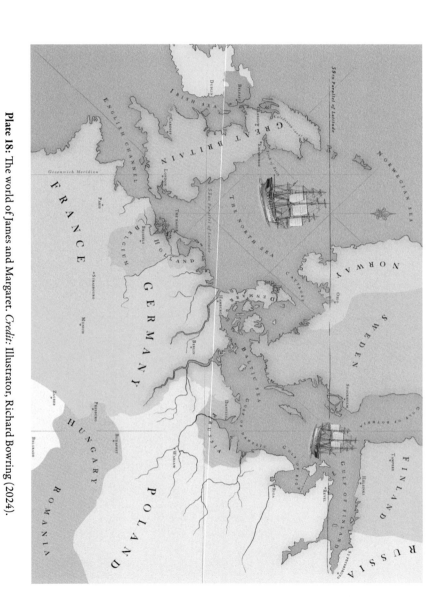

Plate 18: The world of James and Margaret. *Credit:* Illustrator, Richard Bowring (2024).

Whereabouts and weather Tampere Finland

Tampere, Finland, is 395km (245 miles) WNW from Saint Petersburg and a much longer distance by the roads of that time. Since 1809 Finland had been an autonomous Grand Duchy of the Russian Empire and previously in the Kingdom of Sweden. It seems that Dr Paterson's purpose in travelling to Tampere was to investigate the availability of suitable paper for the printing of Bibles, papermaking having started there in 1783, its first industry. A small paper factory was founded south of the Finlayson area. The factory was later taken over by J.C. Frenckell, after whom the factory was renamed. By 1819 James had left his employment under Alexander Wilson and so the chance to get away from Saint Petersburg was maybe opportune, evading for a time any awkward questions about his right to remain in Russia with Margaret without employment.

The destination

Tampere (Latitude 61° 29 '57'N, Longitude 23° 47' 14'E) is about 160km (100 miles) NNW of Helsinki, Finland's capital, and a similar distance NE from Turku (Åbo), the old capital.

It remained a very small settlement until the late eighteenth century when in 1775 it was boosted by being created as a marketplace by Gustav 3rd of Sweden, who later granted it city status. In the nineteenth and twentieth centuries, Tampere grew to become the second most populous city in Finland, after Helsinki, until more recently being displaced into third place by Espoo, just to the west of the capital. Tampere is built on a low ridge of moraine gravel, which averages about 84m (276 feet) above sea level (asl), but rises to 160m asl. Although now spread much more widely, it started wedged between two lakes, Näsijävi on its north side and Pyhäjävi on the south.

The former is at an elevation of 95m asl and the latter 77m asl, the difference of 18m (59feet) creating the rapids between them of Tammerkoski (Tammerfors). Tampere, developing on both sides of the rapids, was quickly recognised as having the potential for water-power, leading to industrialisation. Ample mention is made of the weather in correspondence from Daniel Wheeler and Ferdinand Uhde in the years following the Finlaysons departure. Thunderstorms, snow, rain, heat-waves, drought all occurred, as shown in Table 16. Temperatures are measured according to the Réaumur scale. To convert this to Centigrade, multiply by 1.25 (formula: °C = 1.25 × °R). Weather such as this created problems for the mill and also affected food production. Such severe weather raised the possibility of famine.

Table 16: Weather in Tampere 1839–1853, as described in correspondence

25 October 1839	Odd weather; although very bleak and dull, there was heavy thunder and rain yesterday – today the morning was warm & bright, but evening again rainy
15 January 1840	Frost that we have had in this most mild of climates – for the last 10 days the thermometer has been below the freezing point, and two days ago 9 ½ of Reaumur. Yesterday however the mercury rose & today there are two or three do of heat – there has been next to no snow, that has now vanished – but the ice still bears although the surface is covered with water
29 July 1841	A cool and rainy summer here; the last week however was fine & the rye ripened very fast & promises a good harvest – Now it is again rainy with a temperature of 10° Reaumur in the shade at noon. During the bright weather it never rose above 18° in the shade & most days was not above 15° – the warmest time is about 2 P.M. – I observe much greater difference between noon & night in the bright than in the dull weather.
19 January 1842	A winter as mild as I cannot remember in Russia. Only one cold day 7th Jany [sic] N. S. when we had 20° Ro, but besides 1–3° under zero

12 July 1843	The thermometer reaches 20° every day in the shade, between two and four P.M. and several times has been 21° – yesterday it was 22°, and we hd [sic] a short thunderstorm. In the night, it sinks generally to 13°, but once was not lower than 16° – this was very oppressive. The crops hereaway look very well, but are backward; nearer the coast, they have suffered from drought. On the whole the season (here) has corresponded with what we had in England, namely backward & rainy till midsummer
23 July 1843	Last second day, our fine hot weather gave way to rainy and chilly times, from 20° and 22° Reaumur in the shade at two P.M. the glass has fallen to 14° and 10° at that hour – The change was so sudden as to be much felt.
20 June 1844	The rye crops by the way are most flourishing & the season has been by no means unusually dry.
27 June 1844	Yesterday was excessively wet with the barometer at 28' 33 and today is only very little better. The thermometer was at 6° Reaumur yesterday and today is at 7° at noon
13 July 1844	The weather has been cool and rainy wh [sic] certainly suits me better than the brilliant shadeless exhausting character of our Tammerfors hot weather. Scarcely a day has passed without rain, and the thermometer has ranged from 8° to 12° generally – once it rose to 18°, but a thunder storm effectually checked that demonstration
30 January 1849	As we have seen 30° and even 34° degrees here before, we do not feel surprized at the present cold, but there are frequent changes to extremes this winter which make it unwholesome, for it was only last week when we had rain and 2 degrees of heat.
8 May 1852	Deep snow fell at Tammerfors on 20th April and that they had 14° Re. below freezing a few days before, which kept their ports still shut up and no steamer had started.
23 October 1852	Our winter seems to have set in already. The thermometer a few 5 degrees below freezing point, cold blows from the north over our lake, and now storms, makes it rather uncomfortable now, but having had such an unusual fine summer, we must not complain. We live in latitude 62°, what else can we expect. But all the prognoses tell us, we shall have an unusually early and severe winter. The swallows and birds of passage, amongst others, left us more than a fortnight earlier than usual, which is a sure indication of approaching cold.

| 14 January 1853 | Never before since I live in the north had such early severe frosts set in, and such extraordinary masses of snow fallen. On the 13 Novr the cold reached 20° Reaumur, and we were in expectation December and January would bring us such cold as we never yet had before. We had such beautiful Aurorae Boreales as I have only once before seen. The northern sky was blazing up from the horizon to the zenith in glaring colours, yellow, green and sometimes bloodred. A glorious sight! Soon after however a most unsettled state of the weather began, the barometer sank as low as 28 inches, fearful snow storms; the frost gave way, and during the whole of December up to this day, a succession of dark rainy weather has prevailed so that every trace of snow has disappeared, and things around us look as if we had suddenly advanced to spring, for only in April generally the country assumes the appearance it now has. The fine sledgeroads that we had set in as early as October are long gone, and the stagnation this change has produced in business and agricultural pursuits is very much felt, for if a winter is without sledgeroads it is almost like the failing of crops. Surely there must be somewhere great revolutions going on in nature, besides the eruption of Aetna, for how can such extraordinary state of the atmosphere be explained otherwise? I fully expect to hear of great earthquakes or other phenomena. The sudden melting of the snow has created great floods also in this country, but since we had very low water everywhere on account of the extreme dryness and great heat of last summer, no damage has been done. Indeed to us here individually, no greater benefit could have been done, than this great change. We had much low water in our lake, that when frost set in and the lake became frozen, we looked with dismay how we should get thro' the winter, for only once, 12 years ago, the water had been for a short time so low, and long experience had taught us, never to expect one inch of rise more after the lake is frozen fast. We came so low in November, that we were obliged to set about 1000 spindles at rest, and having the dreary prospect of 5 months winter before us, before, after the commencement of things, the rise of water could be expected, we were fully prepared to set the water falling more yet, so as perhaps to set several thousand spindles and an adequate number of looms and other machinery in a state of inactivity. |

| 12 November ber 1853 | One circumstance in favor is the present mild weather which has continued all along. This day last year our lake froze fast. It then became 200 cold and sledge roads were practicable since 18 October. But this year, not one killing frost has yet been, only rimer frost. We have still pansies and other flowers in our garden, and the people can have their cattle out, by which they save their winter stores. Horses cows and sheep are still kept on pasture, which is a very unusual thing at this season. I am astonished to hear you mention the continual wet. We have had no rain of consequence since the month of May. A parching heat in summer was the cause of our present want of food for the cattle; and though there is no heat now to complain of, yet the dryness of our atmosphere is almost unprecedented. The water in our lake has fallen so considerable, that we suffer from it in our Mill. We have not sufficient power to drive our wheels, and more than 2000 spindles with their needful preparation must stand. This is a twofold loss to us, since the production is so much shorter and we have to pay a good many hands doing nothing. If not soon rain or snow should come, and our lake freezes fast we shall have to suffer under this state of things until next month of April |

Source: Correspondence from Daniel Wheeler and Ferdinand Uhde in Tampere, Finland, Millfield Papers (MIL). Alfred Gillett Trust Archives

Table 17: Population of the City of Tampere 1780–1840

Year	1780	1800	1805	1810	1820	1830	1840
Population	181	463	602	682	956	1,585	1,819

Source: Wallin (later Voionmaa), Väinö. Tampereen Kaupungin Historia: II OSA Tampereen Historia (History of the City of Tampere), 1905. p.393

Table 18: Tampere Climate Data

Month	Mean daily max. °C	Mean daily min. °C	Precipitation mm	Snow depth mm	Precipitation Days = 1mm
January	−2.5	−8.3	41	32.3	10
February	−2.5	−9.1	30	31.4	8
March	2.1	−6.0	29	29.5	8
April	8.8	−0.9	32	13.9	7
May	15.6	4.1	36	1.6	7
June	19.7	9.0	66	0.1	9
July	22.5	12.2	74	0	11
August	20.7	10.8	65	0	9
September	14.9	6.6	55	0	9
October	7.8	2.0	57	3.3	10
November	2.6	−1.5	51	13.1	10
December	−0.5	−5.4	46	27.2	11
Year total	9.1	1.1	582	152.4	109

Figures stated are 30-year long term averages for the years 1991 to 2020 for the airport at an elevation of 119m asl. Source: https://en.ilmatieteenlaitos.fi/statistics-from-1961-onwards

Month	Average temperature °C	Average Precipitation mm	Snow depth mm	Precipitation Days = 1mm
January	−5.2	45	32.3	10
February	−5.8	31	31.4	8
March	−2.1	31	29.5	8
April	3.6	32	13.9	7
May	10.0	36	1.6	7
June	14.6	65	0.1	9
July	17.4	74	0	11
August	15.9	66	0	9
September	10.9	56	0	9
October	5.1	64	3.3	10
November	0.8	53	13.1	10
December	−2.6	49	27.2	11
Year total	5.2	602	152.4	109

Population

The urban area covered by Tampere has very considerably expanded over time as adjacent towns and villages have been absorbed into it. The 2023 population of the municipal city area is estimated at 244,000, with its wider metropolitan urban area, including suburbs etc, estimated at 347,000. Population figures for the municipal city area are:

Climate

In relation to UK, Tampere is on a latitude well north of the Muckle Flugga lighthouse off the north coast of the Shetlands. It is about 130km inland from Finland's coastline, so does not experience much moderation of temperature extremes from proximity to the sea. Tampere has a subarctic climate, with cold winters and cool to warm summers. Temperature average from December to February is below −3°C, with snow cover usually lasting 4–5 months from late November until early April. Since 1980, from figures so far published, the lowest temperature recorded at the airport to the SW of the city was −35.8° C in January 1987 and the highest 32.5° C in July 2010.

Hunger and famine

The climate of Finland, with long harsh winters, seasonally limited daylight hours and short growing seasons has throughout its history been challenging for its people. However, these occurrences had much more serious consequences as the way of life changed from a predominantly rural agrarian economy to urban and industrial. This is exemplified by the rapid growth of Tampere in the nineteenth century, with the advantage initially of water-power and then steam engines, to industrialise papermaking and thread and cloth production, with other industries following.

Dr Andrew G. Newby of the University of Helsinki, with other academic colleagues, has carried out extensive research and published papers on the famines of Finland and Ireland, in particular the 1840s Irish famine and Finland's 'Great Hunger Years' of the 1860s. The latter was after the Finlaysons' lifetime and therefore does not form part of this narrative. During their time in Tampere, however, there were periods of hunger, disease and want and Margaret and James' actions helped to ameliorate peoples' suffering in harsh times.

James and Margaret together in Tampere

James and Margaret were together in Tampere in the spring of 1820, when James was fifty years old. They resided in an old crown distillery, which was renovated as their home. The twenty-two rooms of the house had plenty of space for a childless couple. In 1821, the Finlaysons opened an orphanage where poor children of the neighbourhood received physical care, strict religious education, and training in manual skills such as knitting and weaving and, for older children, light factory work.[4] In their own dwelling, they prepared rooms for some children without means, who might otherwise have resorted to begging and a desolate life. The children must, like the house servants, be present at the daily prayer, in the hosts dining room, morning, afternoon and evening. The worship was most commonly conducted by James, as the head of the household, who thereby from his English Bible read one or more verses, which was translated to Swedish by a 'book-keeper'. The whole day the children were in work. The sabbath day of rest was strict, but any form of leisure was not allowed.

Corporal punishment was not an unknown term in the children's orphanage. Finlayson ordered others both at home and at work, with patriarchal authority. Strict and demanding, but at the same time fair, he was respected by everyone.

In 1821, the new factory began operating on the shores of Tammerkoski. The factory's first buildings were of timber construction, with a foundry and machine shop powered by a 30-horsepower water wheel. In the two furnaces of the foundry, iron was melted in one and brass in the other. The original idea was to make carding and spinning machines for spinning cotton and wool, but it soon became clear that there was not a market for these machines and cash was needed for construction. In 1825 the factory had five employees and in 1830 there were only ten. By 1833, his factory had about fifty people at work; most of them women and children. Finlayson was the first female employer in Finland in the industrial sector. The working day at the factory began at five in the morning, when one of the superiors read a few verses from the New Testament and the morning prayer. Work continued until 7 p.m. or 8 p.m., with only two small food breaks interrupting work.

Margaret Finlayson set up a home weaving and dry laundry in the old distillery building and the orphanage also used a hut there. This orphanage never had a large number of children at a time (a maximum of ten), and children were also used as labour.

Third bankruptcy?

The literature shows that James nearly was bankrupted for a third time by over-extending himself, and without the Imperial loans he would have failed. Lennart Gripenberg (1929) described Finlayson's business management ability, and his incapability of costing his plans and lack of skill in financial management.[5]

At the end of 1823, an order came from the Senate to Niilo Nordenskiöld, a Finnish mineralogist and traveller, to go to Tampere 'without delay' at the expense of the Emperor's treasury to 'fully investigate' the Finlayson plants, to check whether Finlayson had fulfilled all the former conditions imposed on him, to negotiate with him about the future of the factory and then, at the earliest opportunity, to give a 'detailed' report of his observations and of Finlayson's claims and declarations, as well as a proposal and statement on his own behalf.

By 1824, Finlayson's cash shortage reached a crisis. He had already used 26,000 roubles of his own funds to set up his factory. It was almost as much as the loan from the government. Nordenskiöld thought that although James was a skilled artisan, he lacked business skills. One example of the machines, manufactured by James Finlayson in 1824, is a skutching or raw cotton processing machine, (see Plate 6). This was used in the pre-spinning department of Finlayson's "old factory" for 104 years, until 1928. It is in the collections of Tampere museums. It was modelled after the cotton gin, which was patented in the United States in 1794. Finlayson would be allowed to carry on his factory in any way he chose; which might be the most appropriate, he did not have, in spite of his excellent skill, the efficiency required to run a large factory.[6] Finlayson initially believed that the industrial manufacture of yarns and fabrics in Finland would be based on wool and flax. One of the conditions for a second loan was that he used cotton and wool as manufacturing materials. He received an additional loan from the state in 1826. His workshop had been closed for a long time due to lack of funds, but in 1827 one spinning machine for cotton and another spinning machine for wool were completed, as well as the carding and prefabrication machines required for the work required by the project. The production of cotton yarn from the Finlayson mill began with the help of hydropower in 1828, and this year can therefore be considered the birth year of the Finnish cotton industry. As early as 1829, the factory stopped using wool as a material due to weak demand.

Margaret's business ventures in Finland

Whilst James struggled with the management of the factory, Margaret set up three businesses: the orphanage; a weaving and knitting craft industry; and a dry-cleaning business. According to Lindfors, Margaret Finlayson pioneered chemical washing in Finland. In an attic she established a so-called 'sulphur office' or institution for washing delicates with sulphur. There, she washed silk and wool, lace, hats, gloves, plumes etc. The shop was soon famous and generated a large clientele, not only in Finland, but even in Sweden. Additionally, she allowed for knitting of various kinds such as table cloths, gloves, socks, jumpers etc, and she not only hired professional workers, but she also requested her maids to do some knitting every day alongside their usual chores. The working day was long, commonly it began already at 5 o'clock in the morning and could last for 15 to 16 hours. Margaret Finlayson attentively oversaw all the work and scrutinised the final products which she subsequently herself marketed in Tampere as well as in other cities. The enterprise yielded good profits.[7]

In 1842, Uhde referred to Margaret setting up a knitting business as a charitable venture for poor women and for being ahead of her time.

> Mrs Finlayson had in the time of distress where poor
> women had no other work, got such stockings knit
> by them and as the article was new, she had great
> difficulty in selling them so that at one time she had
> several thousands on hand. It was with her a work
> of faith and her faith has not been put to shame.
> For all the large stock has sold long ago and so great
> a demand is now created that the number of poor
> women now cannot supply the needful quantity so
> that we think of doing the rest by machine.[8]

Sarah Wheeler organised the commission of woven and knitted woollen and cotton articles from Margaret's cottage industry, including:

- Yarn workbag & garters.[9]
- Woollen or worsted yarn for stockings.[10]
- Cotton socks (fine) & grey woollen socks (strong).[11]
- Long scarlet sashes[12]
- Vests[13]
- Stockings (coarse, fine)[14]
- Scarlet comfortable (warm quilt?)[15]

James' competencies

Returning to James: if he was a mediocre business-man, what about his mechanical engineering skills? It seems as though he was a highly skilled artisan. Nordenskiöld praised the machines made by Finlayson as 'built with a precision and perfection never before seen in Finland, and testifying to a hand accustomed to such work'. However, Nordenskiöld had noticed that Finlayson's real trade in England had been assembling carding and spinning machines, whereas the casting of the iron pieces needed for the spinning was less familiar to him. Finlayson was well acquainted with the older spinning machines in use, and was skilled in making both wool and linen spinning machines and cotton spinning machines.[16]

Running away?

As the business entered difficulties, and James Finlayson's own health declined, he wanted to return home to Scotland. Perhaps this could be interpreted as running away from his trials. At first, he intended that his nephew, Robert, would continue his own work. Robert lived in James' apartment by the rapids for a year, but he never became a successor. We were unable to identify this nephew and we are not sure that his last name was Finlayson. The story recounts that the character traits of the relatives were very different, and Robert was not ready to humble himself to the command of a strict religious enterprise. Eventually, Robert returned home and James Finlayson's plans lapsed this time.

However, Finlayson had already decided to give up the business, and he even reported in the newspaper in 1829 and, in his own letters to his friends in St. Petersburg, began to propulgate for his cause.

James advertised the sale of the Tampere mill in 1835 in The Scotsman and Northern Whig.

TO MANUFACTURERS, &c.

AN Opening now presents itself to any enterprising individual or company, for carrying on a large manufacturing concern in Tammerfors, about 90 miles north-east from Abo, the capital of Finland. Extensive works, at present employed in Cotton

Spinning, are already erected, and capable of being considerably extended; and the advertiser is convinced that were the situation known, with the established increasing business , and the immense field for export, it would be eagerly, embraced by some of the houses in the manufacturing towns of England or Scotland .

Every inducement is given by the Russian Government to encourage the extension of manufactures, &c. in this place. Free importation of the raw material is allowed. The goods manufactured there are admitted duty free into St Petersburgh — the proprietor and work people exempted from all taxes or public burdens whatsoever. Provision and wages are in general extremely low, and there are a great number of poor children in the neighbourhood, who are willing and anxious to assist for very trifling wages.

The situation is healthy and beautiful, and there is an immense supply of water, more than sufficient for the largest work in Britain, at all seasons of the year. Adjoining the works is a large Dwelling-house, with every convenience, containing 24 fire places, and there are out-houses of every description.

The premises are situated on the margin of a large and deep lake navigable for sloops, for upwards of 30 miles, and in some places of great breadth. The stream, which runs into the lake contains excellent salmon. There is a fall of thirty feet affording power sufficient to impel machinery to any extent. The Mill-house, fitted up with Machinery is about a gunshot from the house, about 100 feet long, two stories high, with well lighted garrets, and is warmed in winter with heated air, at a trifling expense.

There have been two separate loans granted on the works by Government, each for 20 years, free of interest, –the first is due end of April 1841 of 30,000 rubles–the last of 36,000 rubles, 14th March, 1846;

present exchange of 10½d per ruble. Besides paying these loans, the price asked is only 20,000 rubles, or £875. The property might be easily examined, as there is constant steam-communication between Hull and Stockholm, and there are vessels several times every week from Stockholm to Finland.

Household Servants are steady, and wages are low, they frequently remain in their places for 6, 8, 12 years, or more; The highest wages for a woman does not exceed 30s annually, and 50s to .60s for a man. The Swedish language is easily acquired and is understood by most of the inhabitants of Finland.

The town of Tammerfors contains about 2000 inhabitants; 12 merchant's shops, 11 master dyers, several brick works, a saw mill, .3 grain mills, paper mill, extensive works, and apothecary establishment. There are also four large fairs annually attended by a large concourse of people, where much money is circulated.

The situation is well adapted for a Fine Linen Business, as there is a ready demand for this article, and an abundant supply of fine flax. It is also very suitable for the manufacture of Fustians, as there is a great demand for this article for the use of the peasantry. It would be difficult .to enumerate all the advantages of this opening in the compass of an advertisement, but enough has been already mentioned to shew its capabilities. The present proprietor, who has been actively employed for several years, now requires repose, and if a bargain is concluded will give every facility in his power to any company or individual who may be inclined to embark in this thriving concern.

Persons disposed to purchase the works, would of course go out and inspect them; but if farther information is wished in writing, application may be made to Mr James Finlayson, Tammerfors by Abo, Flnland.[17]

[Transcript *The Scotsman*, Wednesday 27 May 1835, p.1]

Despite the search through advertisements, the new investors and management were found for the Tampere works through the personal networks of the Wheeler family. Finlayson's Scottish Quaker friend, William Wheeler, and German businessman Ferdinand Uhde found wealthy venture capitalists for Finlayson for a change of ownership in St. Petersburg; they were Carl Samuel Nottbeck, a merchant from Räävel's (Tallinn) Second Trade Society, and Georg Adolf Rauch, a physician. Neither investor was willing to move to Finland, and they never even visited the factory on site. William Wheeler and Ferdinand Uhde visited Tampere to negotiate and inspect the sites a few times, and on 8 June 1835, James Finlayson made a written offer to hand over to the proposed buyers. The aim was that James would remain until 1838 to help with the transition as an advisor. The Finnish Senate did not oppose the transfer of loans and privileges to the new owners because James had fallen into advanced age and no longer had the energy and capacity to manage the factory.[18]

The deed of sale was signed in St. Petersburg by Carl Nottbeck and Georg Rauch on May 29, 1837. Finlayson left seven spinning machines and 832 spindles in the mill, which were driven by mechanical force. James Finlayson and his wife stayed in Tampere for a little over a couple of years to share advice.

On 20 July 1837, James left Tampere to visit Scotland, perhaps to make arrangements for their repatriation, and returned around midsummer the following year to pick up his wife. Margaret was not enthusiastic about leaving Finland but, in the end, accompanied her husband. Before leaving, Margaret said goodbye to her friends and had dinner with her friend Augusta Lundahl.[19]

The boardroom at the Finlayson factory for a while held

the portrait in oils of James Finlayson (see Plate 7). It is not known when it was commissioned but possibly it was painted at the time of his retirement as an acknowledgement of his contribution to the company.

Its provenance is uncertain. In a letter in August 1836 from Sarah Wheeler to Margaret, she mentions that there was a likeness of Margaret. Perhaps two portraits were done at the same time, as a leaving present from the new owners.[20]

The agreement with the new owners excluded James' horses, carriages, furniture, clothes and books.[21] Finally, on 13 July 1838, the Finlaysons left for Scotland[22] having sent their possessions packed in three wagons.[23] We do not know if the porcelain Margaret brought to St Petersburg was packed in one of the wagons. According to legend, a group of working families with their children gathered in the yard to say goodbye to their former host. After the departure from Tampere, the Wheeler's and Uhde maintained correspondence with each other and mention is made periodically of news concerning James and Margaret. It seems from one of the comments made that Margaret and Ferdinand Uhde had a close relationship.

> C. S. Nottbeck is at Tammerfors, I suppose consoling
> F. U. who is almost inconsolable for the loss of M.
> Finlayson.[24]

There is a drawing of the Finlayson factory in the Library of the Society of Friends (Quakers) in Britain in London (see Plate 8). It is undated but is likely to be drawn after 1842 as it shows the new building with six floors. The building was the first job for the new owners and reached its fifth-floor ceiling height already in the summer of 1837. It is known today as Kuusvooninkinen. The building was designed by the Vyborg architect Lessig. The sixth floor of Kuusvooninkinen was built, covered with an iron roof and put into use in 1842[25].

This could be compared with the building in a drawing by Carl Ferdinand von Kügelgen of Tampere produced 1820 that resides in the State Hermitage Museum in St Petersburg (see Plate 9). According to Antti Liuttunen at the Vapriikki Photo Archives, Kügelgen toured southern Finland in the summer of 1818 and painted sepia etchings. Based on them, he prepared the final versions of the paintings, which were handed over to the emperor Alexander I. In addition, lithographs of fifteen engravings were made in St. Petersburg, which were published in 1823-24 as a three-volume picture publication. Therefore, there are versions of these Kügelgen's paintings dated to different years. However, these originals were made in 1818. After that Kügelgen never revisited Tampere. In 1818, the main building would have been the Crown distillery that the Finlaysons converted into their residence

Uhde and Sarah Wheeler and others from Tampere and St Petersburg kept in touch with James and Margaret. In 1844 Uhde wrote to C. S. Nottbeck:

> From Mr. Wheeler we received news today from Edinburgh, to where he traveled for his sister to recover. Old Finlayson presumably now resides in the vicinity of Edinburgh, and Wheeler wanted to look him up.[26]

NOTES

1 Denoon, B. (1991) James Finlayson of Penicuik 1772–1852: Industrial founder of Finland's second city. Aberdeen University Review, 65(Autumn); Lindfors, G. V. (1938) Finlayson-fabrikerna I Tammerfors Del 1: 1820-1907. Helsingfors: Tilgmann; Peltola, J. (2019) The British contribution to the birth of the Finnish cotton industry (1820–1870). Continuity and Change, 34, pp. 63–89; and Wallin (later Voionmaa),

V. (1905) Tampereen Kaupungin Historia: II OSA Tampereen Historia Aleksanteri I:n ja Nikolai I:n (History of the City of Tampere: PART II History of Tampere under Alexander Ist and Nicholas Ist). Tampere [Finland]: Tampere Kaupungin Kustantama.

2 Denoon, B. (2004) Finlayson, James (1772?–1852?), engineer and cotton manufacturer, Oxford Dictionary of National Biography.

3 Gripenberg, L. (1929) James Finlayson. In: Teoksessa Tampere. Tutkimuksia ja kuvauksia I. (Tampere: Studies and descriptions I.). Tampere [Finland]: Tampereen Historiallinen Seura (Tampere Historical Society). pp. 173–190.

4 Lindfors, G. V. (1938), pp. 87–88.

5 Gripenberg, L. (1929).

6 Wallin (later Voionmaa), V. (1905). p. 109.

7 Lindfors, G. V. (1938), p. 86.

8 Uhde, F. (1842) Letter to Daniel Wheeler, 19 May. Millfield Papers (MIL). Alfred Gillett Trust Archives. MIL_29_7 Uhde 1842-05-19.

9 Wheeler, S. (1821) Letter to Margaret Finlayson, 3 February. Margareta Finlayson Archive/Central Archives for Finnish Business Records (ELKA). ELKA-00427-000001-011. Used with permission from ELKA.

10 Wheeler, S. (1836) Letter to Margaret Finlayson, February. Margareta Finlayson Archive/Central Archives for Finnish Business Records (ELKA). ELKA-00427-000001-018-DOC. Used with permission from ELKA.

11 Wheeler, S. (1836) Letter to Margaret Finlayson, 12 May. Margareta Finlayson Archive/Central Archives for Finnish Business Records (ELKA). ELKA-00427-000001-020-DOC. Used with permission from ELKA.

12 Wheeler, S. (1836) Letter to Margaret Finlayson, 24 September. Margareta Finlayson Archive/Central Archives for Finnish Business Records (ELKA). ELKA-00427-000001-000001-02. Used with permission from ELKA.

13 Wheeler, S. (1837) Letter to Margaret Finlayson, 31 January. Margareta Finlayson Archive/Central Archives for Finnish Business Records (ELKA). ELKA-00427-000001-000001-029. Used with permission from ELKA.

14 Wheeler, S. (1837) Letter to Margaret Finlayson, 11 April. Margareta Finlayson Archive/Central Archives for Finnish Business Records (ELKA). ELKA-00427-000001-000001-030. Used with permission from ELKA.

15 Wheeler, S. (1838) Letter to Margareta Finlayson, 6 April. Margareta Finlayson Archive/Central Archives for Finnish Business Records (ELKA). ELKA-00427-000001-000001-034. Used with permission from ELKA.

16 Wallin (later Voionmaa), V. (1905). p. 102.

17 Advertisement (1835) The Scotsman, 27 May, p. 1; and Northern Whig, 15 June, p. 3 To manufacturers, sale of Tammerfors manufactory. http://www.britishnewspaperarchive.co.uk : accessed 25 July 2023.

18 Wallin (later Voionmaa), V. (1905).

19 Innilä, K. (2008) Augusta Lundahls brev till Fredrika Runeberg 1829–1839. Masters thesis. Tampere University. p. 88.

20 Wheeler, S. (1836) Letter to Margaret Finlayson, 29 August. Margaretta Finlayson Archive, Central Archives for Finnish Business Records (ELKA). ELKA-00427-000001-025. Used with permission from ELKA.

21 Lindfors, G. V. (1938).

22 Uhde, F. (1838) Letter to C. S. Nottbeck, 13 July. Margareta Finlayson Archive/Central Archives for Finnish Business Records (ELKA). 428:IDaa.2. Used with permission from ELKA.

23 Uhde, F. (1838) Letter to: J. C. Aspelund, 13 July. Margareta Finlayson Archive/Central Archives for Finnish Business Records (ELKA). 428:IDaa.2. Used with permission from ELKA.

24 Wheeler, Daniel Jnr (1838) Letter to Sarah Wheeler and Charles Wheeler, 3 August. Millfield Papers (MIL). Alfred Gillett Trust Archives. MIL_29_8 1838-07-22.

25 Määttanen, M. (2020) 'Finlaysonin kukoistus alkoi salaperäisen johtajan komennossa – Lapsityövoima ja orjien tuottamat raaka-aineet olivat tavallisia. (Finlayson's heyday began under the command of a mysterious leader – Child labor and raw materials produced by slaves were commonplace)', Kauppalehti [Preprint]. https://www.kauppalehti.fi/uutiset/finlaysonin-kukoistus-alkoi-salaperaisen-johtajan-komennossa-lapsityovoima-ja-orjien-tuottamat-raaka-aineet-olivat-tavallisia/12b23afb-195f-4caa-8805-24806497fbdc : accessed: 4 January 2024).

26 Uhde, F. (1844) Letter to: C. S. Nottbeck, 28 October. Kotimaahan lähetettyjen kirjeiden toisteet (Letter book of letters sent domestically). Central Archives for Finnish Business Records (ELKA). 428:IDaa.7. Used with permission from ELKA.

— CHAPTER EIGHT —

Their later years

A lthough we know that the Finlaysons left Finland for Scotland in 1838, we do not know whereabouts and when in Scotland they first settled on arrival. The first information we have places them in Govan by May 1839.

Govan

On 4 May 1839 there is this entry in the Quaker meeting minutes of Edinburgh:

> 4th Fifth Month 1839: A communication from James Finlayson residing at Govan, who has for some time attended Friends' Meeting at Glasgow & who has made profession with the Society for a good many years past whilst residing in Russia & in Finland has now been read, expressing a wish to be admitted into Membership with Friends; and the meeting having deliberated, considered the same, appoints the following Friends a Committee to visit James Finlayson, and report viz. John Wigham, William White, Alexander Cruikshank, Wm Smeal.[1]

The reference that he had been attending Glasgow meetings for some time before this application, suggests that Govan might have been their place of residence from the start. The usual process for admission to the Society of Friends was that the applicant would be visited by a delegation to assess their suitability. The committee tasked with this duty visited James and submitted a report to the General Meeting on 13 August 1839.

> The Committee appointed to visit James Finlayson in consequence of his application to be admitted into Membership, have brought in the following report: viz– 'To the Two Months Meeting:- Conformably with our appointment we have paid a visit to James Finlayson which afforded us considerable satisfaction; having reason to believe him to be an upright minded man – one who knows & values the principles & testimonies of Friends. There are some matters of a pecuniary kind connected with his Creditors, which James Finlayson hopes to be able before very long to settle in a satisfactory manner. In the meantime, we recommend that his case be continued under the care of the Committee.' Glasgow 13th of 8th Month 1839 John Wigham, Alex Cruikshank, Wm White, Wm Smeal. ... and the same having now been read and with some verbal explanation solidly considered, the meeting concluded to continue James Finlayson's case under the care of the Committee. [2]

The nature of the pecuniary matters linked to creditors is not known. This might be a new credit problem, as the last sequestration was apparently resolved in 1813. Jarmo Peltola suggested that the difficulties might be explained by two factors.[3] Perhaps Finlayson & Co still owed Finlayson part of the transaction amount in 1839. Or possibly the weak financial situation could be explained at least in part by the information passed by Uhde to Nottbeck in May 1840 that James Finlayson had lost a third of his assets after the insurance company where he had life insurance had gone bankrupt.[4] The nature of the debt and the creditors are not identified. Quakers value financial probity and in their Rules of Discipline concerning trade state that:

> It is the judgment of this meeting, that monthly
> or other meetings ought not to receive collections
> or bequests for use of the poor, or other services of
> the society, of persons who have fallen short in the
> payment of their just debts, though legally discharged
> by their creditors; for until such persons have paid
> the deficiency, what they possess cannot in equity
> be considered as their own. And monthly meetings
> are desired to exercise due caution against too early
> admitting such individuals to take an active part in
> the discipline.[5]

This creates another possibility – that is, the creditors from one or both of the sequestrations had not had their debts met in full despite James being legally discharged. The sequestrations were in the public domain and would have been known by the committee. James may or may not have made a disclosure about the sequestrations. Apparently, the Quakers in Scotland were conservative in their outlook.

> The growth of membership was retarded and its
> decline at times accelerated by the meticulous care
> taken in admission and the readiness to disown for
> minor infractions of discipline. The frequency of the
> 'offence' of bankruptcy is remarkable; a disposition
> neither Quaker nor Scots to 'engage in hazardous and
> unwarrantable speculations' is censured.[6]

The Meeting postponed a decision for two years until finally, on 30 June 1841, the committee was discontinued because James had announced he was moving to Ireland.[7] It was fortunate that the Finlayson couple were enumerated in the 1841 census for Govan as this was held on the night of 6 June 1841. James was described as aged 70, of independent means and born out of the county. Margaret was enumerated as aged 66, of independent means and born within the county of Lanark. Their address was given as Highway within the village of Govan.[8] Highway does not exist today. Colin Quigley identified the road as Greenock Road in the 1841 census. He also located their residence as Napier's Land marked in blue on the map of Govan (Plate 10). 'Land' is used quite often in the early censuses and is an old Scots word for a building of two or more floors with an internal staircase.[9]

Ireland

James moved to Ireland after 30 June 1841. Why did they move to County Armagh, Ireland? A Scottish couple from Glasgow moving to Ireland bucks the trend of that time. According to Cage, writing about the cost of living in Glasgow, the annual increase of Irish matched that of the population as a whole from 1800 to 1840. This changed during the 1840s, when the annual rate of increase of the Irish overtook the population increase by 1.1 per cent.[10]

When he was in Glasgow, James had advertised in the *Belfast Newsletter*, referred to previous work in Ireland. There might also have been connections from his time in Paisley through the Orr family. The Paisley-based partnership W. & J. Orr was responsible for a large share of the finished cotton goods imported into Ireland.[11] Alternatively, he might have wanted to escape from the Glasgow community as he might have perceived them as judgmental through the experience of the Quaker membership application. Another reason for migrating might have been a down-turn in his personal finances following the loss of assets. Ireland might have had the cheaper cost of living. Records for Margaret in Ireland were not located and we cannot know if she remained in Scotland for some of the time or accompanied James. Earlier in her marriage when migrating to Russia and Finland, James preceded her. The letter Margaret wrote to Augusta Lundahl is reputed to come when she was in Ireland.[12] This is a copy as the original is missing and it is undated. However, the letter refers to an 1841 fire that destroyed the old factory buildings on 18 February 1841[13] and this substantiates that it might have been written from Ireland. Further, Margaret writes in the letter that her maid is returning to Finland. Perhaps this was one sign of Margaret and James cutting their expenses, although the maid's departure might have had a different cause.

The first reference to James is in the Society of Friends' Grange, monthly meeting on 18 January 1843, when he makes an application to join them. Grange is a parish in County Armagh, two miles north of Armagh, on the road to Belfast, as shown in the Samuel Lewis map of 1837 (Plate 11). The map shows the location of Lurgan as well as Grange.

> To the monthly meeting to be held on the 18th of the
> 1st mo. at Grange
>
> Beloved friends,
> I have felt for some time no wish to be united with
> you in fellowship of the Gospel, but having for these
> 30 years & upwards been not only standing as one
> idle in the market place but as being tossed up and
> down as the locust like the blind & led in a way they

transport. Yet at the eleventh hour the merciful the divine master's voice seems to me as if saying Why stand ye thereall the day idler go ye also into the vineyard & what is right shall ye have. I can delay no longer. If therefore after solemn waiting for direction the meeting shall feel it their duty to receive me as a member of the Society of Friends it is now my sincere wish. In the meantime I shall tenderly solicit the remembrance of all serious, weighty & sincere friends when to their sweet experience the time of refreshing are felt from the living fountain. James Finlayson[14]

Following two visits from the appointed committee, James was accepted as a member on 22 March 1843.[15] This was a much quicker process than in Scotland. We wonder whether through the 'sin of omission' no mention was made of creditors by James, and the committee were ignorant of the sequestrations. For example, as part of the removal to Moyallon, the Grange Monthly Meeting wrote this:

Dear Friends, James Finlayson a member of this meeting has removed to Moyallon in the compass of yours and upon enquiry made relative to his conduct & respecting debts nothing appears to prevent the issuing of a certificate on his behalf. We therefore recommend him to your Christian care & remain with love your friends.[16]

On 22 Nov 1843, the monthly meeting at Grange was informed that James had removed to Moyallon within the compass of the Lurgan Monthly Meeting.[17] Lurgan and its surroundings had been decimated on the night of 6 January 1839 by one of the worst storms in history, called The Night of the Big Wind. At the time, it was the worst storm to hit Ireland for 500 years. The storm damaged property and killed hundreds of people.[18] It seems unlikely that properties and livelihoods were completely restored by the time James moved into the area. The Great Hunger of 1845 to 1852 is a frequent focus in the subsequent history of Ireland and its diaspora. It started after James and Margaret returned to Scotland. Before 1845, famines existed in Ireland, with consequent food riots. A timeline of Irish famines includes the famine of 1842 where there was widespread distress.[19] All in all, it would have been a difficult time for outsiders to reside in County Armagh. These circumstances might have been the impetus for their migration back home to Scotland. The Lurgan Monthly Meeting of 10 Oct 1844 announced the removal of James from Lurgan Parish to Edinburgh.[20]

Why Edinburgh?

Why did they move here and not to Glasgow or other towns in the west of Scotland? There is no record in the correspondence of reasons for this decision. There might be various alternatives: economic; social networks; climate; public health; status; and/or stigma.

Nenadic argues that although there were similarities between the Glasgow and Edinburgh middling sorts, Edinburgh had the wealthier population and was a centre for professionals and administrators. Glasgow, on the other hand, attracted merchants, bankers and manufacturers.[21]

Perhaps Margaret and James were more suited to the lifestyle of Edinburgh residents. Nenadic goes on to say that Edinburgh people displayed a form of 'conspicuous parsimony'.[22]

Maybe the therapeutic benefit of climate played a part. Her death certificate reports that the cause of death was 'bronchitis senilis' or chronic bronchitis and that she had suffered from this for many years. Widdicombe explains in a history of bronchitis that chronic bronchitis is a progressive disease of the elderly. In the nineteenth century fewer people lived long enough to die from it.[23] Margaret was one of the few who lived long enough.

Glasgow is one of the rainiest cities in the United Kingdom. A recent survey of rainfall between 1981 and 2015 places Glasgow in the top three of wettest cities on a ranking based on its average annual rainfall of 1124.3mm with 170.3 days of rain per year.[24] This compares to Edinburgh having an average annual rainfall of 704.2mm and 124.2 days of rain. However, we wonder if people of the time were aware of this, as measurement of rainfall was not always accurate and depended on the placement of the rain gauge. In fact, the authors of the *New Statistical Account* entry for Glasgow make the claim that Glasgow was drier than Edinburgh.

> The quantity of rain which falls at Glasgow is less than at Edinburgh; this may be accounted for by the circumstance, that the former place is nearly twenty miles inland from the west coast, and is therefore beyond the immediate influence of the Atlantic, which renders some parts of the north-west of England so rainy, while its distance from the east coast, and the high land between it and Edinburgh, screen it from those violent rains, when the east wind blows, which are so common in Edinburgh. The distance of the hills from Glasgow is greater than from Edinburgh, and it is in some degree screened by high ground, both on the east and west.[25]

In addition to damp, both Glasgow and Edinburgh would have suffered from air pollution linked to the burning of coal and this would have not been helpful for chronic bronchitis.

David Stradling and Peter Thorsheim wrote about smoke pollution in British and American cities and observed that Manchester and Glasgow rivalled London for the title of smokiest urban development in the middle of the nineteenth century. The effect the smoke had on respiratory diseases, such as tuberculosis, bronchitis, pneumonia, and asthma was of considerable concern.[26]

It is likely that Margaret would have been aware of the impact of cleaner air on her condition. Not only had she experienced it by living in Tampere, but she also learned about it through her correspondence with Sarah Wheeler and the history of Wheeler deaths from pulmonary diseases. She would have heard about the theories of remediation through environment in connection with tuberculosis or consumption.

Sir James Clark, who was later in 1837 to become 'Physician-in-Ordinary' to Queen Victoria, treated John Keats for his consumption. Clark was particularly of the view that the climate and mineral waters were the most effective treatment in the recovery from consumption and in 1829 published *The Influence of Climate in the Preparation and Cure of Chronic Disease, more particularly of the Chest and Digestive Organs* and drew attention in particular to the south coast of the Isle of Wight as a suitable destination.[27] William Wheeler, Sarah's brother, travelled to the Isle of Wight to help with his bronchitis.[28] Sarah wrote about Louisa Ropes residing in Undercliff in one of her letters.

> From the accounts received from London dear Louisa remains much in the same state as when she left home, & I begin to fear it is doubtful whether she will experience any decided benefit from the change. She has had the care of three London physicians & their first report of the lungs, after examination with the Stethoscope, was that she sounded well; afterwards

they seemed to apprehend that one side of the chest
was diseased; & as her cough remains troublesome,
with oppression of the breathing & other not very
favorable symptoms, I fear their last statement may be
but too correct. They have ordered her to be removed
to Undercliffe in the isle of Wight – a very common
resort for the consumptive patients of our island as
the air & sea bathing are particularly favorable for
diseases of the chest. Happily for her comfort Sarah
Knill had been recommended to pass some time there
on account of her son's health who is very delicate so
it was arranged for them all to go there together. Dr
Wilkie, who passed nearly two years at Petersburg, &
whose very arbitrary banishment out of the country
for his zeal in distributing testaments you would
probably hear of, lives there, & Louisa is confided to
the care of a sister of the late E. Gellibrand, who spent
several years here – so that there will be at least six
individuals collected on one spot who have belonged
to the same circle here & most of whom had often
met during their residence in this city.[29]

Another possibility for the choice of Edinburgh is that
James may have been aware of the stigma of bankruptcies
and wanted to avoid being in a society whose members
knew about his business failures. He had experienced first
hand disapproval through the long-drawn-out application
process to join the Society of Friends that was only resolved
when he moved to Ireland. However, this seems unlikely
as Edinburgh and Glasgow Quakers combined in the two
monthly meeting.

The Finlaysons may have had friends or family in Edinburgh
and they moved to be near close contacts using personal networks. In summary, although economic factors affected the
timing and choice of emigration destination, other important

factors coming into play included the welcoming presence of friends and family and the costs of migration. [30]

A major consideration in the choice of Edinburgh may have been the proximity of two significant families residing in Edinburgh in the 1840s. For a childless couple in later life, moving to be close to friends can be a powerful motivator. Two families, well known to them, already lived in Edinburgh: William and Hannah Swan and John Paterson and his children George and Jean. In St Petersburg, Margaret had been very close to Jane Paterson and her daughter Jean. James had travelled with Paterson when prospecting opportunities in Tampere. Margaret and James met William Swan at the Patersons and maintained correspondence with him over a number of years. William and Hannah arrived in Edinburgh via St Petersburg on 20 June 1841. They remained there until their deaths in 1866 and 1890. John Paterson arrived in Edinburgh in July 1827. He resided in an apartment 10, Elm Row and stayed there until 1850 when he moved to Dundee to be closer to his daughter Jean.[31]

No. 8, Nicholson Square

When Margaret and James moved to Edinburgh they lived in lodgings in Nicolson Square – 0.8 mile from the Swans in St James Place and 1.2 miles from the Patersons in 10, Elm Row. Nicolson Square is on the south side of Edinburgh (see Plate 12). The development of the New Town and south side of Edinburgh signified the move from the medieval heart of Edinburgh where poverty and overcrowding created slum conditions. For a time, the South Side was a fashionable area of Edinburgh but its nineteenth-century development was 'respectable rather than smart'.[32]

At the south-west corner of the square is a Wesleyan Methodist church. It was built in 1814, with a minister's house and schools attached. After James and Margaret moved to Nicolson Square, number 12 was bought in 1846 to be fashioned into public baths for the working class.

PUBLIC BATHS, NICOLSON SQUARE. We are glad to learn that, since the opening of these baths – the result of long agitation and renewed subscriptions – the public have largely availed themselves of the accommodation that they afford. On several occasions, indeed, the number of applications for baths have been so great that the present apparatus has been found insufficient to supply the requisite quantity of hot water. We hope that the directors will soon be enabled to make such arrangements as will meet this deficiency. Saturdays and Mondays are the busiest days; and on some of these days, upward of 150 baths have been given, and nearly as many more unsuccessfully applied for. It is much to be regretted that any should ever be disappointed, and we have no doubt that as soon as the directors can prudently increase the accommodation of the present establishment, they will do so, and also take steps for the erection of new establishments in other quarters of the town. The house in Nicolson Square has the disadvantage of being somewhat obscurely situated, inasmuch as it is not seen from the street, and indeed does not attract attention till the visitor is at the very gate. We venture to say that many hundreds have daily passed along Nicolson Street, within twenty yards of the baths, without being at all aware of their near neighbourhood. If once introduced to them, however, we should think the acquaintance would be speedily and often renewed. All the arrangements are as neat, cleanly, and comfortable as could be desired. The first-class baths are lined with Dutch tiles, and are capacious and well-appointed. The second class are

scarcely inferior to these in any respect, except that
the bath itself is constructed wholly of wood. Nor is
the third class altogether destitute of attraction, for
though wanting some of the elegance of the other
two, the essentials are all there, and the price of course
is proportionally low. It is no slight luxury to be
able to command a comfortable warm bath for the
small sum of three pence. One halfpenny from the
daily earnings of the working man will enable him to
command this luxury every week.[33]

[Transcript *The Scotsman*, 1 December 1847, p.2 of 4]

How did James and Margaret view the footfall in their
square? Perhaps they made use of the facilities. Warm or cold
baths were one of the treatments for mental distress and so
the baths might have been used for their therapeutic effect
and not only for hygiene.[34] Richard Rodger estimated that,
on average, 420 people used the Nicolson Square baths and
washhouses each week between 1848 and 1853.[35]

Social circles in Edinburgh

The Quaker Edinburgh two months meeting on 12 December
1844 noted that James Finlayson was admitted to membership of their meeting, on the recommendation from Lurgan
monthly Meeting in County Armagh.[36] It appears that this
recommendation overcame their earlier concerns about
James' financial position with creditors. However, on 9 May
1846, James sent a letter of resignation to the Edinburgh two
monthly meeting of the Society of Friends.

A letter from James Finlayson of Edinbr, one of our
members has now been received & read tendering
the resignation of his membership in our Society.

The same having obtained some consideration, the
meeting concluded to appoint the following Friends
a Committee to visit him & report. Viz. William
Smeal, William Miller & Robert Mason.[37]

In a letter dated 30 January 1849, Ferdinand Uhde wrote to
Sarah Wheeler and mentions James' writing style. We do not
know what is meant by his 'old style' – maybe they were too
'flowery' and verbose.

I lately got a letter from old Finlayson written in his
old style. He alludes to some letter or letters which he
has published against the Society of friends. Have you
seen them, and what is their contents?[38]

The committee visited James but were unable to persuade
him to withdraw his application:

The Committee appointed to visit James Finlayson
have bro in the following report Viz. 'To the Two
Months Meeting. Agreeably to our appointment we
have had an opportunity with James Finlayson on the
subject of his proposed resignation of Membership
which we think you may say was to some degree of
satisfaction inasmuch as we were impressed with
the opinion that he was disposed to reconsider his
proposal. Two of our number have had another
interview with him which however was not so much
to their satisfaction as James Finlayson distinctly
stated his determination to adhere to his resignation
of membership with Friends – 'Glasgow 11th of 8th
Month 1846 William Miller, William Smeal, Robert
Mason. – Which having been read & considered,
the meeting concluded to accept of James Finlayson's
resignation of his Membership and directed the Clerk
to inform him thereof.[39]

On 13 June 1849, Sarah Wheeler married William Tanner, a Quaker minister, in England. Uhde seemed to have lost touch and wrote to William Tanner, Sarah Wheeler's husband in the same year.

> Pray can you without inconvenience get to know, whether James Finlayson and his wife (our predecessors here) are still living at Edinburgh? For more than a year no accounts have been received from them, and it is feared they are no more amongst the living.[40]

In 1849, James purchased a burial plot or lair at Newington Cemetery in Edinburgh for £1 1/-[41]. It is possible that he felt the intimations of mortality. Uhde wrote to Sarah Tanner in 1850 and told her that James and Margaret were in poor circumstances regarding health and accommodation.

> It appears the Gellibrands have also visited Scotland for I had a letter the other day from Wm Swan mentioning their stay with him. W.S. wrote to inform me that J. & M. Finlayson were in a sinking state of health, and that their lodgings and accommodations were not such as their friends could wish; he therefore wished to know whether the present proprietors of the concern at this place, could not be induced to contribute to alleviate their wants. I wrote to the parties at Petg and trust they will make a remittance. James F. is said to be yet tolerably strong but his wife seems to be drooping most.[42]

1851 census

The 1851 census was taken on the night of 30 March and enumerated James and Margaret with the following details:

James Finlayson (80), Lodger, place of birth Peebles,
Pennycook Annuitant and Margaret Finlayson
(77) place of birth Glasgow, Annuitant. Address 8
Nicolson Square Edinburgh.[43]

As mentioned in previous chapters, Penicuik was in
Edinburghshire or Midlothian county. The mistake is puzzling
and suggests that James was born on a bordering parish with
Peeblesshire. It is unlikely that a Scottish enumerator would
have placed Penicuik in the wrong county. The census entry
also confirms that Margaret was born in Glasgow between 31
March 1773 and 30 March 1774. Being described as an annuitant means that they received some form of pension either
from a previous employer or an insurance company. Taking
in lodgers was common in Edinburgh, as householders sought
to spread housing costs. Rodger analysed occupancy from the
1871 census and found that between a third and a quarter of
all three to eight room houses had lodgers; one fifth of two
room houses had lodgers and they accounted for 30–40% of
the household.[44]

The Post Office Directories for 1851 and following years
only list residents of note and the Finlaysons at 8, Nicolson
Square are not listed. There is an entry for 8, Nicolson Square,
Edinburgh: Finlayson, James, late merchant in the electoral
register.[45] Following the Reform Act (Scotland) in 1832 the
franchise was extended to adult males occupying property
in Scottish Burghs such as Edinburgh, worth at least £10
per annum, provided that they had been in possession of the
property for at least one year; had paid all taxes charged on the
property; and that they had not been in receipt of parish poor
relief during the previous year.[46]

Other electors in Nicolson Square are:

No. 1   Brown, James, teacher (tenant)

No. 2   Deuchar, Robert, solicitor (tenant)

No. 2   Robertson, Alexander, plumber (tenant)

No. 3   Milburn, George, surgeon (tenant)

No. 6   Jamieson, Peter, wine merchant (tenant)

No. 6   Fraser, Andrew, compositor (tenant)

No. 7   Young, John C., bookkeeper (tenant)

No. 7   Leslie, Norman, porter (tenant)

No. 8   Finlayson, James, late merchant (tenant)

No. 11   Steven, William, D.D. (tenant)

No. 12   Little, David, bath-keeper (proprietor)

No. 13   Brunton, William, merchant residence. 40 George Square (proprietor)

No. 14   Paterson, John C. warehouseman (tenant)

An attempt at reconciliation with the Quakers

As James' health failed, he reconsidered his relationship with the Society of Friends and there is a record dated 11 March 1852 in the two-month meeting:

> The following letter from James Finlayson of Edinburgh who some years ago resigned his membership with the Society has now been received and read and is sent to the Womens' meeting to be read there, viz. 'To the Two Months Meeting of Friends intending to meet in their usual place, in Pleasance Edinburgh on 7th day of 5 Month 1852. Beloved Friends. After having withdrawn from religious union and fellowship with you for reasons which at one time appeared in my view sufficient to call for such a step. But after mature reflection and seriously weighing in the 'balance of the Sanctuary', it now appears as my duty thus to come before you and herein seriously solicit your forgiveness for not only leaving the bond of

union and religious fellowship so highly valued at one
period by our progenitors and frequently purchased
with their lives and property – but by injuring the
personal feelings of many among you by the frequent
withdrawing when an accepted ministering Friend
rose to address you, the minds of several may have
been injured. I again solicit your forgiveness. And
from present bodily weakness and age, death is
making hasty approaches; I will at same time entreat
your tender sympathy while breathing for rain to
come down on the new mown grass or as showers
that water the earth that I may steadfastly resist the
many attempts made by our vigilant adversary to turn
away from the belief of a risen Redeemer and seated
on His throne forever. With sentiments of sincere
regard, I am, Dear Friends, your sincere well wisher
James Finlayson' This meeting feeling satisfaction in
the receipt of such an expression of sentiment on the
part of James Finlayson, deems it right to appoint
the following Friends to call upon him and convey to
him the feeling of the meeting thereon, viz. William
Smeal, John Wigham jr, and Robert Mason.[47]

The three Friends visited James and their report was includ-
ed in the records of the meeting on 17 June 1852. John Wigham,
Junior (1781–1862) of Salisbury Road and John Wigham,
Tertius (1784–1864) of Grey Street, both in Edinburgh, were
among the leading Edinburgh Friends. They were cousins and
the former was the uncle and the latter was the father of Eliza
Wigham who visited Margaret in her last years. It was John
Wigham, Jnr who visited James.

John Wigham reports on behalf of himself and other
Friends appointed at last meeting to call on James
Finlayson they attended to the appointment and felt
that the opportunity was one of mutual comfort &

encouragement; James Finlayson having expressed to
them, the cordial & thankful in which he received the
visit[48]

    The visit happened a few months before James died on 18
August 1852.[49] The death is recorded with his age given as 87.
This is incorrect and perhaps is the result of a transcription
error of 87 for 81. His death was at home and the cause of death
was 'decline of life'. His place of birth was given as Penicuik and
the funeral was from his home at 8, Nicolson Square.

Widowhood

Uhde wrote to Sarah Tanner about the death and about
Margaret's abortive plans as his widow.

> No doubt you will have heard that James Finlayson
> died at Edinbg on the 18th August 83 years old.
> I know no further particulars about his death,
> but Catherine got a very pressing invitation from
> Margaret F. to come now and join and nurse her
> immediately. Catherine was at a loss what to do, but I
> represented to her the folly for going out so late in the
> season, and without any certain prospect of getting a
> livelihood in Scotland. M. F. wrote they would work
> together for their bread knitting stocking and socks
> for children and other such work, but how could
> they support themselves with such needle work since
> machines in England will do it cheaper and better?
> Catherine wrote in answer that she must consider the
> proposal till next spring, but that she would suggest
> whether it would not be far better for Marg F. to
> come to Tammerfors and settle here where hundreds
> would be glad to see her, and the little she wants

could be readily supplied. I myself wrote to Wm Swan
on the subject, but have not yet received an answer.
The news of his (J. F.) death has gone through all
the papers in Finland, such an interest was still felt
'for the person who created the first Cotton mill in
Finland, and broke the way to other establishments.'[50]

Presumably, Catherine is Katarina Ekblom, 'a linguistically
adept young woman who came to work as a maid for the
Finlayson family.'[51]

> Katarina Ekblom, known as the 'old maid'. She came
> from Kumlinge in Åland, where she was born on 20th
> December 1800. She had spent the best part of her
> development in the serious pentecostalism of Western
> Finland. In 1833 she entered the service of Finlayson
> and learned the English language in his family. Her
> employers loved her as their own child. Her leisure
> time was spent in reading, and she devoted a compar-
> atively large amount of her time to reading, especially
> on religious and missionary matters. Later, when the
> factory passed into other hands, she was manager of
> the Finlayson yarn shop.[52]

Fortunately, William Swan's intervention led to Finlayson
& Co. providing an annual pension that meant there was no
need to move to Tampere or involve Catherine in setting up
a knitting enterprise.

> But Margaret Finlayson would be told, and in fact
> she never returned an answer to our invitation to
> come over to us, but Wm Swan wrote that she had
> now given up the thought of letting Catherine come
> out to her. As W. S. represented her case to be rather

destitute, having only an annuity of £40. Finlayson
& Co have granted her a yearly pension of £30 which
W. S. thinks will fully cover her all her wants.[53]

Less than three years after being widowed, Margaret died
on 15 February 1855 and was buried with James in Newington
Cemetery on 19 February 1855. The arrangements were made
by the funeral director. As she died in 1855, there is a statutory
death certificate with the following information:

> Margaret Wilkie or Finlayson died aged 82 at 9
> Nicholson Square, Edinburgh. Cause of death
> bronchitis seniles for many years. Doctor saw her on
> the day before she died. Birthplace and parents were
> unknown. 9 years in the district Informant was John
> Smith the undertaker. Burial place was Newington
> Necropolis.[54]

An announcement was made in the local newspaper.

> Margaret Wilkie, relict of the late Mr James Finlayson
> – 8 Nicolson Square, 15th inst.[55]
>
> [Transcript *Edinburgh News and Literary Chronicle*,
> 24 February 1855. British Newspaper Archive.]

The death certificate has the incorrect house number
according to the burial record.[56] Uhde wrote to Sarah Tanner
on the 31 March 1855 sharing that he had been informed of
Margaret's death. The news was rather overshadowed by the
news of the death of Tsar Nicholas I who died on 2 March
1855, during the Crimean War.

> The first came only a week after I had sent off my
> letter, and the second brought the information of the
> death of Margaret Finlayson. The very same mail that

brought that information was also the messenger of the Emperor's death. It was a great shock to receive two such accounts at same time, and so utterly unexpected! But in the case of M. Finlayson we all here saw no cause for mourning. She had attained a very high age, and is now released from every suffering that is the companion of a solitary old age. About her eternal happiness there can neither be any doubt so that in times as these we may adopt the language which you quote: 'then I praised the dead who are already dead'.[57] .... 'I feel particularly obliged to you for the letter of your friend E. Wigham giving a minuter account of the last days and moments of M. F. than I had from Wm Swan whose letter arrived at same time with yours, so that on that night there came from all sides messages of death.[58]

Rather frustratingly, the letters referred to (of William Swan or E. Wigham) appear to be lost. We assume that the latter is Eliza Wigham, a well-known figure in Quaker circles. She was closely involved in the anti-slavery movement.[59] We do not, therefore, have this detailed view of Margaret's last days.

NOTES

1 Religious Society of Friends (Quakers) records (1839). Edinburgh Two Monthly Meeting Minutes. FINLAYSON, James. 4 May. South East & West Scotland Monthly Meeting. p. 140. CH10/1/6. National Records of Scotland, Edinburgh, Scotland. Used with permission from the Clerk.

2 Religious Society of Friends (Quakers) records (1839). Edinburgh Two Monthly Meeting Minutes. FINLAYSON, James. 13 August. South East & West Scotland Monthly Meeting. p. 147. CH10/1/6. National Records of Scotland, Edinburgh, Scotland. Used with permission from the Clerk.

3 Peltola, J. (2020) RE: Finlayson's Bankrupt 1807?' E-mail to Angela Harris, 9 June.

4   Uhde, F. (1840) Letter to: C. S. Nottbeck 11 May. p. 480, Kotimaahan
    lähetettyjen kirjeiden toisteet (Letter book of letters sent domestically),
    428:IDaa.3. ELKA. Used with permission from ELKA.

5   London Yearly Meeting (Society of Friends) (1834) Rules of discipline of
    the Religious Society of Friends, with advices: Being extracts from the
    minutes and epistles of their Yearly Meeting, held in London, from its
    first institution. Third ed. London: Darton and Harvey. p. 276.

6   Marwick, W. H. (1954) Friends in nineteenth century Scotland. The
    Journal of the Friends Historical Society, 46(1), pp. 3–18. p. 7.

7   Religious Society of Friends (Quakers) records (1841). Edinburgh Two
    Monthly Meeting Minutes. FINLAYSON, James. 30 June., South East &
    West Scotland Monthly Meeting.. p. 140. CH10/1/6. National Records
    of Scotland, Edinburgh, Scotland. p. 183. Used with permission from the
    Clerk.

8   Census records. Scotland. Govan village, Lanark. 06 June 1841. FIN-
    LAYSON,James. 646/ 2/ 43. http://www.scotlandspeople.gov.uk :
    accessed 19 March 2020.

9   Quigley, Colin (2020) Govan in 1841. E-mail to Angela Harris 13 April.

10 Cage, R. A. (1983) The standard of living debate: Glasgow, 1800-1850.
    The Journal of Economic History, 43(1). pp. 175–182

11 Nisbet, S. and Foster, J. (2008) Protection, inward investment and the
    early Irish cotton industry: The experience of William and John Orr.
    Irish Economic and Social History, 35(1), pp. 23–50.

12 Kaarninen, M. (2020) Letter from Augusta Lundahl Query. E-mail to
    Angela Harris. 1 June.

13 G. V. Lindfors (1938) Finlayson-fabrikerna I Tammerfors Del 1: 1820-
    1907. Helsingfors: Tilgmann. pp. 175–178.

14 Congregational Records Ireland (1843). Grange Monthly Meeting,
    Congregational Archive (1843) FINLAYSON, James, 18 January. Ulster
    Friends Trustees Ltd Ireland, Society of Friends (Quaker). Archive
    reference: GM5.12. Courtesy of Friends (Quaker) Historical Library,
    Dublin. http://www.findmypast.co.uk : accessed 27 July 2023.

15 Congregational Records, Ireland (1843). Grange Monthly Meeting, Congregational Archive (1843) FINLAYSON, James, 22 March. Ulster Friends Trustees Ltd Ireland, Society of Friends (Quaker) Archive reference: GM5.12. Courtesy of Friends (Quaker) Historical Library, Dublin. http://www.findmypast.co.uk : accessed 27 July 2023.

16 Congregational records, Ireland (1844). Grange Monthly Meeting, Congregational Archive FINLAYSON James. 24 January. Removal Certificate from Grange to Lurgan Monthly Meeting. Ulster Friends Trustees Ltd, Society of Friends (Quaker). LGM5.8. Courtesy of Friends (Quaker) Historical Library, Dublin. http://www.findmypast.co.uk : accessed 28 July 2023.

17 Congregational Records, Ireland (1843). Grange Monthly Meeting, Congregational Archive. FINLAYSON, James. 22 November. Ulster Friends Trustees Ltd, Society of Friends (Quaker). GM1.6 Courtesy of Friends (Quaker) Historical Library, Dublin. http://www.findmypast.co.uk : accessed 28 July 2023.

18 Watters, F. (1994) The Night of the Big Wind, 1839. 'Before I Forget...': Journal of the Poyntzpass and District Local History Society 7. pp. 73–82. https://www.jstor.org/stable/25512111 : accessed 28 July 2023.

19 Kinealy, C. and Moran, G. (eds) (2020) Irish famines before and after the great hunger. Quinnipiac University Press.

20 Congregational Records, Ireland (1844). Lurgan removals. FINLAYSON, James 10 October. Removal from Lurgan Parish to Edinburgh Parish. Ulster Friends Trustees Ltd, Society of Friends (Quaker). Microfilm reel 30 & 32 (Record books held in Lisburn, Ireland). Courtesy of Friends (Quaker) Historical Library, Dublin. http://www.findmypast.co.uk : accessed 28 July 2023.

21 Nenadic, S. (1994) Middle-rank consumers and domestic culture in Edinburgh and Glasgow 1720–1840. Past and Present, 145(1), pp. 122–156.

22 Nenadic, S. (1994).

23 Widdicombe, J. H. (2020) A Brief History of Bronchitis in England and Wales. Chronic Obstructive Pulmonary Diseases, 7(4), pp. 303–314.

24 Walker, E. (2018) Preston ranked in the UK cities to see the most rain. Preston Blog, 21 March. www.blogpreston.co.uk/2018/03/preston-ranked-in-the-uk-cities-to-see-the-most-rain/ : accessed: 21 August 2023.

25 J. Gordon, ed., The New Statistical Account of Scotland / by the Ministers of the Respective Parishes, under the Superintendence of a Committee of the Society for the Benefit of the Sons and Daughters of the Clergy. Glasgow, Lanark. (1999), vol. 6 (Edinburgh: Blackwoods and Sons, 1845), p. 103. https://stataccscot.edina.ac.uk:443/link/nsa-vol6-p101-parish-lanark-glasgow : accessed 20 August 2023.

26 Stradling, D. and Thorsheim, P. (1999) The smoke of great cities: British and American efforts to control air pollution, 1860-1914. Environmental History, 4(1). pp. 6–31.

27 Royal National Hospital for Chest Diseases, The: A Victorian hospital (no date) Isle of Wight Hospitals: A Detailed History of the Island's Hospitals – Past and Present. http://www.iowhospitals.org.uk/index.php : accessed 21 August 2023.

28 Kaarninen, M. (2022) The trials of Sarah Wheeler (1807–1867): Experiencing submission. In: Histories of Experience in the World of Lived Religion. Springer International Publishing. pp. 195–217.

29 Wheeler, S. (1836) Letter to Margaret Finlayson 20th June. The Margareta Finlayson Archive/Central Archives for Finnish Business Records. ELKA-00427-000001-022-DOC. Used with permission from ELKA.

30 Lloyd, A. J. (2007) Emigration, immigration and migration in nineteenth-century Britain. Detroit: Gale (Contextual Essays from Gale Primary Sources. British Library Newspapers) ; 30 July 2023.

31 Alexander, J. M. (1974) John Paterson, Bible Society pioneer; 1776-1855; the later years 1813-55. The Records of the Scottish Church History Society, VIII. pp. 181–200.

32 Gifford, J. et al. (2003) The buildings of Scotland: Edinburgh. London: Yale University Press (Pevsner Architectural Guides: Buildings of Scotland). p. 239.

33 Scotsman, The (1847) 'Public Baths, Nicolson Square', 1 December, p. 2. https://www.britishnewspaperarchive.co.uk : accessed 18 August 2023.

34 Houston, R. A. (1998) Therapies for mental ailments in eighteenth-century Scotland. Journal of the Royal College of Physicians of Edinburgh, 28(4). pp. 555–568.

35 Rodger, R. (2004) The transformation of Edinburgh: Land, property and trust in the nineteenth century. Cambridge: Cambridge University Press. p. 489.

36 Burton, P. F. (2019) James Finlayson. E-mail to Angela Harris 17 December.

37 Religious Society of Friends (Quakers) records (1846). Edinburgh Two Monthly Meeting Minutes. FINLAYSON, James. 9 May. South East & West Scotland Monthly Meeting. CH10/1/6. National Records of Scotland, Edinburgh, Scotland. p. 277. Used with permission from the Clerk.

38 Uhde, F. (1849). Letter to Sarah Wheeler 30 January. Millfield Papers (MIL). Alfred Gillett Trust Archives. MIL_29_5 Uhde 1849-01-30.

39 Religious Society of Friends (Quakers) records (1839). Edinburgh Two Monthly Meeting Minutes. FINLAYSON, James. 13 August. Records of the Religious Society of Friends (Quakers), South East & West Scotland Monthly Meeting. p. 147. CH10/1/6. National Records of Scotland, Edinburgh, Scotland. Used with permission from the Clerk.

40 Uhde, F. (1849). Letter to William Tanner. 30 October. Millfield Papers (MIL). Alfred Gillett Trust Archives. MIL_29_5 Uhde 1849-10-30.

41 Newington Necropolis. Sales Book. James Finlayson 1772–1852.

42 Uhde, F. (1850) Letter to Sarah Tanner. 10 October. Millfield Papers (MIL), Alfred Gillett Trust Archives. MIL_29_5 Uhde 1850-10-10.

43 Census Records, Scotland. St Cuthbert's, Midlothian. 30 March 1851. FINLAYSON, James and Margaret'. 685/2 193/ ScotlandsPeople. ©Crown copyright, National Records of Scotland, [archival reference]. www.scotlandspeople.gov.uk : accessed 24 March 2020.

44 Rodger, R. (2004). p. 279.

45 Poll Books and Electoral Registers, 1538-1893 (1852). Scotland. Street
    list of electors of the City of Edinburgh as in Register after Appeal
    Court 1854, with the voting of each elector at General Election 1852
    (no date). Edinburgh (UK, [database online]). https://www.ancestry.
    co.uk/ : accessed 22 August 2023.

46 Evans, E.J. (1994) The Great Reform Act of 1832. 2nd ed. London:
    Routledge. pp. 68–71.

47 Religious Society of Friends (Quakers) records (1852). Edinburgh Two
    Monthly Meeting Minutes. FINLAYSON, James.11 March. South East
    & West Scotland Monthly Meeting. pp. 65–66. CH10/1/7. National
    Records of Scotland, Edinburgh, Scotland'. Used with permission from
    the Clerk.

48 Religious Society of Friends (Quakers) records (1852). Edinburgh Two
    Monthly Meeting Minutes. FINLAYSON, James.17 June. Records of
    the Religious Society of Friends (Quakers), South East & West Scotland
    Monthly Meeting. pp. 68–69. CH10/1/7. National Records of Scotland,
    Edinburgh, Scotland. Used with permission from the Clerk.

49 Burials (OPR) Scotland. St Cuthbert's Edinburgh. 18 August 1852. FIN-
    LAYSON, James. 685/ 2. http://www.scotlandspeople.gov.uk : accessed
    22 August 2023.

50 Uhde, F. (1852). Letter to Sarah Tanner, 23 October. Millfield Papers
    (MIL), Alfred Gillett Trust Archives. MIL_29_5 Uhde 1850-10-10.

51 Koskinen, K. (2014) Tampere as a translation space. Translation Stud-
    ies, 7(2), pp. 186–202.

52 Hirvonen, Y. (1943) Herätysajan henkilöitä Tampereella (People of
    the Waking Hours). Tammerkoski-lehdessä (Tampere Magazine), 2. p.
    42–43.

53 Uhde, F. (1853). Letter to Sarah Tanner. 14 January. Millfield Papers
    (MIL), Alfred Gillett Trust Archives. MIL_29_5 Uhde 1850-10-10.

54 Deaths (CR) Scotland. Castle and Portsburgh, Edinburgh. FIN-
    LAYSON, Margaret, 15 February 1855. 685/3 124'. http://www.
    scotlandspeople.gov.uk : accessed 24 March 2020. ©Crown copyright,
    National Records of Scotland, [archival reference].

55 Deaths (CR) Scotland. Castle and Portsburgh, Edinburgh. FIN-
    LAYSON, Margaret.

56 Newington Necropolis (1855). Burial Book of Newington Cemetery. 19
    February. WILKIE, Margaret.

57 Uhde, F. (1855) Letter to Sarah Tanner 31 March. Millfield Papers
    (MIL), Alfred Gillett Trust Archives. MIL_30_3 1855-03-31.

58 Uhde, F. (1855) Letter to Sarah Tanner 31 March.

59 Smith, C. J. (1986) Historic South Edinburgh: People, Vol. 3. pp. 25–27.
    Haddington: Charles Skilton Ltd.

– CHAPTER NINE –

Threads in the yarn

So let us today drudge on about our inescapably impossible task of providing every week a first rough draft of history that will never really be completed about a world we can never really understand ... (Philip Leslie Graham, 1963)[1]

❧❦❧

There is no getting it 'right' in history. The past cannot be recaptured and represented 'as it was,' for the writing of history is always about drawing conclusions from insufficient evidence. (Tim Cook, Clio's Warriors, 2011)[2]

❧❦❧

But then this bold judgment is submitted to the critique of the corporation of historians and to the critique of the enlightened public, and the work subjected to an unending process of revision, which makes the writing of history a perpetual rewriting. (Paul Ricoeur, Memory, history, forgetting, 2004)[3]

ᏕᏚᏟᎦ

Sapiens non affirmat quod non probet –
A wise man does not assert that which he cannot
prove. (Latin proverb)

ᏕᏚᏟᎦ

T his final chapter sets James and Margaret in their time
and place. There is a reciprocal connection to the settings described: they were influenced by and they, in
return influenced time and place. This exposition is followed
by a selection of threads or themes that span more than one
part of their life stages. It ends with concluding observations
about the Finlaysons. This is not a conclusion, as there may
well be more to find out about them.

History is a mix of the sources that are available: the stance
of the historian and the times of both the characters studied
and their researchers. Archivists and historians are advised to
be tentative in their declarations, because of the incomplete-
ness of source material.[4] The first quotation was addressed
to news reporters. It could equally apply to the narrators of
the Finlaysons. In the case of the story of James and Margaret
Finlayson, there was limited information easily accessible for
researchers. Prior to this, there was some information in contemporaries' memoirs of the Finlayson's early life. Memoirs of
the time spent in St Petersburg were published by missionaries
such as William Swan (1823),[5] William Allen (1847)[6] and John
Paterson (1858).[7]

Finlayson Oy in Tampere was the first Finnish company
to commission a company history and this publication
provided some of the information in circulation. Inevitably,

the focus was the company and the data on James' earlier years before emigrating to Finland and post Finland were scant. On Margaret, there was very little to say at all. Partly this might reflect the patriarchal perspective of the times. However, as Sivula claimed, until recently commissioned company histories were not regarded as 'proper history' but instead were judged to be applied history.[8]

The unpublished handwritten manuscript of the Finlayson company history by Sigurd Roos was written at the time Vladimir Ilich Lenin died on 21 January 1924. Gustav Lindfors (1938)[9] based the first published history of the company on Roos' manuscript for the James and Margaret's timespan at Tampere.[10] Fewster in 1970 wrote the second published history.[11] All accounts make use of available company archives and oral history of the early lives of James and Margaret. Family historians recognise how repeated oral history can develop into legends. Sullivan argued that legends tend to grow around inessentials, unless they are clearly delineated from facts:

> They have thus left the field to the less meticulous popularizers who have mixed their facts and their fictions into an attractive narrative without so much as a warning as to the difference between the two.[12]:

Legends can be inaccurate for many reasons: the person falsified information deliberately (secrecy and misdirection); exaggeration (to aggrandise the self); embellishment (to make a much more dramatic story); faulty memory; and misinterpretation of conversations. Possible examples of misinterpretation could be: 'I came from Glasgow' translated by the hearer as 'I was born in Glasgow'; 'we left Scotland 20 years ago' translated as 'I spent 20 years in Russia'. Unlike today, the eighteenth and nineteenth century people did not have access to electronic recorders. Sullivan writes about memory:

> As a matter of fact no one in the early nineteenth
> century could recall accurately the very words which
> were spoken.[13]

However, a legend should not be dismissed, as it is possible and even probable that there is a grain of truth in it. By generating and verifying source citations, historians may separate the facts from fiction. They allow others to reverse-engineer legends. Fortunately, three core sources: Selleck,[14] Denoon[15] and Peltola[16] were rigorous about supporting their arguments with sources. However, many authors do not provide sources and even in the three exemplary articles, some data is published without supporting evidence.

In addition to what is written, the historian should also pay attention to what is not written. Silences can be revealing. Silences enter the process of historical production at four crucial moments: the moment of fact creation (the making of *sources*); the moment of fact assembly (the making of *archives*); the moment of fact retrieval (the making of *narratives*); and the moment of retrospective significance (the making of *history* in the final instance).[17]

In summary, several articles claimed: James Finlayson was born in Penicuik in 1772; married Margaret Wilkie in Paisley in 1792; worked in Glasgow and possibly England; the couple emigrated to St Petersburg and James was employed as a chief machinist at the Kolpino works; they moved to Tampere in Finland; he founded a cotton mill and they retired first to Govan and then Edinburgh where he died aged 80 and she died aged 82. He attended meetings and was a member of the Religious Society of Friends (Quakers).

246 \ NINE: THREADS IN THE YARN

The early life in Scotland and Russia was to a large extent unknown.

There was a tendency to over-emphasise James' importance both in Saint Petersburg and Finland. Perhaps this was a result of James' own self-aggrandisement or perhaps it made a more exciting story to retell. If James Finlayson was a man of mystery, Margaret was an even more mysterious woman. Unlike James, no portrait of her has surfaced, although a likeness was made in 1836 according to Sarah Wheeler's letter.[18] It was thought that she was born in 1776 and married James when she was 16 years of age in Paisley.

Historical accounts are skewed by the interests and personal histories of the historians telling the story. This has balanced the weight given to events in Finland and Tampere. Scottish data revealed the emigration from Scotland to St Petersburg. Was it as remarkable as it seemed for this intrepid couple to emigrate to Russia and Finland? Was James' poor health related, either physical or mental, or indeed both? What did he understand about mill construction compared to weaving and spinning machinery? How does James' experience fit with the industrial technology of Britain and Russia? What impact did Margaret's barrenness have on her working and home life? How much did social class bear on their relationships?

New access to primary data sources has been progressive. Drivers for this include the following:

1. In 1991 the Soviet Union collapsed and access to archives improved. The Russian Genealogical Society was established in 1991 and since then interest in Russian genealogy has expanded.

2. 7 July 2011 – Electronic inventories of RGIA were posted on the website and access to electronic records of the

Russian State Historical Archive became possible, including from the official website of Rosarkhiv. Thus, the circle of possible users of this RGIA resource has become much wider.

3. 29 November 2011 the British Newspaper Archive was launched online as a searchable database:

   (a) Caledonian Mercury (1720–1859) was digitised and first made available on the British Newspaper Archive on 10 Feb 2013. The latest issues were added on 25 Feb 2015.

   (b) Perth Courier (1809–22) was digitised and first made available on the British Newspaper Archive on 10 Jul 2015. The latest issues were added on 17 Nov 2015.

4. 2016–2017 digitised Irish Quaker records were added to the Findmypast website, searchable by last name.

5. From 26 June 2017, the official Scottish Government site for searching government records and archives – The ScotlandsPeople website – added baptism records covering the period 1752–1855 from dissenting Presbyterian churches which were outside the established Church of Scotland.

6. August 2017 – DeepL Translator was released to the public, offering free translations between English, German, French, Spanish, Italian, Polish, and Dutch. With never-before-achieved translation quality, DeepL raised the bar for the entire field of machine translation. In December 2018, DeepL Translator saw the addition of Russian. In March 2021, DeepL Translator added Finnish.

As ever, disproof is easier than proof. Table 19 lists some of the sources and where these 'facts' have been disproved, upheld or left as unproven.

Table 19: Proof summaries

Claim	Source(s)	Fact Check – Revise/ Uphold/Suspend Judgment (Not Proven)	See Chapter
James Finlayson			
Birth date 1771	Lindfors (1938): p. 27	Revise: new information	Ch. 2, Penicuik
Birth date 29 August 1772	Denoon (1991): p.122	Revise: new information	Ch. 2, Penicuik
Birth place of Glasgow	Lindfors (1938): p.27	Revise: new information	Ch. 2, Penicuik
Self-trained engineer	MacLean [19]	Suspend judgment: conflicting information	Ch. 2, Penicuik
Quakerism main driving force	Lindfors (1938): p.30; Fewster (1970): p.6;	Revise: new information	Ch. 2, Penicuik & Ch. 9 Threads
Builder of wool and flax machinery	Selleck (1962): p.33	Uphold	Ch. 4 & 5, Glasgow
Set up Alexandrovsky Cotton Mill	Wikipedia[20]	Revise: new information	Ch. 6, Russia
Personal friend of the Tsar Alexander I	Lindfors (1938): p. 28; Denoon (1991): p.120	Revise: new information	Ch. 6, Russia
Weak health	Denoon (1991): p.120	Revise: new information	Ch. 6, Russia
Experienced mill engineer	Geni profile (2018)	Revise: new information	Ch. 4 & 5, Glasgow
Chief machinist at Kolpino	Fewster (1970); Denoon (1991): p.120; Selleck (1962): p33; Nykänen (2018)[21]	Revise: new information	Ch. 6, Russia

Claim	Source(s)	Fact Check – Revise/ Uphold/Suspend Judgment (Not Proven)	See Chapter
Worked in Russia for 20 years	Fewster (1970); Denoon (1991): p.120	Revise: new information	Ch. 6, Russia
Emigrated to Russia in 1800 or 1817	Nykänen (2018)	Revise: new information	Ch. 6, Russia
Worked in England	Selleck (1962): p.33	Revise: new information	Ch. 4 & 5, Glasgow
With Margaret, set up orphanage as charitable concern	Lindfors (1938): p.87	Revise: new information	Ch. 4 & 5, Glasgow; Ch. 6, Russia
Lack of business acumen	Lindfors (1938): p.89	Uphold and new information	Ch. 4 & 5, Glasgow
Margaret Wilkie			
Birth date 5 April 1775	Nykänen (2018)	Suspend judgment: conflicting information	Ch. 3, Paisley
Birth place of Markinch	Nykänen (2018)	Suspend judgment: conflicting information	Ch. 3, Paisley
Parents George Wilkie & Isabel Sibbald	Nykänen (2018)	Suspend judgment: conflicting information	Ch. 3, Paisley
Birth date 12 May 1776	Kaarninen (2019)	Suspend judgment: conflicting information	Ch. 3, Paisley
Birth place of Abbey, Paisley	Kaarninen (2002)	Suspend judgment: conflicting information	Ch. 3, Paisley
Parents Petter Wilkie & Elizabeth Jamison	Kaarninen (2019)	Suspend judgment: conflicting information	Ch. 3, Paisley
Employed destitute people on the land in famine	Denoon (1991): p.124	Uphold	Ch. 7, Finland
Entrepreneur: home industry and sulphur washing	Lindfors (1938): p.86	Uphold	Ch. 7, Finland

Historical context

The fallacy of 'presentism' (also known as the fallacy of 'nunc pro tunc' or 'now for then') concerns the bias of interpreting the past in terms of modern values and concepts. We look at history with the benefit of hindsight that was not available for the characters under review. There is also an arrogance of the assumption of the superiority of the current generation of historians. Hartog concluded that we cannot escape from doing this, as even our selection of evidence is guided by our present-day values. Hartog opines that 'we are always looking both backwards and forwards, but without ever leaving this present (p.203).'[22]

If we cannot avoid presentism, we hope to mitigate it somewhat by considering contextual evidence surrounding the lives of James and Margaret. The preceding chapters are organised by where they lived and, to some extent, how the Finlaysons were influenced by these places and, maybe, how they influenced the places.

> Give me a child until he is seven and I will show you the man.

This quote is attributed to Aristotle. Morris Massey, the sociologist, observed that peoples' values were formed between eight and thirteen by where we live at that time.[23] These values remain relatively fixed but can be changed by significant and painful emotional events. It, therefore, makes a difference if you were around ten years of age living through the London Blitz in World War Two, or in Russia under Stalin.

The period covered by this account of the lives of the Finlaysons is from about 1770 to the 1850s, a time of very great change and revolution. A number of historians have identified armed conflicts in the eighteenth and early nineteenth century as promoting a sense of British identity among the Scots.[24] The period includes the War of American Independence (1775–1783); the French Revolution (1789–1799) and the French Revolutionary and Napoleonic Wars (1792–1815). Many Scots identified themselves with a 'radical Covenanting Presbyterian vision' according to Finlay.[25] This vision was deeply antagonistic to episcopacy, Anglicanism and Catholicism. The French were seen as the great enemy, although the list of enemies was fluid, with Russia stepping between being an enemy and ally, for example. As is often the case, the enemy is caricatured where Protestantism and economic prosperity of Britain were contrasted with Catholicism and poverty in France.[26]

There is no evidence that James served in the armed forces. However, the effects of the war would be all around him. Soldiers, sailors and militiamen mixed with citizens and would be plentiful. The Baltic trade supplied timber for ships and textile manufacturers produced materials for uniforms and sailcloth. Migration journeys were affected by brigands, smugglers, convoys and enemy shipping. Impressment through the deployment of press gangs was used by the Royal Navy during the eighteenth and early nineteenth centuries as a means of crewing warships as there was a shortage of willing manpower.

The Age of Revolution

James and Margaret lived most of their lives through what Hobsbawm in his book delineated as the Age of Revolution.[27] This is a period in history between about 1775 to 1848. Over the course of these years, society in Europe and the Americas underwent a series of revolutions in almost all theatres of life:

political, war, social and cultural, and economic and technological. The probable impact of some of these on the lives of
Margaret and James are described below.

The following published timeline,[28] provide some key
events up until 1855, the year Margaret died.

1709 – **Abraham Darby** (1678–1717) converts furnace to smelt iron
with coke instead of charcoal

1712 – **Thomas Newcomen** (1663–1729) builds the first commercially successful steam engine known as the Atmospheric Steam
Engine

1733 – **John Kay** (1704–64) develops the flying shuttle which
weaves yarn mechanically rather than by hand., thereby allowing
weavers to weave faster

1742 – Cotton mills first opened in England

1764 – **James Hargreaves** (1772–78) is credited inventing the
spinning jenny to improve the spinning wheel

1769 – **Josiah Wedgwood** (1730–95) opens a pottery-making factory
near Stoke-on-Trent in Staffordshire, England

1769 – **Richard Arkwright** (1732–92) patents his water frame, a
spinning machine powered by water

1769 – **James Watt** (1736–1819) develops an improved steam engine
which features a separate condenser.

1770 – **Hargreaves** patents his spinning jenny

1771 – **Richard Arkwright** opens a water-powered mill in Cromford, England

1773 – A group of brokers establishes a stock exchange in London

1775 – **Matthew Boulton** (1728–1809) and James Watt begin
manufacturing and marketing an improved steam engine in
Birmingham, England

1776 – **Thomas Paine** published *Common Sense*

1776 – **Adam Smith** (1723–1790), Scotsman and founder of modern
economics gets his An *Inquiry into the Nature and Causes of the
Wealth of Nations* published

1776 – **Captain Cook** begins last of three voyages of exploration

1776 – **Declaration of Independence** is ratified on 4th July in
Philadelphia

1779 – **Samuel Crompton** (1753–1827) invents the spinning mule which is a cross between Hargreaves' spinning jenny and Arkwright's water frame

1780 – **The Gordon Riots**: anti-Catholic protests paralyse London

1781 – **James Watt** invents a rotary motion device for his steam engine

1783 – First balloon flight in Paris

1784 – **Andrew Meikle** (1719–1811) Scottish engineer develops a water-powered threshing machine

1785 –**Watt's** steam engine is first used to power a cotton mill

1785 – **Edmund Cartwright** (1743–1823) patents his water-powered loom.

1786 – **New Lanark Cotton Mill** was built

1786 – **Matthew Boulton** develops steam-powered coin-minting machinery.

1786 – **Richard Arkwright** uses a Watt engine in a cotton mill

1787 – **Thomas Clarkson** commissions diagram of slave ship *Brooks*

1788 – **Robert Burns** pens Auld Lang Syne

1789 – **George Washington** becomes first president of the United States

1789 – **Olaudah Equiano' narrative** about his life in slavery was published

1789 – **Storming of the Bastille, Paris**

1790 – **Forth and Clyde Navigation** is opened

1791 – **Thomas Paine** published *Rights of Man*

1791 – A Manchester mill orders 400 of **Edmund Cartwright's** power looms, but workers burn down the mill because they fear losing their jobs

1792 – **Hannah Wollstonecraft** published *A Vindication of the Rights of Woman*

1792 – **Thomas Muir** co-founds the Scottish Association of the friends of the People

1793 – **King Louis XVI and Queen Marie Antoinette** executed

1793 – **Edward Jenner** discovers smallpox vaccine

1798 – **Irish Uprising** by the Society of United Irishmen

1799–1800 – New Combination Acts outlaw trade unions which are repealed in 1824

1801 – **Act of Union** creating the United Kingdom of Britain and Ireland comes into force

1801 – **Richard Trevithick** (1771–1833) builds a steam carriage

1802 – **Macadamisation of British roads**

1803 – **John Dalton,** theory of atomic structure developed

1804 – **Trevithick** runs a steam locomotive on rails in an ironworks

1804 – **Joseph Marie Jacquard** develops Jaquard Loom

1804 – **Napoleon Bonaparte** declared himself Emperor of France

1805 – **Battle of Trafalgar**

1806–59 – **Isambard Kingdom Brunel** builds many railroad lines, tunnels, bridges and steamships during his lifetime

1807 – **William Wilberforce,** bill to outlaw slave trade in Britain passed on 25 March

1811–16 – During Luddite riots, workers destroy machines they fear will replace them

1814 – **Koenig & Bauer printing press** trialled by the *Times* newspaper

1815 – **Battle of Waterloo**

1815 – **First of the Corn Laws** passed

1817 – **Baron Karl von Drais** invented the bicycle in Germany

1818 – **Mary Shelley** published *Frankenstein* or *The Modern Prometheus*

1819 – **Peterloo Massacre** in Manchester

1823 – **Charles Babbage** (1791–1871), an English mathematician, develops his difference engine, a mechanical computing machine

1825 – **George Stephenson** (1781–1848) builds the 25-mile-long Stockton & Darlington railway

1829 – **Stephenson's** *Rocket* locomotive travels at 29 mph

1831 – **Michael Faraday** (1791–1867) discovers the principle of electromagnetic induction, later used in electric generators

1833 – **Adrian Stephens** invents the steam whistle

1833 – **The Slavery Act** abolished slavery across the British Empire

1837 – **William Fothergille Cooke and Charles Wheatstone** develop the first commercial electric telegraph

1838 – The Liverpool & Manchester Railway is extended south to London, thereby making 500 miles of railroad track in Britain

1838 – **William Lovett** published the *People's Charter*, supporters of the cause were named Chartists

1839 – Louis Daguerre publicised his 'daguerreotype'

1840 – Rowland Hill (1795–1879) introduces prepaid mail and the first postage stamps, the Penny Black

1843 – Isambard Kingdom Brunel's iron-hulled steamship SS *Great Britain* is launched

1843 – Ada Lovelace works on algorithms for Charles Babbage's 'calculating machine'

1845 – Great Famine in Ireland

1847 – Dr James Simpson discovered anaesthetic properties of chloroform

1847–1848 – Bronte sisters published their novels: *Wuthering Heights, Jane Eyre* and *Tenant of Wildfell Hall*

1848 – Karl Marx and Friedrich Engels published the *Communist Manifesto*

1848 – February Revolution, France becomes a republic

1851 – The Great Exhibition opens on May 1 in Hyde Park, London, and runs until October 11. More than 6 million people pay to visit the exhibition

1855 – Henry Bessemer (1813–98) patents his process for converting pig iron into steel

Industrial Revolution

Not all sources agree on the dates of the Industrial Revolution, but do agree on where it started – Great Britain. It roughly spanned a century between 1760 and 1860. What a time for a Scottish mechanic to be alive! It started in UK in the late eighteenth century with the increasing use of fossil fuels, initially coal for steam-power, supplementing water-power, then later oil and gas, to power transport and drive indus-trialisation. One of the earliest uses of coal for steam-power was in water pumping to drain mines, closely followed by steam-power driving textile spinning and weaving machinery, replacing hand loom weaving. The demand for linen, for ships sails and then domestic uses, drove the growth of flax mills in Scotland and elsewhere, closely followed by cotton mills, initially using waterpower and then steam engines. Powered spinning and weaving mills initially had to be located close to lively perennial streams, the source of their power, but when steam power took over the need was for these mills and other industries to be close to coal mines to reduce the cost of moving this bulky fuel. Where both circumstances occurred together, as in some parts of the central belt of Scotland, a mill's competitive edge could be maintained, helped by a skilled workforce, until other economic and international factors determined otherwise. One interesting observation has been made by Hobsbawm about the relative simplicity of the British inventions and small start-up capital required for factories and mills. These inventions repaid their costs almost immediately due to increased output and could be funded out of current profits.

> The new inventions which revolutionized it – the spinning-jenny, the water-frame, the mule in spinning, a little later the power-loom in weaving — were sufficiently simple and cheap, and paid for themselves almost immediately in terms of higher output. They could be installed, if need be piecemeal, by small men who started off with a few borrowed pounds, for the men who controlled the great accumulations of eighteenth-century wealth were not greatly inclined to invest large amounts in industry. The expansion of the industry could be financed easily out of current profits, for the combination of its vast market conquests and a steady price-inflation produced fantastic rates of profit.[29]

We do not know whether Margaret's parents were wealthy but James started his business life with very little capital to start his business and fortune was on his side if he did not need much to set up. James specialised in machine tools for homes and cotton mills. It was only later that he moved on to hosiery and woollen goods. Hobsbawm explained that the term 'factory' or 'mill' was used for spinning, carding establishments and related industries using power-operated machinery from 1780 to 1815 and then later for weaving.[30]

American Revolution 1775–83

Even though James and Margaret were children at the time of the American Revolution, it is likely that their families were aware of the conflict across the Atlantic, because it captured the public's imagination and caused a media frenzy in the local press and had a major impact on Glasgow's cotton trade.

> Between 1763 and 1789 there was a significant
> expansion of the Scottish press; the developing
> quarrel with the colonies was partly responsible. So
> great was the interest in the course of the American
> crises that good American coverage was essential to
> the success of a paper[31].

Opinion was divided, according to Fagerstrom, amongst key intellectuals such as Adam Smith, the author of *An inquiry into the nature and causes of the wealth of nations*,[32] and within the Churches in Scotland.

> The views of Adam Smith on the colonies and
> towards the war have been examined frequently,
> but cannot be ignored here. His associations with
> the Glasgow merchants during his professorship in
> the city from 1751 to 1764, his close friendship with

Franklin, and his extensive consideration of colonial trade in the Wealth of Nations made his interest in the American crisis inevitable.[33]

Fagerstrom goes on to observe that:

Perhaps the most interesting and certainly the sharpest division of opinion on the war was to be found in the Scottish Church, where the division into Evangelical and Moderate factions based on theological emphases and church practices was carried over into the debate on the American question. Leaders of the Moderate party supported the government. A number of Evangelical or Popular clergymen and lay leaders openly expressed their opposition.[34]

We cannot know which side the Antiburghers of Howgate supported. Tom Devine made the case that the Scots as a whole supported the British side.[35]

Another author, Brad Jones, argued that the American Revolution acted as a catalyst for Glasgow's emergence as the 'Second City of Empire and that the public's response solidified their identity as British.[36] Jones asserted that the print culture was ideologically important in allowing Glaswegians to express themselves as loyal British subjects. The number of Scottish newspapers rose in the second half of the eighteenth century. Although the field was dominated by Edinburgh-based newspapers, Glasgow began to compete. Eight newspapers and twelve magazines were published during the Revolutionary War, including the *Caledonian Mercury, Edinburgh Advertiser, Edinburgh Evening Courant* and Ruddiman's *Weekly Journal.*[37]

Perhaps this explains the reason for James using the Edinburgh paper, the *Caledonian Mercury* to advertise his services and products in Shuttle Street and Havannah Street in Glasgow.

The impact of the American Revolution on Glasgow's trade was significant. The success of the Clyde ports of Glasgow (Port Glasgow and Greenock) in Atlantic commerce attracted the attention of historians.[38] It was based largely on sugar, tobacco and cotton. The American Revolution ended Glasgow's status as the tobacco entrepôt (an intermediary centre of trade). Until the end of the war, Scottish trade showed considerable annual fluctuation.

Even though Margaret and James' adulthood started after the American Revolution had ended, it is likely that the consequences of it reverberated in their working personal lives.

French Revolution 1789–1799

The French Revolution and its message of 'Liberté, Egalité, an Fraternité' sparked change round the world and especially in Scotland.

> Throughout Great Britain the controversy excited by the French Revolution embittered social as well as political life; but in Scotland its influence knew no bounds. 'Everything,' it has been said, 'not this or that thing, but literally everything, was soaked in this one event.' [39]

It resonated with the mood amongst the Scottish people and church followers, whether of the establishment or the seceders. This was linked with the antipathy to Church patronage and the conduct of authority.[40]

Although many did not support the subsequent violence, the egalitarian principles were welcomed in Scotland. Emma Vincent also noted that in 1782 the number of newspapers published in Scotland increased until in 1790, there were twenty-seven and Thomas Paine's *Rights of Man*, published two years after the revolution in 1791, was widely read. Later, she also argued that the French Revolution triggered an enthusiasm for missions, both at home and abroad. It is probable that the evangelism of Margaret and James and of their friends, the Wheelers, Swans and Patersons, would have been influenced by an event of such magnitude.

Protest movements

As a primary Quaker belief is that all human beings are equal and worthy of respect, the fight for human rights has also extended to many other areas of society, including the emancipation of women and the abolition of slavery movements. James was a member of the Quakers in Edinburgh and might have listened to the thoughts of people such as William Smeal and his daughter, Jane Smeal. Smeal was a Gallowgate tea merchant and Quaker who founded the Glasgow Anti-Slavery Society in 1822. Jane founded the Glasgow Ladies Emancipation Society in the 1830s and remarked that her cause did not have universal appeal. In a letter to Elizabeth Pease in December, 1836, Jane Smeal wrote that their subscribers were from the middling and working classes rather than the elite classes of nobles, rich and educated.[41]

We do not know the Finlaysons' personal opinions on any of these matters. Margaret's role, if any, is not specified, but Scottish Quaker women played a significant part in the movements. For example, Elizabeth Pease Nichol, Priscilla Bright McLaren, Jane Smeal and Eliza Wigham were four Edinburgh Quaker women who fought in protest movements for the abolition of slavery and votes for women.[42]

On 25 March 1807, the slave trade was abolished in British

possessions – how much impact would that have had on the Finlaysons? Maybe very little for people such as them, struggling to make a living under the shadow of war.[43] In addition, the Finlaysons were dealing with the first sequestration of 1807. Their financial ruin must have been in the forefront of their minds.

Although James and Margaret may not have been directly affected by this legislation, the City of Glasgow's wealth was partly based on the slave trade and there would have been indirect consequences. Also, their Quaker friends in St Petersburg would have been strong slave trade abolitionists. In a letter from Ferdinand Uhde, we learn that Sarah Wheeler was involved in the campaigns against slavery:

> I should be glad to hear, what progress the Slavery
> abolition Society has been making, and what
> prospects there are of seeing the abominable Slave
> trade entirely crushed. How is the civilisation of
> Africa going on? Excuse these questions, but knowing
> you take a part in those efforts to put down these
> horrors, I make free to ask you.[44]

Towards the end of Margaret's life, she was supported by Eliza Wigham, the step-daughter of Jane Wigham née Smeal, who was deeply involved in the anti-slavery movement.[45]

They also had first-hand experience of a different type of bondage in the serfdom present in Russia. Both the Russian serf and the American slave were under the total domination of their respective masters. By the nineteenth century when both institutions were fully developed, neither serfs nor slaves had any civil or legal rights. They could not acquire property nor contract a loan. Marriages were sanctioned by their masters, as was any effort to "hire out." They were chattels subject to whatever whims, idiosyncrasies and duties the masters might desire the bondsmen to carry out. Serfdom and slavery were systems of absolute control.[46]

Wars

French Revolutionary Wars & Napoleonic Wars 1792–1815

Georges Lefebvre wrote that the conflict between Bonaparte and Britain was 'a clash between two imperialisms.'[47]

> Moreover, the almost continuous fighting between 1792 and 1815 was not one single conflict, but a great number of wars, insurrections, and revolts that differed in kind as well as in chronology. Even if only the wars between the major European powers are considered, they are divided into seven separate coalitions during which, at one point or the other, all of the states, except for Great Britain, were opponents or allies of the French, joining or leaving coalitions, and on occasion changing sides, under different circumstances and for differing reasons. If there is wide agreement that these wars can be considered a single historical episode, with a division between the revolutionary and the Napoleonic era, this view prevails because the major political and military developments provided continuity. Wars changed from the affairs of kings to the wars of nations [48]

The news was part of daily life for many middle-class families.[49] In these times, cycles of boom and bust were exacerbated in the short term by restrictions in trade through embargos, tariffs and smuggling. In the mid-term Britain was able to work around the Continental System imposed against British exports to Continental Europe and Russia in 1806 by Napoleon through lax controls and the use of neutral shipping.

No point in Britain is more than 70 miles from the sea, and all the chief industrial areas of the nineteenth century, with one exception (Birmingham), were either on the sea or within easy reach of it. Transport by sea was cheaper and faster than by land and this facilitated James and Margaret in trading with Ireland and migrating to Russia.[50] After the Battle of Trafalgar, the only way of defeating Britain was through the Continental System of blockades. Napoleon had no chance of invading Britain by crossing the Channel.[51]

Napoleon Bonaparte has divided opinion for two hundred years and is considered by some as a military genius and by others as an obsessive tyrant and bogeyman.

The wars lasted for over twenty years and would have shaped James and Margaret's values and beliefs. Everyone in Britain shared in the wars in one way or another.

The Battle of Waterloo in 1815 brought to an end the years of armed conflict and fears and James and Margaret probably shared in the sense of pride in Britannia as Britain emerged as the leading nation in control of the seas and commerce.[52]

Admiral Nelson and the Duke of Wellington were the opposing British heroes to Napoleon. Just before James died, a memorial was unveiled in Edinburgh to Wellington (see Plate 13).

> The statue of the Duke of Wellington outside Register House was unveiled in a highly patriotic ceremony on 18 June 1852, the thirty-seventh anniversary of his greatest victory at Waterloo. The old general, by then 83, was not present, but many veterans he commanded in the battle were there to hear him hailed as an outstanding British military hero. He died in September that year ... The proposal for a public

statue in Edinburgh was carried out by a committee of Tory landowners and supporters. Other landowners, who were their political opponents, contributed funds. They also had a high regard for Wellington's military prowess and leadership, although they deplored his conservative politics. ... In 1842 the commission went to John Steell, from Edinburgh, who depicted Wellington mounted on his favourite horse, Copenhagen, firmly but calmly directing his forces in battle. His magnificent bronze sculpture is regarded as among the best of the duke, and one of his greatest works... The proposal for a public statue in Edinburgh was carried out by a committee of Tory landowners and supporters. Other landowners, who were their political opponents, contributed funds. They also had a high regard for Wellington's military prowess and leadership, although they deplored his conservative politics.[53]

Plague, Pox and Pestilence – disease and public health

We were struck by the longevity of both the Finlaysons and thought originally that it was exceptional to be alive in the 1850s in your eighties. As the statutory recording of births, marriages and deaths was not introduced until in Scotland in 1855, life expectancy data are estimations. There are records for the Church of Scotland, known as the 'old parish registers', but these can be incomplete and dissenting parishes did not always record life events. Houston estimates that the life expectancy for Scottish adults at birth was close to thirty years of age around 1755.[54] He goes on to explain that a fifth to a quarter of all babies born alive in the mid eighteenth century died before their first birthday. Deadly infections were the most common cause of death. If you survived childhood and childbirth, your life expectancy increased. As far as we know, Margaret did not experience childbirth as the records state she was childless. James Cleland collated mortality statistics from 1820 for Glasgow that are reliable. In the period 1821–1825, life expectancy was 35 years of age. Simon Szreter and Graham Mooney argued that the main industrial cities of England had poorer life expectancy in the 1840s onwards.

In the previous section, we described how many of Napoleon's soldiers in Russia died of disease – specifically typhus, dysentery and diphtheria. Typhus is a name given to three different types of infectious disease, one of which is epidemic louse-born typhus (the type experienced by Napoleon's army).[55] In this case disease worked to the advantage of Britain. Cleland discovered from the mortality bills of 1783–1812 that 50% of all deaths occurred in children of under 10 years. More specifically, smallpox accounted for 19 per cent of all deaths under age 10.[56]

Following the introduction of the Jennerian vaccine against smallpox in 1798, there was a great reduction in smallpox mortality. Other lethal diseases were measles, scarlet fever, typhus, whooping cough and cholera (from 13 February 1832).[57] Cholera first started to spread world-wide in 1817 and, slowly but surely, reached all cities in the 1830s and Moscow by 1831.[58] Tuberculosis (TB) or consumption was another main killer although it was not understood that it was contagious and caused by a bacillus. The Finlaysons were well aware of the devastating effect of the disease through the contact with the Wheeler family and correspondence with Sarah Tanner, née Wheeler.

However, health is not just about disease. Mood disorders relate to the spectrum of emotions with two extreme poles of elation and melancholia and were known about in ancient times. They were first systematically described by Hippocrates

(460–337 BCE). Later the cyclical nature of what is now known as bipolar disorder was identified by Jean-Pierre Falret which he termed "folie circulaire" in 1851. It is characterised by a perpetual cycle of depression and mania with varying intervals in between.[59].

Houston describes what mental therapies were available in Scotland in the eighteenth and early nineteenth centuries.[60]

> A formidable array of remedies was available to sufferers. These included evacuations, blood-letting, cathartics, purgatives, emetics, blistering agents, camphor, opium, warm and cold bathing, mercury, anti-spasmodics, belladonna, and digitalis. Most of these derived from the tradition of heroic therapeutics and were an attempt to restore the balance of 'humours' in the body.[61]

Other treatments included confinement (at home, in strait jackets or in lunatic asylums); self-medication with alcohol; travel; conversational interrogation and confrontation; and religious or moral interventions.

Longevity is a product of genetics, the environment and lifestyle.[62] For the Finlaysons to have lived into their eighties is a tribute to their physical resilience and perhaps their residence in Finland and Russia as well as their probable abstemious lifestyle.

How might it feel, to be a minority as it regards old age? In 1840 an analysis was given of the ages of the people who completed the 1831 census in Glasgow.[63] It is possible that the statistics from the census in Edinburgh might have been somewhat different.

Table 20: The ages of persons in Glasgow, Barony and Gorbals in 1831 census

Ages	Males	Females	Total
Under 5	15,422	14,855	30,277
From 5 to 10	13,127	12,580	25,707
From 10 to 15	10,491	10,720	21,211
From 15 to 20	8,489	12,256	20,745
From 20 to 30	15,177	23,008	38,185
From 30 to 40	12,179	14,240	26,419
From 40 to 50	8,685	9,329	18,014
From 50 to 60	5,549	6,099	11,648
From 60 to 70	3,228	3,692	6,920
From 70 to 80	1,090	1,502	2,592
From 80 to 90	260	385	645
From 90 to 100	26	32	58
From 100 and upwards	1	4	5
Total	93,724	108,702	202,426

Source: Cowan, Robert. 'Vital Statistics of Glasgow, Illustrating the Sanatory Condition of the Population.' Journal of the Statistical Society of London 3, no. 3 (1840): 257–92.

As global trade increased in the eighteenth and nineteenth centuries, so too did the business of actuaries and life assurance companies. A number of the latter were insecurely funded and became bankrupt. This happened to the firm that James invested in and he lost a third of his assets in May 1840.[64]

What are the threads?

Who were James and Margaret Finlayson? What have we learned? There are still intriguing gaps in the narrative. However, there are story threads that run consistently through their lives. As well as evidence, we come away with strong impressions. Future historians are likely to refute some of these tentative conclusions as they trawl the world for missing pieces in the story. The Finlaysons left behind no diaries, very few of their own letters, and little detail in the archives of their day-to-day lives and beliefs. We include speculation in the threads where we are unable to meet the Genealogical Proof Standard (GPS), which is the guideline for establishing the reliability or 'proof' of a genealogical conclusion with reasonable certainty. Our impressions reflect our own prejudices and lifetimes, after all.

We were able to find a correct date of birth and details of James' life in Glasgow and Russia. At the start of this research, our hope was to find out more about Margaret and we have not been totally successful with that. We have contested the birth information with alternative suggestions. We now know where she was buried – with James. We have discovered some letters written to her from William Swan and Sarah Wheeler. We have been able to discover information about James' early life in response to Väinö Wallin's claim that James was a man of mystery.

> The person himself was already mysterious. He came
> from Scotland (Glasgow) and was born in 1771. Very
> little is known about his earlier life, and even that is
> anecdotal. But his deeds testify to him and the rest we
> can guess from the time in which he lived [65]

Margaret remains a woman of mystery.

Class and education

Our impression is that Margaret was of a higher status and educational attainment level than James. Both people seem firmly situated in the 'middling sort'. James was the son of a village tailor and we do not know Margaret's lineage for sure. We have no knowledge of their education although they were both literate and, in James' case, numerate. Margaret and James alluded to religious writings in correspondence and seems to have devoured religious texts.

Epistolary literacy of James and Margaret

The Central Archives for Finnish Business Records (ELKA) holds an archive for Finlayson Oy and Margaret Finlayson. There are 34 letters that have survived, written to Margaret while she and James were in Tampere; they were from Sarah Wheeler, William Swan and Sally Stallybrass. Sadly, we can only have a one-sided view of the correspondence as the letters Margaret sent have been lost and we only have copies of the letters she received. Nevertheless, we can deduce that Margaret was a diligent correspondent with people of the middle-class intelligentsia. Margaret kept in touch with St. Petersburg friends through letters. All the ones she received are religious in tone. Mervi Kaarninen has analysed the letters that Sarah Wheeler wrote from 1821–1838 from the perspective of Quakerism.[66]

Sarah started writing to Margaret when she was thirteen years old. She made reference to the age gap:

> Tho' our ages may not agree perhaps our tastes &
> feelings might for I generally find by far the most
> solid satisfaction in associating with those who have
> advanced farther than myself & especially who have
> travelled farther & longer than I in that strict &
> narrow path that leadeth to the kingdom in which it
> is my earnest wish to be focused.[67]

Though Margaret may not have liked being called elderly in the following letter when in her fifties!

> Now my dear Friend, tho' it would give me much pleasure to hear from thee. I must request thee on no account to write to me unless it be perfectly convenient to do this as I know it is less easy for an elderly person to write than for one who is younger.[68]

Both Margaret and Sarah Wheeler had moved across continents because the men in their lives made the decision to emigrate for business or religious reasons. With Margaret in Tampere, Finland and Sarah in Shoosharry, near St Petersburg, they must have experienced loneliness. Sarah writes about 'the extreme seclusion in which you live'.[69] Also letters mention times when James in St Petersburg.

> It gave us great pleasure to see J Finlayson & it would have been a still greater gratification to us to have seen thee also but I suppose from your large family this is at present not very likely. Well my dear Friend, thy lot is indeed a solitary one & must sometime feel rather discouraging but seeing it is in the appointment of a gracious & merciful Father doubtless He will support under it.[70]

The letters could be passed around within an assembled group of family and as such they were public. Sarah mentioned that she was sharing her correspondence.

In the correspondence that has survived, Margaret engaged with elite men and women such as Jane Paterson, William Swan, Augusta Lundahl and Sarah Tanner, née Wheeler. Although Margaret's letters are lost to us, the one-sided conversations suggest an intellectual depth that is missing in James' more flowery turns of phrase. By flowery, we mean the traditional 'flowers of rhetoric' where devices use imagery drawn from nature, often portraying cataclysmic events such as storms, volcanoes, earthquakes and fire.

> ... not only standing as one idle in the market place
> but as being tossed up and down as the locust like the
> blind & led in a way they transport.[71]

Also, the court case papers against the Incorporation of Wrights in Glasgow, James submitted rather cursory arguments when compared with the detail of William Dunn versus the Wrights.

Depression or normal reaction to adverse events?

Many people experience sadness or distress related to grief and other life stresses, including the stress of physical illness. Sarah Wheeler endured the illnesses and deaths of her mother, brothers and sister while she lived in Shoosharry and she expresses her grief through her letters. Margaret too seemed to experience low moods, according to William Swan's letters. At first, he attributes it to grief following the death of Jean Paterson.

> But I must attend more particularly to your letter –
> that you complain of yourself dullness & stupidity I
> can account for in my own mind although I cannot
> explain. You have been stunned – but by the time you
> receive this you will be recovered, and able to look
> back calmly & see distinctly what before seemed all
> dim & confused.[72]

In 1823, Swan seems to suggest that her ennui is part of the human condition that will only be resolved by death.

> You complain however of weakness – languor slowness in spiritual things – and I hope will always complain till you are cured – that is till you arrive at the land where the inhabitant shall not say 'I am sick.'[73]

James seemed to suffer low moods and had difficult times. In the history of Tampere, we learn that 1824 was 'particularly unhappy for Finlayson'.

> In the spring, his cash shortage had already become permanent; he had, according to his own words, put nearly 26,000 banknotes into the factory from his private funds, and yet he had been forced to dismiss his workers. In the summer he fell ill, and no wonder. Information came from Scotland that 4 crates of goods coming to Finlayson, presumably machine parts, had been seized in Liverpool and that the workers Finlayson had called in were not coming from there either.[74]

Was this illness the same as the one he experienced at the end of his employment at Alexandrovsk? There is some suggestion that James suffered from recurrent depression. Apparently, James had been spending his time in bed for some time.[75] We could not find the original source to confirm this. In view of his bursts of activity between bouts of low mood, we hypothesise that James had bipolar disorder. He describes this shift in a letter to Daniel Wheeler.

> That arch and unceasing deceiver; who in every age has so uniformly tried, either to exalt above

measure, or to cast down in despair, has been of late uncommonly busy here; so much so, as cannot be express [sic][76]

According to a letter in 1826, from Daniel Wheeler, James suffered a bout of depression in 1826:

> This, and thy doubts, whether thou art right, in taking up thy residence in Finland, must not be suffered to aggravate thy already depressed situation of mind, lest the unwearied adversary should gain an advantage by directing its attention with those things which are but temporal, from others, incomparably superior, though now unseen, which are eternal. I fully believe thy present situation to be a peculiarly trying one; and such an one, as no mortal can render thee any help.[77]

This depression was also mentioned in 1827 according to another letter from Wheeler.

> I sincerely hope by this time thy bodily complaints have taken a favorable turn, and that losing a little blood, has contributed to thy relief – It often happens that when the poor body is indisposed, the mind at the same time suffers from additional depression, so that every thing seems combined to weigh down the tribulates christian traveller and darken with heavy clouds of dismay, the path he has to tread ... I am therefore not surprised to learn from thy last letter, that thou art plunged again into Jordan.[78]

Part of his treatment appeared to have been blood-letting. This treatment was practised through the eighteenth and nineteenth centuries in Europe for fever, hypertension, pulmonary inflammation, and pulmonary oedema. Its therapeutic value was beginning to be challenged, especially by Pierre Charles Alexandre Louise in 1834. The most famous of these disputes between proponents and sceptics erupted in Edinburgh between Dr William P. Alison and Dr John Hughes Bennett in the 1840s.[79]

The mental and physical weakness provided an impetus for James to transfer ownership of the business and to seek help from Daniel Wheeler in finding investors from St. Petersburg.

> I have of late been sometimes from my bodily
> weakness, led to think of trying to lett off the works
> for the remaining years; because from this weakness,
> and the failure of recollection, amidst so many giddy
> and light heads, it is farr from being unlike that the
> advantages of the situation are not only unoccupied
> as they should, but that even, those gained may be
> squandered or abused. – It is perhaps likely if some in
> Petersburg knew of the place, they will at last take a
> part in it, and assist me. – When a spare hour occurs,
> please think over it, and let me hear thy opinions.[80]

James lived to a good age of 82 and, based on his letters and biographies, there is evidence of depression. Considering the stress of almost three bankruptcies in Glasgow and Tampere, and forced emigration to St Petersburg, it seems that the depression could be situational. However, it does not seem that depression alone was the problem. There also are signs of recurrent emotional distress of a cyclothymic type. A novel methodology, combining psychiatric and literary approaches, was used to assess the feasibility of using Robert Burns' extensive personal correspondence as a source of evidence for assessing the presence of symptoms of a clinically significant mood disorder. This study engaged in retrospective diagnosis and attracts some debate.

> Thus, while a historical disease may not be directly equated with a modern condition, the modern label is a useful framework for assisting modern understanding of the historic individual.[81]

The authors used diagnostic criteria corresponding to those conditions and symptomatic descriptors for the depressed, hypomanic and manic mood states of bipolar disorder in a table.[82]

We would have to be very careful to retrospectively diagnose James as having a mood disorder. For a start, the body of evidence to Burns' mental health comprises more than 800 letters and 400 entries in journals and commonplace books written by Burns, alongside various sketches and accounts from those who knew him in life. We only have a handful of letters and contemporaneous accounts for James. Therefore, we lightly hold that there is some evidence concerning irritability, aggression, grandiosity, over-optimism and extravagant schemes that suggests mania or hypomania. In historical accounts, these qualities have been attributed to personality and poor business skills. Robert Burns is known for his consumption of alcohol and his rampant romantic relationships with the 'lassies'. In past times, people self-medicated with alcohol and laudanum. However, it seems unlikely that James would have used these due to his puritanical behaviours and any mood disorders he experienced would have had to run their course. We have no information about his sexual appetite and assume it was controlled – unlike that of his father's 'unclean behaviour' in Howgate. James appeared to be on an emotional roller-coaster and this volatility must have been difficult for his friends, business colleagues and mostly for his wife, Margaret.

Table 21: Diagnostic criteria and their means of identification

	Symptom	Mania	Hypomania	Depression
Mood	Mood level	Elevated, incongruent to circumstance	Mildly elevated	Lowered, little change in response to circumstances
	Pleasure	Elevated	Mildly elevated	Anhedonia
	Attitude	Irritable, aggressive	Mildly irritable	Anxious
Cognition and perception	Self esteem	Increased to grandiosity	Sense of well-being, some grandiosity	Guilty and worthless
	Outlook	Overly optimistic	Optimistic	Pervasively gloomy, fearful, morbid and/or suicidal
	Thought processes	Pressured, flight of ideas, incoherence of ideas, impulsive	Mentally efficient, fluency of ideas, distractible	Struggles to keep train of thought, inefficient, indecisive
	Speech	Pressured, incoherent	Talkative with fluency	Reduced, stilted
Activity and behaviour	Energy and activity levels	Overactive and increased energy, restlessness	Increased activity and energy, degree of restlessness	Fatigue, psycho-motor agitation or retardation
	Sleep	Reduced need but feels refreshed	Reduced need, feels refreshed	Disturbed (insomnia, hypersomnia, disturbing dreams), doesn't feel rested regardless of duration
	Social skills	Reduced inhibitions, possibly improper, over-familiar	Sociable, pushing limits of propriety, overly familiar	Socially withdrawn

	Symptom	Mania	Hypomania	Depression
	Participation and risk	Extravagant schemes, reckless and/or risky activities	Multiple tasks started but not all completed, some risky and/or reckless behaviour	Withdrawal from regular activities, reluctance to participate
	Libido	Greatly increased, inappropriate encounters	Increased, inappropriate encounters	Reduced, even lost

Source: Hansen, M, D J Smith, and G Carruthers p.168

Business acumen

Whether James' business failures should be attributed to mood disorder or lack of skill, he could not be described as a successful businessman. We found it interesting when considering James' business skills to compare and contrast his life with that of William Dunn. Dunn was celebrated as a man who raised himself from poverty to considerable wealth through his own efforts. The French sociologist Gustave d'Eichtal visited Britain in 1828 and noted that William Dunn, a Scotsman in Glasgow, had raised himself from nothing.[83]

Both men were born in 1770, a month apart. William was born in Gartclash, in the parish of Kirkintilloch, Dumbartonshire, on 31 October and, as we described earlier in the chapter on Penicuik, James was born in Penicuik near Edinburgh on 27 November. William died on 13 March 1849 a wealthy man aged 78. He was buried in Glasgow Necropolis and the substantial monument of Irish granite was commissioned by his surviving brother, Alexander Dunn from the architect John Thomas Rochead (Plate 14). James died on 18 August 1852, aged 81, a man of limited means. He was buried in Newington Cemetery in Edinburgh without a headstone. The headstone was commissioned by Oy Finlayson-Forssa AB of Finland on the occasion of the 150th anniversary of their company (Plate 15). He left no will.

William's biography provides details of his early life.[84] He was educated in the local parish school and partly at the neighbouring village of Campsie. He showed evidence of mechanical skills and his first situation was in the establishment of a cotton-spinner named Waddington, at Stockingfield, near Glasgow. Here he learned iron-turning and machine-making. Three or four years later he was in Messrs. Black & Hastie's works at Bridge of Weir, from which he went to Pollokshaws, to the factories of John Monteith. William was orphaned in 1798 and assumed responsibility for four brothers and one sister. He sold his father's estate for a few hundred pounds. With this capital, opened a manufactory of machines in High John Street, Glasgow.

James' biography is silent on his early years. We could assume that his education and apprenticeship was similar to that of William in that he could have been educated in a parish school and then learned his craft under one or two masters. We suppose that he also showed mechanical aptitude at an early age. The only significant divergence was that James was not orphaned at a young age and did not take responsibility for his siblings. He also did not have a few hundred pounds as capital to invest in setting up a business.

The lives of these men converged in Glasgow, where they both set themselves as machine makers for the cotton industry. James advertised heavily in the local newspapers and so we have evidence of attempted diversification. We could not find evidence that Dunn placed advertisements and so we do not know what his products were. Both men were included in the post-office directory of 1801.[85]

Dun, William, machinery-maker, John-street

Finlayson, James, machinery maker, Shuttle-street

William Dunn entered the Incorporation of Hammermen in Glasgow in August 1801. He became the Collector for the Hammermen in 1806 but never became Deacon. James entered the Hammermen two years later, in August 1803, and did not serve office as Collector or Deacon.

In January 1804, the Incorporation of Wrights in Glasgow petitioned the Magistrates to restrict William manufacturing Spinning Jennies, as they claimed that they fell under the jurisdiction of Wrights. On 7 June 1805, the Wrights made a similar claim against James Finlayson. Although Dunn and Finlayson lost the case at first, Dunn later appealed and won the argument. Finlayson 'piggy-backed' on Dunn's case and the case notes do not demonstrate the same attention to detail shown by Dunn. In fact, Dunn was well-known for his excessive liking for law pleas and he was constantly in the Court of Session making them with his neighbours.[86]

When James was entering his first bankruptcy in 1806, William was going from strength to strength:

In 1808 William Dunn, eldest son of William Dunn,
proprietor of Gartclash, parish of Kirkintilloch,
acquired the mill at Duntocher, then idle, and which
had previously been used only for spinning wool
and cotton yarn. Having succeeded to the Gartclash

property on the death of his father, Mr. Dunn, even
at the time spoken of, had made a fair start with
those machine-works in Glasgow, which afterwards
became so famous throughout Britain. He fitted up
the Duntocher mill with his own machinery, and
succeeded so well that in a few years he purchased the
neighbouring Faifley mill from the Faifley Spinning
Company. These mills he continued to enlarge and
improve till his business reached a point far beyond
their powers of production. He was then compelled
not only to extend the old but to erect entirely new
works. About 1813 he acquired from Messrs. Den-
nistoun the Dalnotter ironworks, used principally for
slitting and rolling iron, and, eight years afterwards,
erected upon their site the Milton mill.[87]

Although James experienced severe setbacks in the form of
sequestrations, William also had setbacks – from a series of fires
that burned his premises to the ground. The factory in John
Street Glasgow was ravaged by fire in 1805 and 1814.[88] There
was another fire there in 1835.[89] Milton Mill at Duntocher was
also destroyed by fire in 1846.[90] These setbacks might have been
catastrophic but William had insured the premises. Despite
making a loss, there were advantages to the fires. As one of
Escher's letters recounts the words of his host concerning the
1814 conflagration:

'Do not take it to heart so much. In four or six weeks
Mr. D(unn) will have a far better factory than the
one which has been destroyed. He won't lose a penny
for he will know how to recompense himself for the
loss of the business while his works are being rebuilt.
In fact the whole affair may be regarded as proper
punishment for his own carelessness and for the
carelessness of his workmen. The factory has been
burned down twice on the same spot and each time

it has arisen like a phoenix from the ashes, a finer building than before.'[91]

The lives of Dunn and Finlayson diverged in terms of wealth and international experience and Dunn remained in Scotland. Although we believe they knew each other in Glasgow, we do not know if they maintained contact throughout their lives. Was it just a matter of luck that Dunn became so wealthy and James did not? Luck might have played a part but we believe that skill was also involved. William seemed a more detail-conscious man in terms of his case against the Wrights. He made good use of the few hundred pounds from the sale of his patrimony. He invested in land and businesses.

There are many reasons why businesses fail. In current years, research gives the following reasons why small businesses fail and these reasons seem also to apply to James.

Why small businesses fail

According to research done by U.S. Bank and cited on the SCORE/Counselors to America's Small Business, the reason small businesses fail overwhelmingly includes cash flow issues. This includes poor cash flow management and poor understanding of cash flow, starting out with too little money, and lack of a developed business plan.

82% – Poor cash flow management skills/poor understanding of cash flow

79% – Starting out with too little money

78% – Lack of a well-developed business plan, including insufficient research on the business before starting it

77% – Not pricing properly or failure to include all necessary items when setting prices

73% – Being overly optimistic about achievable sales, money required, and about what needs to be done to be successful

70% – Not recognizing or ignoring what they don't do well and not seeking help from those who do.[92]

Whereas William navigated these issues with skill, apart from pricing, it would appear that all of the points formed part of James' failures. For example, Lindfors wrote about his time in Tampere:

> While it must be said that James Finlayson was enterprising and careful in the planning of his enterprises, as well as being undoubtedly a very skilful professional in his trade. However, he did not have an industrial leader's eye for business question. He could not draw up reliable calculations for future costs. He could not even evaluate his next business venture in relation to his current finances. This lack of capability in financial planning almost caused the company to collapse.
>
> Finlayson worked systematically but his calculations and assumptions did not add up. For example, he had imagined that his machine manufacturing would be a large income source, he was going to build all sorts of machines for other people. Thanks to the commercial profit this would be able to provide, he also imagined he would be able to supply his own spinning mill with the required machinery. But when he had his buildings erected and was ready to start manufacturing machines, it turned out that he had miscalculated. He did not receive a single machine order.[93]

It is interesting to note that William supplied his own machinery for his mills and, thus the two men's business models were similar. However, Tampere was a more immature market than Glasgow. The difficulties of cash flow management and poor management are put in perspective when the successes of Daniel Wheeler and Ferdinand Uhde are compared to James. Wheeler provided access to capital and Uhde demonstrated fine business acumen over the years he acted as manager.

James Finlayson's technical skills

In the account of the founding of the Tampere factory, there is no mention of the millwright who designed and built the original concern. There is no evidence that Finlayson became a millwright and it seems unlikely that he designed and built the mill on his own. James was a machine tool maker and assembler of spinning and carding machines. Joel Mokyr distinguishes between macroinventors and microinventors. The former made transformational changes in their field of expertise that transformed the economic and social landscape. Macroinventors would include in their number James Hargreaves (inventor of the spinning jenny), Richard Arkwright (inventor of the water frame), and Samuel Crompton (inventor of the mule). The microinventors make incremental improvements using their competence to advance in small steps.

> Competence is defined here as the high-quality workmanship and materials needed to implement an innovation; that is, to follow the blueprint with a high level of accuracy, carry out the instructions embodied in the technique, and to have the ability to install, operate, adapt, and repair the machinery and equipment under a variety of circumstances. Beyond

those, competence often involved minor improvements and refinements of a technique, which may not
have qualified as a 'microinvention' stricto sensu, but
clearly enhanced the innovative effort in economy.[94]

James seems to fit amongst the myriad of microinventors.
He had built up his craft in Glasgow, St Petersburg and now
Tampere. Nordenskiöld wrote:

> Otherwise, in the opinion of the proposer, the main
> emphasis should be on woollen work, which seemed
> to have a special chance of success. 'Since,' he said, 'the
> wool spinning machines which Finlayson has perfect
> skill in making are of a better construction than those
> imported from Sweden, especially as Finlayson's
> machines will probably produce a smoother and
> finer yarn, and with less waste give a larger output
> in a shorter time and with fewer men, it seems to be
> most important for the country that such a spinning
> mill should be established.' The first step towards a
> better use of the country's woollen resources would
> thus have been taken, and no doubt other woollen
> manufacturers in the country would sooner or later
> acquire for themselves similar machines which
> Finlayson could manufacture for them.[95]

However, as is often the case, his skills became outdated as
he became out of touch with centres of excellence, according
to Nordenskiöld.[96]

In the 1813 sequestration in Glasgow, James is referred to as
a 'hosier and woolen manufacturer', whereas in that of 1807
he is a 'machine maker' and in earlier advertisements in the
Caledonian Mercury of 16 October 1802 he advertises 'Cotton
and Flax Machinery' and in the same paper of 19 June 1800 he
describes himself as 'machine maker and turner'.

On 16 August 1803 James joined the Hammermen of Glasgow, as perhaps his easiest way into a trade guild in Glasgow to allow him to conduct his business there in Shuttle Street. From 1804 to 1809 he was associated with William Dunn in a dispute with the Wrights of Glasgow, another trade guild, as to whether the building of a spinning jenny and its wooden packaging were exclusively the preserve of the its Members, as being 'square wright work – that is, they are made under the plane and chisel, and not with the turning loom'. If the latter it would be 'excepted by the Act of Parliament from the exclusive priviledges [sic] of Incorporation.' After the Magistrates of Glasgow agreed with the Wrights, Dunn appealed this decision and the House of Lords reversed it on 21 February 1809.

The rather different 1813 description of James's business may be self-styled in an attempt to avoid drawing too much attention to his previous financial trouble in 1807. However, the list of machinery etc advertised for sale at his 'Havannah Street Woollen Spinning Factory' on Thursday 3 June 1813 indicates the wide range of his activities. This list included:

A steam engine of 6HP with all appurtenancies.
Six woollen carding machines
Eleven Spinning Jeanies (*Jennies*)
Two Roving Billies
Two Twining Mills
Two Wauk Mills

A list of tools, utensils and equipment advertised for another later sale on 26 August 1813 of 'Manufacturing Utensils', 'lately possessed Mr James Finlayson woollen manufacturer, and belonging to his sequestered Estate', did not include any of the above items, but did list:

A Skutching Machine
Four Stocking Frames, one 28 inches, one 20 inches, one 16 inches, and one 9.
A roving frame, Head and Cans
60 Mill Bobbins, and many other utensils and pieces of equipment and materials.

The sale of 'Cotton Machinery & Tools' auctioned on Wednesday 16 August 1807 and arising from the Sequestration of that year, included the following:

13 Carding Engines, of various breadths, with Cast iron Framing.
1 Drawing Frame, four Heads, with Doublers.
1 Roving Frame, with eight Cans.
8 Mules, of 192 Spindles, adapted for coarse numbers.
1 Stretching Frame of 96 Spindles.

Margaret's skills

As well as her looking after their employees and their families, it is clear from her activities in Tampere and surviving letters to her, that Margaret had a considerable knowledge of hosiery making and in Tampere was producing stockings to order. The way her stockings were made is not known in detail, but involved employing local women outworkers and, given the available technology of the time, would probably have been hand-knitted or produced on a stocking frame. It seems unlikely that her stockings would have been produced in tubular form and the complex shaped stocking machines developed later in the nineteenth century were not then around. Whatever methods Margaret used, she was able to organise and manage the production of cotton and woollen stockings of a quality greatly appreciated by her customers.

Evangelicalism

In the Finlaysons' lifetime, the history of Presbyterianism was turbulent worldwide. Evangelicalism grew and Christian churches splintered. Bebbington's book, *Evangelicalism in Modern Britain* is a useful source. Bebbington explained that four priorities underpin all evangelical sects:

1. Conversionism, the belief that lives need to be changed;
2. Activism, the expression of the gospel in effort;
3. Biblicism, a particular regard for the Bible; and
4. Crucientrism, a stress on the sacrifice of Christ on the cross

In 1793, the *Evangelical Magazine* was founded. Adherents to the Evangelical Movement in Britain included: Methodists, Quakers, Calvanistic Dissenters, Baptists, Independents (also known as Congregationalists and were largely based on Puritanism). After 1800, the majority of Quakers in Britain gradually embraced the evangelical revival, based on Jesus Christ's sacrifice as the effective source of salvation.[97] Quakers believed in 'an inward light' and this belief along with their distinctive calendar, clothes and language set them apart from other Dissenters.[98] The Puritan legacy in the eighteenth century was greater in Scotland than in England. The Evangelical communities in Britain were largely composed of artisans and tradesmen such as shoemakers, carpenters and coopers. Even some of the clergy in the Established churches of England and Scotland were Evangelical.

As we discovered, both Margaret and James were Evangelical in their allegiances. James' father was a tailor in Penicuik and attended the Antiburgher church in Howgate that would have been part of the Evangelical movement. The main contentious issue for seceders in Scotland was the issue of patronage – the right of a patron to appoint the minister in each parish. It is perhaps not surprising that clergy and followers were uncompromising people who believed in following their own consciences. Various schisms were started in 1732 when Ebenezer Erskine and three other ministers seceded from the Established Church to form the Associated Presbytery. This Presbytery then split again in 1747:

> **Burghers and Antiburghers:** The ministers of these
> secession movements were uncompromising men
> and so tended to be difficult to work with and it is
> no surprise that it did not take long for dissension
> to arise amongst them. A split occurred in 1745.
> The bone of contention was a religious clause in the
> oaths that burgesses had to take in the royal burghs
> of Edinburgh, Glasgow and Perth. In 1744, the more
> extreme seceders had argued that they could not in
> all conscience take the oath because this would mean
> that they approved of the Church of Scotland. The
> outcome was the establishment of two churches – the
> General Associate Synod (Antiburghers) and the
> Associate Synod (Burghers).[99]

The schisms within Presbyterianism in Scotland from sixteenth to twenty-first century are illustrated in Plate 16. A detailed history of the Presbyterian Secession Church and the reasons for the schism can be found in John McKerrow's book on the *History of the Secession Church*.[100]

In addition to the Presbyterian churches splintering during

the lives of the Finlaysons, there was also a burgeoning of Protestant missionary activity.

> In fact, the revolutionary and Napoleonic decades saw the beginning of systematic Protestant missionary activity mostly by Anglo-Saxons. The Baptist Missionary Society (1792), the interdenominational London Missionary Society (1795), the evangelical Church Missionary Society (1799), the British and Foreign Bible Society (1804) were followed by the American Board of Commissioners for Foreign Missions (1810), by the American Baptists (1814), Wesleyans (1813–18), the American Bible Society (1816), the Church of Scotland (1824), the United Presbyterians (1835), the American Methodist Episcopalians (1819) and the rest. Continental Protestants, in spite of some pioneering by the Netherlands Missionary Society (1797) and the Basel Missionaries (1815), developed somewhat later: the Berlin and Rhenish societies in the 1820s, the Swedish, Leipzig and Bremen societies in the thirties, the Norwegian in 1842. Roman Catholicism, whose missions were stagnant and neglected, revived even later. The reasons for this outpouring of bibles and trade over the heathen belong both to the religious, social and economic histories of Europe and America.[101]

The previous biographies of James and Margaret ascribe many of their behaviours to a Quaker faith and we have challenged that assumption. Gripenberg repetitively claims that James was a Quaker and attributes his behaviour to this allegiance.[102] Why is that? Perhaps commentators made this assumption based on the relationship of the factory with the Wheelers, William, Daniel, Junior and Sarah. The histories of the company attribute James' rigid religious practices and habits as due to Quakerism. For example, in Tampere, James was described as a 'queer, gruff and quiet gentleman in the wide-brimmed hat'.[103] His refusal to remove his hat in the presence of city magistrates in Tampere and his religious services at home are offered as evidence of Quakerism. James openly challenged the convention that 'inferiors' should render 'hat honour', baring their heads to their 'superiors'.[104] Quakers were renowned for their refusal to doff their hats. There seems to be no records of other sects sharing this behaviour. James was probably influenced by his upbringing as an Antiburgher. Antiburghers would have been aligned with the egalitarianism of Quaker beliefs through their shared puritanical roots. After all, they were the sect that refused to honour the burgher oath. This secession church held similar beliefs to the Society of Friends in terms of plainness and puritanism. We could not find any references to the style of hats Antiburgher men wore. It is possible that James adopted the broad-brimmed hat of the Quakers and equally their defiance of social, political and religious norms. In terms of attitudes to clothing and family worship, Andrew Holmes, author of *The shaping of Ulster Presbyterian belief and practice, 1770–1840* advised us that 'there is virtually no significant difference between Quakers and Seceders. After all, they are both products of a puritan / presbyterian tradition that exemplifies simplicity.'[105]

Another piece of evidence pointing to Quaker leaning is the exemptions that James gained from Emperor Alexander I.

Privilege granted at Tammerfors

... H. M. besides grants the Petition of J. Finlayson that such of these manufacturers as belong to the sect of Quakers may now and in future be freed from war taxes and all taxes for the support of Military, as well

as from all charges and pay to the Finnish Clergy.
But in case they should buy land or estates in the
country or if they get in some other way in possession
thereof such cannot avoid to bear the onera (charge)
or pay the demands on behalf of the Military or
the Clergy, but for such landed property which the
members of that Sect may possess in the town of
Tammerfors they shall for the present have nothing to
pay for such. Likewise as to the making an oath H. M.
has upon Finlaysons request in behalf of the Quakers,
been pleased to declare that their written declaration
which they deliver to the respective authorities
shall be considered, as respects not only the oath of
allegiance, but in all cases where the laws direct an
oath to be made to have the same virtue and power as
if they had confirmed their declaration with an oath
in form.[106]

In 1832, James wrote that he was considering translating
the book *Grounds of a Holy Life* by Hugh Turford.[107] Turford
was a Quaker writer. His book became a classic, appealing to
a broad spectrum of readers because it was non-sectarian.[108]
This provides equivocal evidence of James' affiliation with the
Society of Friends.

Mervi Kaarinen provides conflicting information about the
plainness of Margaret's dress. Apparently she wore a brownish
grey Quaker dress when she was in town, whereas servants
recalled that she dressed festively for dinner and changed her
clothes up to three times a day. When she left Tampere in 1838,
the four-year-old daughter of her maid described silk ribbons
adorning her bonnet.[109]

Although her plain dress was attributed to a Quaker faith,
this was not necessarily the case. Plain dress was adopted by
a number of Puritan-based faith communities. Plain dress
for Quaker women used to mean going without any sort of

adornment, and especially dressing modestly. Given the embellishment on her hat and the dinner clothes, the plain dress Margaret wore to market may have been worn for practicality rather than fashion.

Sarah Wheeler's letters are modelled on a Quaker writing style and it is easy to think that Margaret was merely a recipient of Sarah's belief. However, there is evidence that Margaret sought theological biographies and literature and Sarah supplied them as it was easier to organise that from St Petersburg. The texts include:

- *Polynesian Researches* by William Ellis (1794–1872) a member of the London Missionary society
- *Life and character of Gerhard Tersteegen: With extracts from his letters and writings.* Translated from the German by Samuel Jackson. First edition 1832.[110] Gerhard Tersteegen (25 November 1697 – 3 April 1769), was a German Reformed religious writer and hymnist.
- *The Evangelical Magazine*[111]
- *Journal of voyages and travels* by the Rev. Daniel Tyerman and George Bennet, esq. Deputed from the London missionary society, to visit their various stations in the South Sea Islands, China, India, etc., between the years 1821 and 1829 / Compiled from original documents by James Montgomery. 1831[112]
- Memoir of Sarah Stallybrass[113]
- *A Memoir of the Rev. Legh Richmond, A.M.* by T S Grimshawe 1829.[114]
- John Bunyan, *A Pilgrim's Progress.*[115]

Perhaps this type of reading was not only a means of improvement but also a distraction from the isolation and loneliness of Margaret's life.

Our research discovered that although James attended

meetings with Daniel Wheeler, he did not become a member of the Society of Friends until he returned to Ireland. In his chapter on 'Family Worship, Prayer Meetings, and Lay Involvement in Church Life', Andrew Holmes wrote about Presbyterianism as a whole in Ulster and that is closely linked to the Presbyterian sects in Scotland.

> The head of the family was to ensure that all members of the household observed family worship, which consisted of prayer, praise, catechizing, and Bible reading. Family worship was deemed an indispensable component of the religious instruction and development of the young, and, therefore, the church as a whole.[116]

Not all Christian believers adhered to family worship but evangelical Presbyterians were zealous in holding family prayers twice a day. Thus, the adherence to family worship should not be viewed as evidence of Quakerism.

Although James joined the Quakers late in life, there are no records that Margaret was a member of the Society of Friends. She is not listed in the Women's meetings of Edinburgh. Every piece of evidence suggests that they followed an evangelical religious doctrine and that Margaret was aligned to the Congregational Church through Rev. John and Jane Paterson and William Swan. We have no records of them attending congregations.

Childlessness

The lack of known descendants makes genealogical research harder as there are no inheritors to preserve their private papers for archives. [117] In addition, inheritors or descendants provide information about their parents through their own recorded life events such as baptisms, marriages and census data. James and Margaret were married for nearly sixty years. The narratives on their lives stated that they had no children. Infertility is a modern term and in earlier times 'barren or barrenness' were the terms used for when a woman was unable to give birth of a viable child.[118] How common was barrenness? According to Trussell and Wilson, approximately 4.6% of women who married between the ages of 20 and 24 in the period of their study never gave birth to a living child.[119] The evidence is silent about this in the Finlaysons' lives and so we do not know the causes: celibacy; impotence; fertility problems or miscarriages. Miscarriages were not recorded although still births sometimes were. Miscarriages create their own levels of distress. Nor do we know about James and Margaret's reaction to infertility: was their childless state voluntary or involuntary? Margaret maintained friendships with at least two other childless married couples: William Tanner/ Sarah Wheeler and William Swan/Hannah Cullen. However, unlike Sarah and William who married their spouses later in their lives, Margaret married as a young woman in her teens.

During the Victorian period:

> Women's fertility was emphasized and women were
> destined to devote themselves to motherhood,
> a task for which they were clearly designed. The
> belief that motherhood was a woman's fulfilment
> also had a material basis as economic functions left
> the household. Motherhood remained as the most
> creative part of a woman's life and an important part
> of her self-esteem. Married women who were infertile
> were left in an undesirable position of being perceived
> as less feminine and with few socially-sanctioned
> activities to occupy them. In addition, infertile

women were judged to have brought their condition upon themselves. And finally, the medical literature predicted a dire future for her because of her malfunctioning reproductive organs.[120]

Benninghaus writes about the reticence of Americans when they were unable to have children. She argued that this reticence is evidence of the stigmatisation of childlessness and possibly piety as religion encouraged a quiet acceptance of fate.[121] There is no reason to believe this would not be the same for a Scottish woman.

Childlessness affects men and women in different ways over their lifespan. In the early years of marriage, infertility can impact multiple trajectories and shifting identities over the life course.[122] What does childlessness mean in the context of growing older? Being childless also means being grand-childless.

Hoffman and Hoffman in 1973[123] theorised the motivations for having children in that they satisfied nine psychological needs for parents:

1. Adult status and social identity (included here is the concept that motherhood is woman's major role)
2. Expansion of the self, tie to larger entity, 'immortality'
3. Morality: religion, altruism, good of the group, regarding sexuality, impulsivity, virtue, character norms building
4. Primary group ties, affection
5. Stimulation, novelty, fun
6. Achievement, competence, creativity
7. Power, influence, effectance
8. Social comparison, competition
9. Economic-utility[124]

The term 'childless' has negative connotations as it represents a lack or deficit. A more positive term might be 'child-free'.

> Motherhood was a defining moment for nine-
> teenth-century women and to be excluded from such
> a moment would have been not only heartbreaking
> but a blow to their self-confidence. ... Many women
> began to search for alternatives to mothering, such as
> adoption, while others found alternatives in careers
> such as teaching, nursing, and writing children's
> novels.[125]

Perhaps Margaret found an alternate form of mothering in the establishment of an orphanage in Tampere.

> While there was much continuity between Catholic
> and Protestant England, and many ideas about gender
> and sexuality circulated throughout all of Europe
> in this period, the Reformed theology did more to
> highlight childbearing as the main avenue for female
> piety. Catholic women had, at least in theory, two
> avenues for performing their religious duty: the more
> common avenue of marriage and childbirth, and the
> 'sacred' avenue of virginity. By contrast, Protestantism
> highlighted marriage as 'the best Christian life' and
> objected to celibacy as impractical for most.[126]

In the history of Tampere, James is described as a strict disciplinarian whereas Margaret was prized for her maternal nature:

> ... and it was said that Mrs Finlayson was a gentle
> mother and mistress. She educated the children as
> carefully as she fed them, and the Christianity which
> animated this couple sometimes influenced for life
> the few who attended this peculiar school.[127]

Philanthropy

We argue that the historical accounts of the Finlayson Factory seem to give too much weight to the novelty of philanthropic gestures of setting up an orphanage in Tampere in the early nineteenth century. We should remember that James may already have been exposed to two philanthropic ventures: New Lanark Mills under David Dale (founded 1786) and Alexandrovsk manufactory under the patronage of Empress Maria Feodorovna. Benevolent entrepreneurs such as Strutt at Belper and Arkwright at Cromford established Sunday schools in 1784 and 1785 respectively.[128] All of them provided education for poor children and disciplined living conditions despite their use of child labour in the mills. Although current attitudes view child factory employment as abhorrent, it is perhaps more nuanced than that. Undoubtedly, there is evidence of gross abuse. For example, the study of 'bio-archaeological' evidence for pauper apprentices in nineteenth century England and the health consequences of child labour.

> Most of the children exhibited distinctive 'non-local' isotope signatures and a diet low in animal protein when compared to the named local individuals. These children also showed severe growth delays and pathological lesions indicative of early life adversity, as well as respiratory disease, which is a known occupational hazard of mill work. This study has provided unique insights into the harrowing lives of these children; born into poverty and forced to work long hours in dangerous conditions. This analysis provides a stark testimony of the impacts of industrial labour on the health, growth and mortality risk of children, with implications for the present as well as our understanding of the past.[129]

However, some mill owners and patrons employed children for more philanthropic reasons. For example, Empress Maria Feodorovna had two objects in view:

> First, to find an additional field of industry in which to employ a large number of the foundlings, whom she rears with so much maternal care and regard almost from their birth, till they become men and women; and secondly, to obtain fresh means of increasing the enormous capital which is necessary to defray the annual expenditure of an institution of such magnitude as that of the Foundling. From what I have seen, it appeared to me that the two objects had been most completely accomplished.[130]

In Russia and across Europe the numbers of abandoned children were a social problem. The rates of child mortality were high whether in the community or in foundling homes. Employment was one way to address this, through providing socialization, personal development, structure, opportunities to contribute and sometimes education, meals and lodging. In some cases, it was better than the alternatives of prostitution, crime and starvation. However, the costs that must be weighed against these benefits are: health problems, abuse (physical, sexual and psychological); workplace hazards; slave-like employment; long working hours and deprivation of education, when not provided by the employer.[131]

Apart from the working hours, mill conditions and punishments, diet played an important role in the health of the children. David Dale responded to the questions of T. B. Bayley in 1796 with details of the social conditions operating at New Lanark Mills.[132] Although the food was plain, it was plentiful for those times.

The provisions are dressed in cast iron boilers and consist of oatmeal porridge for breakfast and supper, and milk with it in season. In winter its substitute is a composition of molasses, fermented with some new beer, which is called swats. For dinner, the whole of them have every day, in all seasons, barley broth made from fresh beef. The beef itself is divided among half of the children, in quantities of about seven ounces English to each; the other half is served with cheese in quantities of about five ounces English each; so that they have alternately beef and cheese for dinner, excepting no and then a dinner of herrings in winter, and fresh butter in summer. To the beef and cheese is added a plentiful allowance of potatoes or barley bread, of which last they have also an allowance every morning before going to work.[133]

Visitors to the Alexandrovsk Manufactory provide descriptions of feeding the children. For example, Augustus Bozzi Granville writes:

The dinner consists of plain or cabbage soup (shchi), beef and kascha [buckwheat porridge], and rye bread, five days in the week; and of fish (sniatky,), in their cabbage soup, the other two days in the week. Kvass is their beverage ad libitum, according to the season of the year. They again work from half past one or two, till half past seven; and at four o'clock receive a second half-pound of rye bread. Supper is prepared at eight, consisting of soup, and kascha of buck-wheat, kroupa (grits), in winter, or milk in summer.[134]

It is probable, therefore, that James and Margaret were following in the footsteps of David Dale and Alexander Wilson. The Finlayson orphanage was established in 1821 and was the first of its kind in Finland. Their aim was to bring up poor and orphaned children with a religious and moral conduct, with a sense of diligent purpose through their work life. In their own house, they prepared rooms for some children without means, who might otherwise have resorted to begging. Destitute, begging children were everywhere in that time in Finland. It was therefore completely natural that Finlayson's orphanage came to draw public attention. Among others, the General Governor, Count Steinheil embraced this philanthropic business with particular warmth. For the orphanage in Tampere, he even helped obtained a state grant.[135] Perhaps the orphanage also filled an empty part of this childless couple's lives by providing an outlet for their desire to nurture close to home.

Concluding observations

> What people regard as vanity – leaving great works, having children, acting in such a way as to prevent one's name from being forgotten – I regard as the highest expression of human dignity.
> Paulo Coelho, *The Pilgrimage*

In the 1980s, Michael Dixon, Education Correspondent and Jobs Columnist for the *Financial Times*, listed the 'Common Laws of Stupidity'.[136] One of these was the Peter Principle, coined by Dr Laurence J. Peter (1919–1990) in his book with co-author, Raymond Hull, *The Peter Principle*: that in any hierarchy, every employee tends to rise to his level of incompetence. [137]

Peter and Hull go on to describe the method people reach their level of incompetence is through 'pull' or 'push' mechanisms. The pull mechanism is the stronger and is frequently enabled through patronage. Peter and Hull also differentiate incompetence into four types: physical, social, emotional and mental. James' record shows he was mentally incompetent in terms of financial acumen. His career was not strictly as an employee within a hierarchy apart from his time working for Alexander Wilson in Russia. However, his successes and failures can be understood by the application of the Peter Principle. James was, at heart, a machine maker of textile machinery. Whether it was the push factor of personal ambition and drive, or the pull factor of patronage by John Napier, Tsar Alexander I or John Paterson, James arrived in positions of business management to which he was ill-suited. James was better at starting businesses than implementing sound management and finishing the projects. James also showed social incompetence in his relationships. His character style could be abrasive, as shown with the Quakers in Edinburgh. He did seem to make long term relationships with men such as John Napier and Daniel Wheeler. Were these friendships or patronage? There is no evidence to suggest one more than the other. Whether James showed physical or emotional incompetence, it is probable that it was a mix of the two and led to cyclical bouts of 'illness'. He was affected by events such as John Napier's ill-health but he was possibly self-destructive and, thereby, not reaching his full potential. Nevertheless, he was a remarkable man who took advantage of the opportunities presented to him. Religious integrity was a core part of him.

Margaret is more of an enigma. She demonstrated social competence with long-term friendships with men and women, such as Ferdinand Uhde, William Swan, Sarah Wheeler and Augusta Lundahl. There are memories of her kindness to the orphans in Tampere. She was industrious and, even when a widow in her eighties, she was thinking of supporting herself through setting up a knitting business with her friend Katriona Ekblom. She was James' worthy partner for nearly sixty years and supported him through his travails, following him from place to place. This must have been difficult as she left friends behind.

James Finlayson ensured his legacy by his demand that the new owners of the Tampere mill continued to use his name. Otherwise, James and Margaret might have been forgotten figures in Scotland's story. Nottbeck, Wheeler and Uhde surely achieved more than James. We compared James Finlayson with a contemporary, William Dun, earlier. Despite the latter being a more successful businessman, we would argue that Dun is relatively unknown compared with Finlayson. Any visitor to Tampere will have seen the sign in massive Gothic lettering above the old mill, shown in Plate 17.

Both Margaret and James were Scots worthy of remembrance.

NOTES

1 Graham, P. L. (1963) Speech to the Newsweek foreign correspondents. London. April.

2 Cook, T. (2011) Clio's warriors: Canadian historians and the writing of the world wars. Vancouver: UBC Press. p. 234.

3 Ricoeur, P. (2004) Memory, history, forgetting. Translated by K. Blamey and D. Pellauer. Chicago and London: The University of Chicago Press. p. 320.

4 Peek, M. (2021). Comment on Lois Leveen, "Best Guess or Worst Doubt: What's the Role of Conjecture in Writing Biography and History?" in David Prior, et al., The H-CivWar Author's Blog, 24 August 2021 https://networks.h-net.org/node/4113/blog/h-civwar-authors-blog/8089270/best-guess-or-worst-doubt-whats-role-conjecture : accessed 24 November 2023.

5 Swan, W. (1823) Memoir of the late Mrs Paterson, wife of the Rev. Dr Paterson, St Petersburg, Containing Extracts from Her Diary and Correspondence, 2nd edn. Edinburgh: Waugh & Innes.

6 Allen, W. (1847) Life of William Allen: With selections from his correspondence. in two volumes. Philadelphia: H. Longstreth.

7 Paterson, J. and Alexander, W. L. (Ed) (1857) The book for every land: Reminiscences of labour and adventure in the work of bible circulation in the North of Europe and in Russia. London: John Snow.

8 Sivula, A. (2014) Corporate history culture and useful industrial past: A case study on history management in Finnish cotton company Porin Puuvilla Oy. Folklore, 57. pp. 29–54.

9 Lindfors, G. V. (1938) Finlayson-fabrikerna I Tammerfors Del 1: 1820-1907. Helsingfors: Tilgmann.

10 Peltola, J. (2020) RE: Finlayson's Bankrupt 1807? E-mail to Angela Harris, 9 June 2020.

11 Fewster, F. A. (1970) Finlayson 1820-1970. Tampere, Finland: Oy Finlayson Ab.

12 Sullivan, J. (1929) Legend, anecdote and history. The Quarterly Journal of the New York State Historical Association, 10(1), pp. 29–44, p.30.

13 Sullivan, J. (1929). p. 39.

14 Selleck, R. G. (1962) Quaker pioneers in Finnish economic development: James Finlayson and the Wheeler Family. Quaker History, 51(1), pp. 32–42.

15 Denoon, B. (1991) James Finlayson of Penicuik 1772–1852: Industrial founder of Finland's second city. Aberdeen University Review, 65(Autumn).

16 Peltola, J. (2019) The British contribution to the birth of the Finnish cotton industry (1820–1870). Continuity and Change, 34, pp. 63–89.

17 Trouillot, M-R. (2015) Silencing the past: Power and the production of history. Beacon Press.

18 Wheeler, S. (1836) Letter to Margaret Finlayson. 29 August. Margareta Finlayson Archive/Central Archives for Finnish Business Records (ELKA) ELKA-00427-000001-000001-025. Used with permission from ELKA.

19 Maclean, K. (2017) Finland, Finlayson and Finno-Scottish Links. Royal Scottish Geographical Society Media Blog, 5 December. http://www.rsgs.org/blog/finland-finlayson-and-finno-scottish-links : accessed: 31 August 2023).

20 Wikipedia contributors. James Finlayson (industrialist). Wikipedia, The Free Encyclopedia. 14 Nov. 2023. Web : accessed 30 Jan. 2024.

21 Nykänen, P. (2000) Finlayson, James and Margaret: Founders of the Finlayson cotton spinning mill. Kansallisbiografia online, pp. 786–787.

22 Hartog, F. (2015) Regimes of historicity: Presentism and experiences of time. Columbia University Press. p. 203.

23 Massey, M. (1979) The people puzzle: Understanding yourself and others. Reston, VA: Reston Publishing Company.

24 Conway, S. (2001) 'War and national identity in the mid-eighteenth-century British Isles', The English Historical Review, 116(468), pp. 863–893. Conway, S. (2001) War and national identity in the mid-eighteenth-century British Isles. The English Historical Review, 116(468). pp. 863–893.

25 Finlay, R. J. (1999) Keeping the Covenant: Scottish national identity. In: Eighteenth-Century Scotland: New perspectives. East Linton: Tuckwell Press, pp. 121–133.

26 Conway, S. (2001). p. 886.

27 Hobsbawm, E. (1962) Age of revolution: 1789-1848 [Kindle]. London: Phoenix Press.

28 Morris, Neil (2010). Timeline adapted by Concordia International School from The Industrial Revolution. Heinemann/Raintree, 2010. pp 12-14. https://library.concordiashanghai.org/c.php?g=393491 : accessed 8 September 2023.

29 Hobsbawm, E. (1962), p.59. Copyright © Hobsbawm, E. (1962). Reproduced with permission of the Licensor through PLSclear.

30 Hobsbawm, E. (1962)

31 Fagerstrom, D. I. (1954) Scottish opinion and the American Revolution. The William and Mary Quarterly, 11(2), pp. 252–275. p. 252.

32 Smith, A. (2008) An inquiry into the nature and causes of the wealth of nations. London: Oxford University Press (Oxford World's Classics).

33 Fagerstrom, D. I. (1954). p.259.

34 Fagerstrom, D. I. (1954). p. 265.

35 Devine, T. M. (2008) Scotland and the Union 1707-2007. Edinburgh University Press. p. 6.

36 Jones, B. A. (2006) The American Revolution, Glasgow, and the making of the second city of the empire. In: Europe's American Revolution. London: Palgrave Macmillan, pp. 1–25.

37 Jones, B. A. (2006). p. 6.

38 Devine, T. M. (1976) The colonial trades and industrial investment in Scotland, c. 1700-1815. The Economic History Review, 29(1). pp. 1–13.

39 Mathieson, W. L. (1910) The awakening of Scotland: A history from 1747 to 1797. J. Maclehose and sons. p. 141.

40 Vincent, E. (1994) The Responses of Scottish Churchmen to the French Revolution, 1789-1802. The Scottish Historical Review, 73(196, Part 2), pp. 191–215. p. 191.

41 Morton, V. (1991) Quaker politics and industrial change c.1800-1850: Jane Smeal letter to Elizabeth Pease December 1836. PhD Thesis. Open University. p. 116.

42 DRBs Scottish Women's History Group (no date) Women on the platform. https://theedinburghreporter.co.uk/wp-content/uploads/2014/01/DRB-Exhibition-Booklet.pdf : accessed: 15 October 2023).

43 Uglow, J. (2014) In these times: Living in Britain through Napoleon's Wars, 1793–1815 [Kindle]. Faber & Faber. loc. 7425.

44 Uhde, F. (1849) Letter to Sarah Wheeler 30 January. Millfield Papers (MIL). Alfred Gillett Trust Archives. MIL_29_5 Uhde 1849-01-30.

45 Smith, C. J. (1986) Historic South Edinburgh: People. Haddington: Charles Skilton Ltd.; Uhde, F. (1855) Letter to Sarah Tanner 31 March. MIL_30_3 1855-03-31. Millfield Papers (MIL). Alfred Gillett Trust Archives.

46 Hine, W. C. (1975) American slavery and Russian serfdom: A preliminary comparison. Phylon, 36(4), pp. 378–384. p. 379.

47 Lefebvre, G. (1969) Napoleon: From Brumaire to Tilsit: 1799-1807. London: Routledge & Paul. p. 179.

48 Rothenberg, G. E. (1988) The origins, causes, and extension of the wars of the French Revolution and Napoleon. The Journal of Interdisciplinary History, 18(4), pp. 771–793. p. 773. Used with permission from The MIT Press.

49 Uglow, J. (2014). loc. 128

50 Hobsbawm, E. (1962)

51 Hobsbawm, E. (1962). p. 132.

52 Uglow, J. (2014). loc. 10749.

53 National Records of Scotland. The Duke of Wellington statue at Register House, https://www.nrscotland.gov.uk/research/learning/features/the-duke-of-wellington-statue-at-register-house : accessed 27 September 2023.

54 Houston, R. A. (1988) The demographic regime. In: People and society in Scotland. Edinburgh: John Donald (A social history of modern Scotland), pp. 9–26. p. 13.

55 Allen, B. M. (1998) The effects of infectious disease on Napoleon's Russian campaign. A Research Report Submitted to the Faculty in Partial Fulfillment of the Graduation Requirements. Maxwell Air Force Base, Alabama: Air Command and Staff College, Air University, p. 48.

56 Szreter, S. and Mooney, G. (1998) Urbanization, mortality, and the standard of living debate: New estimates of the expectation of life at birth in nineteenth-century British cities. The Economic History Review, 51(1). pp. 84–112. p. 98.

57 Cowan, R. (1840) Vital statistics of Glasgow, illustrating the sanatory condition of the population. Journal of the Statistical Society of London, 3(3). pp. 257–292.

58 Kiple, K. F. (1999) Plague, pox & pestilence: Disease in history. London: Phoenix Illustrated.

59 Mason, B., Brown, E.S. and Croarkin, P.E. (2016) Historical underpinnings of bipolar disorder diagnostic criteria. Behavioral Sciences. 6(3), pp. 1–19. p. 2.

60 Houston, R. A. (1998) 'Therapies for mental ailments in eighteenth-century Scotland', Journal of the Royal College of Physicians of Edinburgh, 28(4), pp. 555–568.

61 Houston, R. A. (1998)

62 Bin-Jumah, M. N. et al. (2022) Genes and Longevity of Lifespan. International Journal of Molecular Sciences, 23(3).

63 Cowan, R. (1840). p. 261

64 Uhde, F. (1840) Letter to C. S. Nottbeck, 11 May. Kotimaahan lähetettyjen kirjeiden toisteet (Letter book of letters sent domestically). Central Archives for Finnish Business Records (ELKA). 428:IDaa.3. Used with permission from ELKA.

65 Wallin (later Voionmaa), V. (1905) Tampereen Kaupungin Historia: II OSA Tampereen Historia Aleksanteri I:n ja Nikolai I:n (History of the City of Tampere: PART II History of Tampere under Alexander Ist and Nicholas Ist). Tampere [Finland]: Tampere Kaupungin Kustantama. p. 84.

66 Kaarninen, M. (2022) The trials of Sarah Wheeler (1807–1867): Experiencing submission. In: Histories of Experience in the World of Lived Religion. Springer International Publishing, pp. 195–217.

67 Wheeler, S. (1836). Letter to Margaret Finlayson February. The Margareta Finlayson Archive/Central Archives for Finnish Business Records. ELKA-00427-000001-018-DOC. Used with permission from ELKA.

68 Wheeler, S. (1832). Letter to Margaret Finlayson 5 November. The Margareta Finlayson Archive/Central Archives for Finnish Business Records. ELKA-00427-000001-015-DOC. Used with permission from ELKA.

69 Wheeler, S. (1832).

70 Wheeler, S. (1830). Letter to Margaret Finlayson 22 August. The Marga-
    reta Finlayson Archive/Central Archives for Finnish Business Records.
    ELKA-00427-000001-011. Used with permission from ELKA.

71 Society of Friends (Quaker) Congregational Records. Grange Monthly
    Meeting, Congregational Archive: Ulster Friends Trustees Ltd Ireland.
    Archive reference: GM5.12. Courtesy of Friends (Quaker) Historical
    Library, Dublin.

72 Swan, W. (1820). Letter to Margaret Finlayson 27 March. The Marga-
    reta Finlayson Archive/Central Archives for Finnish Business Records.
    ELKA-00427-000001-001-DOC. Used with permission from ELKA.

73 Swan, W. (1823). Letter to Margaret Finlayson 26 December. The
    Margareta Finlayson Archive/Central Archives for Finnish Business
    Records. ELKA-00427-000001-005. Used with permission from ELKA.

74 Wallin (later Voionmaa), V. (1905). p. 107. Translated with www.
    DeepL.com/Translator (free version).

75 Hakala, E. (2015) James Finlayson. avainsijoitus, 31 October : accessed
    10 March 2023.

76 Finlayson, J. (1832) Letter to Daniel Wheeler 30 June. Daniel Wheeler
    Papers, London Society of Friends Library, TEMP MSS 366 Volume 1
    Item 88.

77 Wheeler, D. (1826). Letter to James Finlayson 9 February. Daniel
    Wheeler Papers. London Society of Friends Library. LSF MSS 366
    Volume 1 Life in Russia Item 56.

78 Wheeler, D. (1827) Letter to James Finlayson 5 June. Daniel Wheeler
    Papers. London Society of Friends Library. LSF MSS 366 Volume 1 Life
    in Russia Item 63, page 1.

79 Bell, T. M. (2016) A brief history of bloodletting. The Journal of Lan-
    caster General Hospital, 11(4). pp. 119–123

80 Finlayson, J. (1832)

81 Hansen, M., Smith, D. and Carruthers, G. (2018) Mood disorder in
    the personal correspondence of Robert Burns: Testing a novel inter-
    disciplinary approach. Journal of the Royal College of Physicians of
    Edinburgh, 48(2). pp. 165–174. doi:10.4997/jrcpe.2018.212. p. 167.
    Used with permission from the Royal College of Physicians of
    Edinburgh.

82 Hansen, M., Smith, D. and Carruthers, G. (2018). p. 168.

83 d'Eichthal, G. (1977) A French sociologist looks at Britain: Gustave
    d'Eichthal and British society in 1828. Edited by B.M. Ratcliffe and
    W.H. Chaloner. Manchester: Manchester University Press. p. 103.

84 Goodwin, G. (no date). William Dunn (1770-1849). Dictionary of
    National Biography 1885-1900.

85 Glasgow Directory (1801). Directories. Scotland. Scottish Post Office
    Directory of Glasgow. p. 33. https://digital.nls.uk/directories/ :
    accessed 27 April 2023.

86 Watson, T. (1894) Kirkintilloch: Town and parish. Glasgow: John
    Smith and Sons.

87 Watson, T. (1894), pp.330–31.

88 Henderson, W. O. (1968) Industrial Britain under the Regency: The
    diaries of Escher, Bodmer, May and de Gallois. London: Cass.

89 Perthshire Courier (1835) Dreadful fire at Glasgow, 11 June. https://
    www.britishnewspaperarchive.co.uk/ : accessed 30 August 2023.

90 Dundee, Perth, and Cupar Advertiser (1846). Destruction by Fire of
    Milton Mill at Duntocher. 31 July. https://www.britishnewspaperar
    chive.co.uk/ : accessed 30 August 2023.

91 Henderson, W. O. (1968). p. 42.

92 Vance, J. (2023) Why business fails. Small business cash flow manage-
    ment: strategies for success by Nov 29, 2023 Financial Strategy. https://
    preferredcfo.com/cash-flow-reason-small-businesses-fail/ : accessed 31
    January 2024.

93 Lindfors, G. V. (1938) pp. 89–90. Translated by Anna McIvor.

94 Meisenzahl, R. R. and Mokyr, J. (2011) The rate and direction of invention in the British Industrial Revolution incentives and institutions, Working Paper 16993. National Bureau of Economic Research. © 2011 by Ralf Meisenzahl and Joel Mokyr. All rights reserved. p. 445.

95 Wallin (later Voionmaa), V. (1905). p. 107. Translated with www. DeepL.com/Translator (free version). , p. 105.

96 Peltola, J. (2019)

97 Kennedy, T. C. (2017) Quakers. In: T. Larsen and M. Ledger-Lomas (eds) The Oxford History of Protestant Dissenting Traditions, Volume III: The Nineteenth Century. Oxford University Press.

98 Bebbington, D. W. (1989) Evangelicalism in modern Britain: A history from the 1730s to the 1980s. London: Routledge.

99 Baptie, D. (2014) A short history of the Secession churches in Scotland. https://scotsarchivesearch.co.uk/short-history-secession-churches-scotland/ : accessed: 30 September 2023). Used with permission.

100 McKerrow, J. (1839) History of the Secession Church. Edinburgh: William Oliphant and Son.

101 Hobsbawm, E. (1962), p.328. Copyright © Hobsbawm, E. (1962). Reproduced with permission of the Licensor through PLSclear.

102 Gripenberg, L. (1929) James Finlayson. In: Teoksessa Tampere. Tutkimuksia ja kuvauksia I. (Tampere: Studies and descriptions I.). Tampere [Finland]: Tampereen Historiallinen Seura (Tampere Historical Society), pp. 173–190.

103 Wallin (later Voionmaa), V. (1905). p. 107. Translated with www. DeepL.com/Translator (free version).

104 Corfield, P. J. (1989) Dress for deference and dissent: Hats and the decline of hat honour. Costume, 23(1). pp. 64–79.

105 Holmes, A. (2023) Scottish anti-burgher practices. E-mail to Angela Harris, 15 February.

106 Finlayson, J. (1832)

107 Finlayson, J. (1832)

108 Barbour, H. (2004) Turford, Hugh (d. 1713), religious writer. In: Oxford Dictionary of National Biography online.

109 Kaarninen, M. (2019) Margaret Finlayson, In: Global Tampere: An economic history of the city from the 18th century to the present. Tampere [Finland]: Vapriiikki Tampere Museums, pp. 30–31. p. 31.

110 Wheeler, S. (1836) Letter to Margaret Finlayson, 11 April. The Margareta Finlayson Archive/Central Archives for Finnish Business Records. ELKA-00427-000001-013-DOC. Used with permission from ELKA.

111 Wheeler, S. (1836) Letter to Margaret Finlayson 29 August. The Margareta Finlayson Archive/Central Archives for Finnish Business Records. ELKA-00427-000001-000001-02. Used with permission from ELKA.

112 Wheeler, S. (1836) Letter to Margaret Finlayson 22 February. The Margareta Finlayson Archive/Central Archives for Finnish Business Records. ELKA-00427-000001-019-DOC. Used with permission from ELKA.

113 Wheeler, S. (1836) Letter to Margaret Finlayson 17 November. The Margareta Finlayson Archive/Central Archives for Finnish Business Records. ELKA-00427-000001-000001-027. Used with permission from ELKA.

114 Wheeler, S. (1836) Letter to Margaret Finlayson 24 September. The Margareta Finlayson Archive/Central Archives for Finnish Business Records. ELKA-00427-000001-000001-026. Used with permission from ELKA.

115 Wheeler, S. (1830) Letter to Margaret Finlayson 22 August. The Margareta Finlayson Archive/Central Archives for Finnish Business Records. ELKA-00427-000001-011. Used with permission from ELKA.

116 Holmes, A. R. (2006) The shaping of Ulster Presbyterian belief and practice, 1770-1840. Oxford: Oxford University Press. p. 285. Reproduced with permission of Oxford Publishing Limited through PLSclear.

117 Benninghaus, C. (2017) Silences: Coping with infertility in nineteenth-century Germany. In: The Palgrave Handbook of Infertility in History: Approaches, Contexts and Perspectives, pp. 99–122. p. 100.

118 Oren-Magidor, D. (2017) Infertility in Early Modern England. Palgrave Macmillan UK. Reproduced with permission

119 Trussell, J. and Wilson, C. (1985) Sterility in a population with natural fertility. Population Studies, 39(2). pp. 269–286.

120 Rhodes, R. (1988) Women, motherhood, and infertility: The social and historical context. In: Infertility and adoption: A guide for social work practice. Routledge. pp. 5–20. Copyright © 1988 by Routledge. Reproduced by permission of Taylor & Francis Group.

121 Benninghaus, C. (2017). p. 115.

122 Allen, R. E. S. and Wiles, J. L. (2013) How older people position their late-life childlessness: A qualitative study. Journal of Marriage and Family, 75(1). pp. 206–220.

123 Hoffman, L. W. (1975) The value of children to parents and the decrease in family size. Proceedings of the American Philosophical Society, 119(6). pp. 430–438. Reproduced by permission of the American Philosophical Society.

124 Hoffman, L.W. (1975) p. 431

125 Butler, A. (2020) A Unique Type of Loneliness: Infertility in Nineteenth-Century America" (2020). Arkansas Tech University Theses and Dissertations from 2020. 7. https://orc.library.atu.edu/etds_2020/7. pp. 7–9.

126 Oren-Magidor, D. (2017). p. 20.

127 Wallin (later Voionmaa), V. (1905). Translated with www.DeepL.com/Translator (free version). p. 114.

128 McLaren, D. J. (2015) David Dale: A Life. Stenlake Publishing. Permission granted from David McLaren and Stenlake Publishing.

129 Gowland, R. L. et al. (2023) The expendables: Bioarchaeological evidence for pauper apprentices in 19th century England and the health consequences of child labour. PLOS ONE. Edited by S. E. Halcrow, 18(5). https://doi.org/10.1371/journal.pone.0284970 : accessed: 22 July 2023). p.1. Open access article distributed under the terms of the Creative Commons Attribution License.

130 Granville, A. B. (1829) St. Petersburgh, A journal of travels to and from that capital; through Flanders, the Rhenich Provinces, Prussia, Russia, Poland, Silesia, Saxony, the Federated States of Germany, and France. London: Henry Colburn. p. 321.

131 Krummel, D. and Siegfried, P. (2021) Child labour ethics through the prism of utilitarianism and deontology. Open Access Library Journal (OALJ), 8(2), pp. 1–14. https://doi.org/10.4236/oalib.1107140 : accessed 22 July 2023.

132 McLaren, D. J. (2015) Appendix 7: Dale's Letter to T. B. Bayley, 1796.

133 McLaren, D. J. (2015) Appendix 7. p. 252.

134 Granville, A. B. (1829) pp. 320–21.

135 Lindfors, G. V. (1938).

136 Dixon, M. (1986) The Common Laws of Organizational Stupidity: How organisations lose touch with reality. Jobs Column, Financial Times. 3 April; 4 September; and 10 December.

137 Peter, L. J. and Hull, R. (1970) The Peter Principle. London: Pan Books. p. 22.

Chronology

Table 22: Timeline of James Finlayson and Margaret Wilkie

James' age	Date	Event
	1759	Robert Burns, the poet, born in Alloway, Ayrshire
	1764	James Hargreaves invented Spinning Jenny or multi-spool spinning frame
	1769	Richard Arkwright invented the Water Frame
	1770	James Finlayson born 27 November and baptised Howgate Associate, to James Finlayson and Margaret McClaren
	1776	Margaret Wilkie baptised in Abbey Parish, Renfrewshire, to Peter Wilkie and Elizabeth Jamieson (disputed)
5	1776, 9 March	Adam Smith, Scotsman and founder of modern economics, published An *Inquiry into the Nature and Causes of the Wealth of Nations*
	1776, 4 July	American Declaration of Independence
8	1779	Samuel Crompton invented the spinning mule based on the Spinning Jenny and the Water Frame
14	1785	David Dale and Richard Arkwright established New Lanark village
18–28	1789–1799	French Revolution

James' age	Date	Event
22	1792, 1 December	James Finlayson married Margaret Wilkie in Abbey Parish
21–44	1792–1815	French Revolutionary and Napoleonic Wars started 20 April 1792 and ended 20 November 1815.
25	1796, 21 July	Robert Burns, the poet, died in Dumfriesshire
28	1799	Alexandrovsk textile manufactory established
	Bef 1800	James Finlayson in Shuttle Street, Glasgow
32	1803, 26 August	James Finlayson entered Incorporation of Hammermen in Glasgow
32–33	1803–1804	James Finlayson moved to Havannah Street, Glasgow
34	1805, 7 June	Petition by Incorporation of Wrights of Glasgow
35	1806, 21 November	The Continental System, inaugurated by the Berlin decrees, was meant to prohibit all trade, even by neutral countries, with Britain
36	1807, 13 February	First sequestration (bankruptcy) of James Finlayson
36–39	1807–1810	Partnership between John Napier and James Finlayson
37	1808, 5 June	Tsar Alexander I issued Manifesto declaring Finland part of Russia during the 1808–9 Russia-Sweden War in Finland
39	1810, 14 May	Property on Havannah Street conveyed to John Napier and James Finlayson
40	1811, 21 January	Partnership between John Napier and James Finlayson dissolved
	1811	John Napier conveyed his half interest in the property to James Finlayson
42	1813, 13 February	Second sequestration of James Finlayson
	1813	James Finlayson conveyed his property to his creditors

James' age	Date	Event
	1813, 8 July	James Finlayson closed his business
	1813, 29 July	John Napier died in Glasgow
	1813	James Finlayson emigrated to St Petersburg in Russia and was employed by Alexander Wilson at the Alexandrovsk Manufactory as a Master mechanic
44		Margaret emigrated to St Petersburg, Russia
48	1819, 22 July	Left St Petersburg and travelled to Tampere with Rev. John Paterson
49	1820, 10 May	James Finlayson granted letters patent, along with land, customs facilities, freedom of worship and use of Tammerfors water power. May 10 1820 is regarded as the date the Finlayson Company started
	1820	James and Margaret Finlayson moved to Tampere separately
50	1821	James and Margaret set up orphanage at Tampere
65	1836	James sold the Finlayson manufactory to C. S. Nottbeck, G. A. Rauch, and the Wheelers
67	1838	James and Margaret left Tampere for Scotland
68	1839	James, residing with Margaret in Govan, Lanarkshire applied for membership to the Society of Friends but the application was deferred due to issues with creditors
69	1840	James Finlayson lost one third of his assets due to bankruptcy of Life Insurance company
	1840	Daniel Wheeler, Snr died in New York
70	1841	James and Margaret moved to Ireland
72	1843, 22 March	James applied for membership to Society of Friends in Grange, County Armagh, Ireland and was accepted as a member
	1843	James and Margaret moved to Moyallon in County Armagh

James' age	Date	Event
73	1844	James and Margaret moved to Nicolson Square, Edinburgh
75	1846, 9 May	James tendered his resignation from the Society of Friends in Edinburgh
	1846, 17 November	Daniel Wheeler, Jnr and Sarah Wheeler withdraw their interest in Finlaysons
78	1849	James purchases a lair in Newington Cemetery, Edinburgh
81	1852, 18 August	James died at 8, Nicolson Square, Edinburgh aged 81 and was buried in Newington Cemetery
	1855, 15 February	Margaret died at 8, Nicolson Square aged 82 and was buried with her husband

Acknowledgements and thanks

There are many people who have helped us in the decade since we started work on this book, including the staff in archives, museums, libraries and online in Glasgow, Edinburgh, London, Finland and Russia. For their helpful responses to our questions, many thanks to:

Olli Alm, Information Services and Development Manager, Central Archives for Finnish Business Records (ELKA), Mikkeli, Finland

Diane Baptie, researcher in archives

Elena Bobrova, Journalist and tour guide from St. Petersburg, Russia.

Craig Bryce, Honorary Archivist of the Trades House of Glasgow

Paul F. Burton, Academic author of 'A Social History of Quakers in Scotland, 1800–2000'

Andrew R. Holmes , Reader in History at Queen's University Belfast

Lorna Kinnaird, of DunEdin Links Genealogy, Family history researcher in Scotland

Antti Liuttunen, Researcher at Vapriikki Photo Archives

Yuriy Longuinoff, Publisher at Paleograph Press

Rosemary Marwick, co-author of Stories from an Edinburghshire Village: Howgate

Julie Mather, Archivist at Alfred Gillett Trust, Street, Somerset

Henrik Mattjus, Secretary of The Historical Society of Tampere

Juho Mattila, Research Officer, The National Archives, Hämeenlinna, Tavastehus, Finland

Stuart Nisbet, freelance researcher

Roy Pearson, Executive Committee Member of the Quaker Historical Library

Colin Quigley, Founder of 'acumfaegovan' website

Lucy Saint-Smith, Library Assistant, The Library of the Society of Friends, London

Marita Viinamäki, Researcher, The Finnish Labour Museum Werstas

David Whitford, Social Media Manager, Anglican Church in St Petersburg, Russia

Hanna Yli-Hinkkala, Museum Educator, The Finnish Labour Museum Werstas

We would like to extend our sincere thanks to Anton Pilvinskii, museum curator at State Museum Reserve Peterhof for finding documents within the St Petersburg archives. He was able to illuminate the time the Finlaysons spent in Russia.

We must also thank Janet Sidaway for reading an early draft of our book. Her enthusiasm and wise counsel were just what we needed. Thanks to our editorial and production team, Duncan Lockerbie and Stephen Cashmore for guiding and encouraging us through the process of bringing our book to fruition. Also, we thank our illustrator, Richard Bowring for the cover design and map of South Side Edinburgh. He took our preliminary ideas and made them work.

We acknowledge the contribution made by Jarmo Peltola, University Researcher from University of Helsinki, and Mervi Kaarninen, University Lecturer from Tampere University. Their published research gave us a sound foundation to work from.

We would like to extend our gratitude to Brian Denoon who started our interest in the Finlaysons in Edinburgh. We enjoyed meeting up with him and his wife, Sheila, in the Newington Cemetery.

List of Tables, Figures and Plates

* * *

Abbreviations

Source types for vital records (births, baptisms, marriages, deaths and burials

CR   Civil records
NCR   Non-conformist records
OPR   Old parish records (Scotland)

Appendix: Textile technology
This discussion of technology is limited for the purposes of this narrative

Yarn Spinning

This description of the processes does not purport to be an authoritative account of textile history or technology. Its purpose is just to try to explain briefly to a non-technical reader the processes described. It uses data from multiple sources.

What started it?

The phrase 'Spinning a yarn' may well have evolved to describe bored sailors on-board ship telling a tale, quite possibly not true or highly elaborated, to while away hours spent repairing ropes. nets or sails. The origin of yarn spinning from animal or plant fibres to form a long twisted stronger thread or yarn is lost in pre-history. Hand spinning using simple tools, the spindle and distaff, continued for thousands of years until the invention of the spinning wheel in the Islamic world in the eleventh century AD speeded up production, with this invention later spreading to China, India and Europe by about 1300. From the eighteenth century onwards increasing mechanisation and then automation successively improved yarn and thread output, quality and consistency.

Yarn or Thread?

These terms are used somewhat interchangeably, but 'yarn', as in spinning fibres, tends to be used to describe strands of fibres or filaments twisted together to form a long, strong, rather coarse strand which can be woven into cloth, whereas 'thread' usually denotes the same, but is finer, smoother and more consistent, suitable for use as sewing thread or for weaving into fine cloth. Many natural filaments can be spun into yarn or thread, but all need pre-treatment to make them suitable for spinning and then weaving into cloth and this depends on the natural materials being used. Some yarn may undergo further processing after being woven, such as cleaning, bleaching, dyeing or printing. All these processes spawned over many centuries, domestic-scale industries to carry them out, leading to aggregation into large complex manufactories, spearheading the Industrial Revolution and urbanisation.

Weaving into cloth

Weaving to produce cloth or textile is where two sets of yarn or thread are interlaced at right angles to each other to form a woven cloth or fabric, with the warp being longitudinal parallel threads and the weft (woof in old usage) those crossing at right angles. The way the weft interlaces with the warp – that is, over and under the warp – defines the weave. Plain weave is where each weft thread crosses each warp thread alternately over and under, produced by a shuttle thrown from side to side by the weaver or moved automatically by machinery. There are many other forms of weave, which can be carried out on a simple hand loom, later powered by a horse-gin, or waterwheel and then steam and electricity. The history of weaving from simple beginnings to large industrial enterprises is of great interest in itself, but as far as we know James Finlayson's knowledge and experience was in spinning and related processes and so weaving is not considered in detail in this account. However, from records of her activities in Finland, we can see that Margaret Finlayson knew a great deal about the practices then in use to wash, bleach and dye woven and knitted fabrics.

Knitting into hosiery

Around the time of the Elizabethan court, male courtiers and diplomats had need of full-length hosiery to show off a shapely leg, whereas women, with their long concealing dresses, did not. In the UK in the seventeenth and eighteenth centuries, fashion and the way the country was governed evolved, so that men of rank and business no longer needed long hosiery, but women did as their dresses got shorter.

The stocking frame, a knitting machine invented by William Lee of Calverton near Nottingham UK in 1589, was widely known and used by those in the eighteenth century hosiery trade. It was a speedier form of hand knitting, producing cloth in strips to be shaped and seamed by other skilled workers. It was progressively adapted to produce ribbed and fine cloth including silk.

The spinning bottleneck

Weaving uses a lot of yarn or thread for even a modest length of cloth and historically a simple hand-loom could outpace the availability of yarn or thread of consistent quality, a shortfall exacerbated by the increasing mechanisation of weaving. Efforts, therefore, concentrated on trying to improve the output and quality of yarn and thread and their related processes. James Finlayson initially concentrated on making machines and their components for these spinning processes, claiming to have improved many of those then commercially available. He later moved into yarn or thread production when the market for his machines did not come up to expectations, focusing on linen from flax, wool from sheep and cotton.

Linen from flax

The flax plant (*Linum usitatissimum*) has in its stem long, quite strong, fibres, which for thousands of years have been spun and woven into durable, rot resistant linen cloth. It can also be grown for its seeds, which after processing yield linseed oil. Carbon dating shows that linen cloth was in use in Egypt 8000 years ago. In 3000 BC finely woven linen cloth was being used to wrap the mummies of ancient Egyptian pharaohs. Flax has also been grown in northern Europe for centuries and, provided it has sufficient water, it will thrive in a wide range of climates. The Nile Delta in Egypt, with its annual inundation and supply of nutrients from the Nile, was an ideal habitat.

The linen fibres are embedded in cellulose pith under the skin of the stem of the flax plant and all this has to be removed to allow the fibres to be spun into yarn or thread. Historically, this was done by **retting**, steeping the harvested flax in water to allow natural pectins to break down by partial decomposition the material surrounding the fibres, allowing them to be released. The retting took place in a bog, or slow-moving watercourses, ponds or dammed up streams, but in suitable areas less polluting dew retting can be carried out. All methods of retting require skilled and experienced judgement to assess when the process has continued long enough to allow the fibres to be released, but not so long as to damage them.

After drying, the next stage is **scutching,** getting the fibres to part from the surrounding material and removing any other impurities in preparation for spinning. Traditionally, scutching flax by hand meant repeatedly using a scutching knife to scrape down the fibres while they hung vertically, to pull away pieces of stalk without damaging the fibres, leaving them smooth and silky. This was hard, tedious, labour-intensive work and machines were developed to take on this task, with varying degrees of success and efficiency. Many machines used a system of rollers to crush and break away the material from the fibres, but wastage from fibre damage continued to be a problem until relatively recent times. A '*skutching machine*' is itemised in the sale of James' manufacturing utensils advertisement in 1813.[1]

The last stage before spinning is **heckling (carding)** to separate and straighten the flax fibres and remove any remaining impurities. The flax is pulled through sets of combs or mounted prongs of increasing fineness or closer pitch. From combs on boards for hand heckling, machines were developed with metal prongs mounted on a series of rollers, with each roller having prongs progressively closer together between which the slivers of flax were pulled. The short fibres that remained on the combs could still be spun into inferior yarn and woven bags or twisted into cord or used as fuel or manure.

Wool from sheep

Wool spun into yarn from hair on the coat of sheep is possibly the most widely used animal fibre in the world and woollen knitted, knotted or woven fabric, clothing, carpets and blankets have been around for thousands of years. Wool offers protection, insulation and comfort, as does yarn spun from the coat of other animals, such as mohair from the Angora goat, alpaca from a small breed of llama, the yak and rabbits. Sheep's wool when dry is light, slightly elastic, springy and soft, which is why it is a good insulator. The fleece has an oily or greasy feel, due to wax secreted from sebaceous glands in the animal's skin. Most pre-spinning treatment removes this wax, which can be purified as lanolin and used to protect and treat human skin.

Prior to spinning into yarn, the usual treatment for shorn fleece is **scouring** to remove grease and impurities. The clean fibres are then combed or **carded** to disentangle them and ensure the fibres are parallel to each other ready for spinning. Blending different varieties of wool may then take place also and the fibres may be differently prepared dependent on whether the worsted or woollen or other process is being used.

Sheep's fleece retains grease, skin particles, shed hair and other organic material such as faeces, parasites and twigs acquired during grazing. Scouring is washing to remove these impurities, traditionally hand washing in bowls or tanks using a naturally derived detergent such as soap, or latterly using complex synthetic detergents in washing machines. The wash (effluent) from wool scouring can be highly polluting. After scouring the wool fibres are then dried and carded.

Carding wool may involve several processes, a preliminary one being picking or teasing, traditionally carried out by hand using natural teazle heads, to open up the fibres and tease out remaining debris. This involves pulling a lock of wool apart gently by hand to fluff it up into a 'cloud' or using hand combs or coarse teeth on boards, such as nails. Picking machines have been around since the late eighteenth century and commercially this task has been taken over by modern machinery. Carding continues this process using a series of boards or adjacent drums or rollers carrying on them meshing hard and flexible teeth to achieve by firm brushing a mat of clean, separated fibres, the output or 'roving' required dependent on the weaving system to be used. The 1813 sale of items from Finlayson's Woollen Manufactory' included 'a Skutching Machine', but it is not known of what type. The carded Rovings are then divided and collected on spools ready for spinning into cloth, a roving frame also being included in the same 1813 sequestration sale. James Finlayson both made and operated the machines then available, or made their components, so his expertise in wool would have been an asset in his employment in St Petersburg. However, not all sheep's wool is the same. Russian wool differs from English wool, as William Sherwood to his cost found in Alexandrovsk Manufactory in October 1802 when he had to remake the carding machine in a timescale of six months.

Cotton

The cotton shrub, of the genus *Gossypium*, has a number of species or hybrids grown commercially for different characteristics of its fibre, which is the seed head of the plant. It requires a hot and humid, tropical or subtropical climate, with a long sunny season and a copious supply of water. The fluffy head allows the seeds it contains to be spread widely by being blown on the wind. The plant grows naturally and is cultivated commercially in many parts of the world, such as China, Iran (Persia), the Indian sub-continent, the Americas, and Africa including Egypt and Australia. The plant was independently domesticated for its fibre in the Old and New Worlds and is usually spun into fabric, which is light, cool, breathable and durable. When wet the fabric is much lighter than wool, which can take time to dry, is prone to shrinkage and loss of shape. Using cotton for fabric has been known since prehistoric times and scraps of fabric have been dated to around 4000 BC. As with flax, cotton grown in the Nile Delta was historically well-known for being of high quality and is widely used for towelling.

Cotton is ready for harvesting when the seed head (boll) splits open, revealing fluffy white fibres (lint). Harvesting is by removing the boll from the shrub, by hand a tedious, arduous, labour-intensive task, in places and former times sometimes carried out by slave labour to maximise the planation owner's return. Reliable and effective cotton-picking machines or harvesters were not invented until many decades after the Finlaysons' time. They began to be used in the USA from the1920s, being improved from an initial capability of picking one row of shrubs to a modern self-propelled machine able to deal with six rows of shrubs at a time. There are broadly two types of cotton harvester in use. The first is the 'picker', which as well as removing the bolls also takes away quite a bit of the plant as well, which is then separated out by a dropping process before the lint is gathered in a basket at the back of the machine. The second type is the 'spindle picker', which has rows of barbed spindles rotating at high speed to whip the lint from the plant. The lint is then removed from the spindle by a counter-rotating 'doffer and then blown into a gathering basket. In some cotton producing areas, the non-commercial growing of cotton shrubs, in gardens for example, is regulated to try to limit the spread of diseases and pests, such as the boll weevil, which can ruin a crop.

In the seventeenth century, the East India Company introduced into Britain highly coloured cheap cotton fabrics, supplementing and eventually overtaking its spice trade. However between the late seventeenth century and the early eighteenth , the UK Parliament, seeing a threat to its domestic textile businesses, adopted protectionist policies, banning the importation into UK of finished cotton goods, but allowing raw cotton imports. This spawned the development in UK of mechanical means of preparing yarn for spinning and spinning and weaving machinery, concentrated in cotton mills, an environment which the Finlaysons experienced and worked in, part of the Industrial Revolution.

At that time raw cotton was exported in wrapped bales, each weighing about 500lbs (225kg), but bale standards varied. Some initial scutching or ginning was carried out prior to shipping, but as well as cotton fibres, each bale also included unwanted material, husks, cottonseeds, plant remains and insects, which had to be removed prior to spinning, the **scutching** or **ginning** stage.

Hand scutching of raw cotton was traditionally carried out by spreading it on a mesh and beating the fibres with sticks or purpose-made wooden tools, so that the impurities dropped through the mesh. Hand-held roller gins were in use in the Indian sub-continent by about 500AD and the Indian worm-gear roller gin was invented around the sixteenth century, still in use in some places. The earlier version consisted of a single wooden or iron roller and a flat wiper of stone or wood. The later sixteenth-century Indian worm gear gin could have a hand crank to operate it or be water-powered and was exported widely, including to the USA. Familiarity with this machine may well have created the impetus in 1793 for Eli Whitney to invent the modern mechanical gin, patented the following year.

In general. this mechanical gin had two rotating cylinders. The first had lines of teeth around its circumference and angled against it is a metal plate with small holes in it, ginning ribs, through which the teeth can fit with only slight gaps between them, so the teeth grip the cotton as it rotates, dragging it through the small holes. The seeds and other residues are too big to pass through the holes and are removed by the plate, falling into a collecting pot. On the other side of the first cylinder is a second one, also rotating, with brushes on it to wipe the cotton from the first cylinder and deposit it in a receptacle. Specifically, Whitney's gin employed a wooden cylinder covered by rows of wires to catch the boll fibres. Each row of wires passed through a comb-like grid, pulling the fibres through the grid. The teeth of the grid were closely spaced to stop the seeds and other debris from passing through it and this debris was then removed by a second roller covered with brushes to stop the mechanism from clogging. Others improved or modified Whitney's gin, in some cases to try to evade the patent. A modern industrial-scale automated gin plant has multiple powered cylinders offering far greater productivity and produces compressed larger bales or rolls of cotton equal to several standard bales.

In the Finlaysons' time, imported cotton bales, usually from USA, has first to be broken open to continue the carding stage by scutching or ginning as already described. The 1807 sale of Finlayson's cotton machinery included '13 Carding Engines, of various breadths', but it is not clear what type they were.

After the various carding processes, which may also include combing and drawing stages, the output is a narrow bundle of smooth, parallel fibres, usually slightly twisted, suitable for spinning, known as a **roving,** which can also mean a small roll of these strands.

Yarn Spinning

For thousands of years natural fibre was spun by hand using a stick as a spindle, until output was greatly increased by the invention of the spinning wheel. However, this did not change the basic way in which a human finger and thumb were used to form into yarn narrow strands of wool or other fibre, giving strength and continuity to it by twisting imparted by the whirling of the spindle by the spinner or by the spinning wheel. The addition to a hand spindle of a weighted disc or whorl with a hole in it (a distaff) imparted momentum, allowing it to spin longer and produce a greater length of yarn spun with each cycle of operation. In wheel spinning a distaff can also be mounted near the bobbin, rotated by the wheel. Many variants of this procedure evolved over the centuries, dependent on the fibre being spun and the local physical and social environment. The term 'distaff' may also describe the female side of a family, the male term being 'spear' side.

The addition of a flyer in the form an inverted U to the spindle allowed continuous spinning on a spinning wheel, but it remained a rather tedious process until the 1730s onwards, when a number of inventions enabled spinning, in particular of cotton, 'without the intervention of the human fingers'.[2] Specifically in 1764/5 James Hargreaves of Lancashire invented the **Spinning Jenny**, a multi-spindle spinning frame, with a worker able to tend more than 8 spools at once, growing to 120, but the yarn produced was not very strong or consistent. Then Richard Arkwright in the 1770s developed the **Water Frame**, which simulated better the action of hand spinning by stretching the roving using drafting rollers and twisting it by winding onto a spindle. This was a big, heavy machine which had to be driven by water-power, hence its name. In 1779, Samuel Crompton created a hybrid of these two machines, the **Spinning Mule,** so-called because it was a hybrid or cross-breed. The Mule consisted of a fixed frame with a creel of bobbins holding the roving connected through a headstock to a parallel movable carriage carrying the spindles. The was an intermittent process, so on the outward traverse the rovings were paid out and twisted and on its return the rovings were clamped and the spindles reversed to take up the newly spun yarn. Many improvements were made over the following years to enable the Mule to automatically produce large quantities of consistent high yarn, especially Lancashire cotton, with the machine supervisor needing fewer skills than before, replacing empty roving bobbins or full yarn ones as necessary and repairing any breaks in the thread.

Another rival spinning process is the throstle frame or **Ring Frame**, invented and developed in the USA in the nineteenth century, in which the roving is drawn, twisted and wrapped in a single continuous operation. The roving is first attenuated by drawing rollers, then spun and wound around a rotating spindle, which in turn is contained within an independently rotating ring flyer. Whilst the Spinning Mule was more versatile in being able to be readily adapted to different fibres and tasks, it required more skilled attention than the Ring Frame, which could be looked after by semi-skilled workers. Progressive development and technological improvements in the twentieth century led to this method of spinning becoming the principal means of producing yarn and thread world-wide commercially, also using automation.

The sequestration sales of 1807 and 1813 give some insight into yarn spinning and the associated activities of James Finlayson in his business. The sale of August 1807 included '8 Mules of 192 spindles, adapted for coarse numbers'. These may be quite large machines for their time, set up to produce coarser cotton, rather a than fine sewing thread, 'coarse numbers' probably referring to a low number of twists per inch. The other machines in that sale were probably all connected with successive cotton carding stages to produce rovings of a quality suitable for spinning into yarn. On the other hand, the machines in the 1813 sales, including the

'Eleven Spinning Jeanies' seem to have been more to do with wool, but it is not clear whether with this is solely related to stocking manufacture.

Final Stages

Generally bleaching and dyeing are carried out after the prepared yarn is woven into cloth, except where it is used for sewing or knitting. For wool, **Fulling (Waulking** in Scottish English) of woven cloth is a cleaning, shrinking and thickening (milling) process to remove oil (lanolin) any remaining dirt etc. still in the cloth after weaving, by washing, kneading and pounding the cloth, preceded by bleaching. Chemical means, traditionally using stale urine for the ammonium salts in it, but also manufactured bleaching agents were increasingly used. From her correspondence, Margaret Finlayson clearly had a good understanding of the chemicals then in use for bleaching. In Scotland in particular, bleaching of woven cloth was often carried by spreading it on a bleachfield. Stuart Nisbet has an illustration of Bleachfields near Paisley of about 1800.[3]

The June 1813 sale at James's 'Havannah Street Woollen Spinning Factory' lists 'Two Waulk Mills'. Waulking could be a collective activity carried out by groups of women, the kneading and working of the woollen cloth in the waulk mill requiring a rhythmic beat, slow at first and then the beat quickened. Waulking Songs to encourage the performance of this tedious and arduous task were a feature of rural life in Gaelic Scotland, especially in tweed producing localities, the songs themselves becoming part of Gaelic heritage.

NOTES

1 Advertisement (1813) Glasgow Courier (1813) Manufacturing utensils for sale. 21 August.

2 Baines, E. (1835) History of the Cotton Manufacture in Great Britain. H. Fisher, R. Fisher, and P. Jackson. p. 134.

3 Nisbet, S. (2009) The development of the cotton industry in Paisley. Renfrewshire Local History Forum (RLHF) Journal, 15. p. 8.

Bibliography and sources

ARCHIVAL SOURCES
Alfred Gillett Trust Archives
Millfield Papers (MIL).
Ancestry.com
Finland Communion Books 1825–1838.
England, Select Marriages, 1538–1973.
UK, Poll Books and Electoral Registers, 1538–1893.
Archives & Special Collections, University of Glasgow
New Lanark Mills' Visitors Book 1795–1799.
Central Archives for Finnish Business Records (ELKA)
Chancery of the Governor General.
Finlayson Oy Letter book of letters sent domestically 1836–1852 ID: 428.
Margareta Finlayson archive.
Edinburgh Central Library
Edinburgh Room, cemetery prospectuses.
Edinburgh Cemeteries and Crematoria, Bereavement Services, Edinburgh
Newington Necropolis records (Sales book / Burial book)
FindmyPast.com
Congregational Archive, Ireland, Society of Friends (Quaker)

Gazetteer for Scotland

Glasgow City Archives, Mitchell Library, Glasgow

Register of Sasines.

Register of the Incorporation of Hammermen in Glasgow (1766-1816).

HathiTrust Digital Library

Lloyds List.

Library of the Society of Friends, Friends House, London

Daniel Wheeler Papers, Volume 1 Life in Russia LSF MSS 366.

Extracts from the letters of Daniel Wheeler MS Box X2/14.

National Archives of Britain (TNA)

Research Guides

National Archives of Finland. Helsinki, Finland

Finland Communion Books 1670–1917.

National Library of Scotland, Edinburgh (NLS)

1799–1828 Glasgow Post Office Directory.

1805–1834 Edinburgh Post Office Annual Directory.

Metropolitan Cemetery Association.

National Records of Scotland, Edinburgh

Consolidated Schedules of Assessed Taxes: Volume 28 Tax Payers in the City of Glasgow, from 5 April 1798 – 5 April 1799.

Court of Session Unextracted Processes, 1st Arrangement, Innes-Durie Office 1669–1837 CS234

Court of Session Register of Acts and Decreets, 3rd Series, Dalrymple's Office, 2nd Division 1810–1821 CS33.

Court of Session: Unextracted Processes, 1st Arrangement, Inglis Office 1657–1863 CS233.

Court of Session: Bill Chamber Processes, Old Series 1670–1852 CS271.

High Court of Justiciary processes JC26/1809.

Religious Society of Friends (Quakers) records, Edinburgh.

The Russian State Historical Archive (RGIA), St Petersburg, Russia

> Office for institutions of Empress Maria Fedorovna Funds 758 & 759.
>
> Cases in the Alexander Manufactory

ScotlandsPeople

> Baptisms (NCR) Scotland
>
> Baptisms (OCR) Scotland.
>
> Baptisms (OPR) Scotland
>
> Bellshill Relief Church Scotland, North Lanarkshire (baptisms and burials)
>
> Burials (OPR) Scotland
>
> Census Records, 1841–1851 Scotland.
>
> Communion roll 1796–1826 Scotland. Antiburgher Associate Session, Howgate.
>
> Deaths (CR) Scotland.
>
> Free Church Minutes, Scotland
>
> Greyfriars baptismal register, Scotland, Glasgow, Shuttle Street.
>
> Kirk Session Minutes, Scotland.
>
> Marriages (OPR) Scotland
>
> Presbytery Minutes, Scotland
>
> Record Guides
>
> Testamentary records. Scotland.

University of Edinburgh Library, (https://stataccscot.edina.ac.uk)

> The Statistical Accounts of Scotland 1791–1845.
>
> The Old Statistical Account 1791–1799, Penicuik, Edinburghshire.
>
> The New Statistical Account, Penicuik, Edinburghshire

Newspapers

Belfast Newsletter (1828–1900).

Caledonian Mercury (1720–1867.)

Dundee, Perth, and Cupar Advertiser (1839–1864).

Edinburgh Advertiser (1772–1826).

Edinburgh Gazette, The (1699–present).

Edinburgh News and Literary Chronicle (1848–1863).

Gazette, The, Official Public Record (1665–present)

Glasgow Courier (1791–1866).

Hull Packet (1800–1886).

Perthshire Courier (1809–1916).

Scots Magazine, The (1739–1900).

Scotsman, The (1817–2002).

Texts

Adams, J. Q. and Adams, C. F. (1874) *Memoirs of John Quincy Adams: Comprising Portions of His Diary from 1795 to 1848.* Philadelphia: J.B. Lippincott & Co.

Age of Revolution. *Timeline.* http://www.ageofrevolution.org.

Ahonen, P. (2006) The Inevitability of Globalization and Its Costs: The Voikkaa Paper Mill Shutdown and Forest Industry Restructuring in the Newspapers Torkkeli, M. In: *Regional Revival: Perspectives on Industrial and Corporate Change.*, Research Report 178. Lappeenranta University of Technology. pp. 34–47.

Aikin, J., (ed) (1807) *The Atheneum: A Magazine of Literary and Miscellaneous Information (Published Monthly). January to June 1807.* Vol. 1. Longmans, Hurst, Rees, and Orme.

Aksenov, A.I. (2016) An Essay on the History of Genealogy in Russia. *Russian Studies in History* 55(1). pp. 26–52.

Alexander, D.; Bogdan, N. Q.; Grounsell, J.; Gallagher, D.; Haggerety, G.; Murdoch, K. R. and Thoms, J. (1999) A Late Medieval Hall-House at Uttershill Castle, Penicuik, Midlothian. *Proceedings of the Society of Antiquaries of Scotland* 128. pp. 1017–1046.

Alexander, J. M. (1972) John Paterson, Bible Society Pioneer, 1776–1855. The Earlier Years:1776–1813. *The Records of the Scottish Church History Society* XVII. pp. 131–53.

Alexander, J. M. (1974) John Paterson, Bible Society Pioneer; 1776–1855. The Later Years 1813–55. *The Records of the Scottish Church History Society* VIII. pp. 181–200.

Allen, B. M. (1998) *The Effects of Infectious Disease on Napoleon's Russian Campaign.* A Research Report Submitted to the Faculty in Partial Fulfillment of the Graduation Requirements. Maxwell Air Force Base, Alabama: Air Command and Staff College, Air University. Defense Technical Information Center.

Allen, R. E. S., and Wiles, J. L. (2013) How Older People Position Their Late-Life Childlessness: A Qualitative Study. *Journal of Marriage and Family* 75(1). pp. 206–220.

Allen, W. (1847) *Life of William Allen: With Selections from His Correspondence. in Two Volumes.* Vol. 1. Philadelphia: H. Longstreth.

Alvarez-Palau, E. J. and Dunn, O. (2019) Database of Historic Ports and Coastal Sailing Routes in England and Wales. *Data in Brief.*

Anderson, M. S. (1960) Some British Influences on Russian Intellectual Life and Society in the 18th Century. *The Slavonic and East European Review* 39(92). pp. 148–63.

Andreycheva, V. F. (2014) A Scottish Trace in the Territory of Nevsky District'. *New Toponymic Journal* 2 pp. 50–67.

Ankarloo, D. (2002) New Institutional Economics and Economic History. *Capital & Class* 26(3). pp. 9–36.

Annual Monitor (1868) William Tanner and Sarah Tanner. *Annual Monitor: Obituary of the Members of the Society of Friends in Great Britain and Ireland for the Year 1867,* 26: pp. 219–33.

Annual Register (1858) *The Annual Register or a View of the History and Politics of the Year 1857.* Chronicle: Conviction and Sentence for Will Forgery. London: F. & J. Rivington

Anon (1825) *The Scottish Tourist and Itinerary; or, a Guide to the Scenery and Antiquities of Scotland and the Western Islands; with a Description of the Principal Steam-Boat Tours.* Edinburgh: Stirling & Kenney.

Anon (1847) *The Topographical, Statistical, and Historical Gazetteer of Scotland*. Vol. 1. Edinburgh: A. Fullarton and Co.

Anon. (1870) Obituary. Engineer-General Alexander Wilson (Imperial Russian Service), 1776–1866. *Minutes of the Proceedings of the Institution of Civil Engineers* 30(1870). pp. 461–65.

Anon. (1931) History of the Firm Finlayson & Co., Aktiebolag, Tammerfors, Finland. *Transactions of the Newcomen Society* 12(1) pp. 108–109.

Argent, A. (2017) A Congregational Church in Revolutionary Petrograd. *The Congregational History Society Magazine* 8(4). pp. 57–64.

Aristotle and Heath, M. (1996). *Poetics*. London: Penguin Books.

Associate Congregation at Howgate. (1795) Call to Mr William McEwan, Preacher of the Gospel in Kilmarnock to Be Pastor. 1 December. Howgate Kirk.

Baines, E. (1835) *History of the Cotton Manufacture in Great Britain*. H. Fisher, R. Fisher, and P. Jackson.

Baptie, D. (2014) A Short History of the Secession Churches in Scotland. *Diane Baptie* (blog).

Barbour, H. (2004) Turford, Hugh (d. 1713), Religious Writer. In *Oxford Dictionary of National Biography Online*.

Barclay, K. and Simonton, D. (2013) *Women in Eighteenth-century Scotland: Intimate, Intellectual and Public Lives*. Farnham: Ashgate.

Barney, J. (2009) North Sea and Baltic Convoy 1793–1814: As Experienced by Merchant Masters Employed by Michael Henley & Son. *The Mariner's Mirror* 95(4). pp. 429–440.

Barry, J. and Brooks, C., (eds) (1994) *The Middling Sort of People: Culture, Society and Politics in England, 1550–1800*. Basingstoke: Macmillan.

Bartlett, R. (2023) Quakers in Russia – a Longer History: The Religious Society of Friends (Quakers) and Russia. *Friends House Moscow* (blog).

Baskerville, B. (1968) 19th Century Burlesque of Oratory. *American Quarterly* 20(4). pp. 726–743.

Bawden, C. R. (1980) The English Missionaries in Siberia and Their Translation of the Bible into Mongolian. *Mongolian Studies* 6. pp. 5–39.

Bebbington, D. W. (1989) *Evangelicalism in Modern Britain: A History from the 1730s to the 1980s*. London: Routledge.

Bebbington, D. W. (2004) Evangelical Theology in the English-Speaking World during the Nineteenth Century (Finlayson Memorial Lecture. *The Scottish Bulletin of Evangelical Theology* 22. pp. 133–150.

Beckert, S. (2015) *Empire of Cotton: A New History of Global Capitalism*. UK: Penguin Books.

Bell, G. J. (1810) *Commentaries on the Laws of Scotland, and on the Principles of Mercantile Jurisprudence, Considered in Relation to Bankruptcy; Competitions of Creditors; and Imprisonment for Debt* ... 2nd ed. Edinburgh: Archibald Constable & Company.

Bell, R. (1817) *A System of the Forms of Deeds Used in Scotland*. 3rd ed. Vol. 7. 19th-Century Legal Treatises.

Bell, T. M. (2016) A Brief History of Bloodletting. *The Journal of Lancaster General Hospital* 11(4). pp. 119–123.

Benninghaus, C. (2017) Silences: Coping with Infertility in Nineteenth-Century Germany. In: Gayle Davis and Tracey Loughran (eds) *The Palgrave Handbook of Infertility in History: Approaches, Contexts and Perspectives*. pp. 99–122.

Bensimon, F. (2019) Special Issue on British Labour and Migration to Europe during the Industrial Revolution Introduction to the Special Issue. *Continuity and Change* 34(1). pp. 1–13.

Bensimon, F. (2023) *Artisans Abroad: British Migrant Workers in Industrialising Europe, 1815–1870*. Oxford University Press.

Bernstein, L. (2002) Merchant "Correspondence" and Russian Letter-Writing Manuals: Petr Ivanovich Bogdanovich and His Pis'movnik for Merchants. *The Slavic and East European Journal* 46(4). pp. 659–682.

Bin-Jumah, M. N.; Nadeem, M. S.; Gilani, S. J.; Al-Abbasi, F. A.; Ullah, I.; Alzarea, S. I.; Ghoneim, M. M.; et al. (2022) Genes and Longevity of Lifespan. *International Journal of Molecular Sciences* 23(3).

Birrell, C. M. (1859) *The Life of the Rev. Richard Knill of St. Petersburg.* London: The Religious Tract Society.

Black, J. (2015) The Middling Sort of People in the Eighteenth-Century English-Speaking World. *Sociology XVII-XVIII*, no. 72. pp. 41–56.

Boldorf. M. (2015) The Ulster Linen Triangle: An Industrial Cluster Emerging from a Proto-Industrial Region. In: Thorade N. Czierpka J., Oerters K. (eds) *Regions, Industries, and Heritage. Palgrave Studies in the History of Social Movements.* London: Palgrave Macmillan.

Bottomley, Sean. (2014) Patenting in England, Scotland and Ireland during the Industrial Revolution, 1700–1852. *Explorations in Economic History* 54. pp. 48–63.

Bremner, D. (1869) *The Industries of Scotland: Their Rise, Progress and Current Condition.* Edinburgh: Adam and Charles Black.

Brown, R. (1886) *The History of Paisley, from the Roman Period down to 1884.* Vol. 2. J. & J. Cook.

Buck, C. (2023) Entry for "Seceders". In: *Charles Buck Theological Dictionary.*

Business Historical Society (1932) Textile Material Again. *Bulletin of the Business Historical Society* 6(3). pp. 6–12.

Burim, L. D. (2002) Engineer-General Alexander Wilson and His Activities in St. Petersburg and Kolpino. *History of St. Petersburg* 3(7). pp. 41–46.

Burnett, J. C. (1883) Obituary: Wielobycki, Dionysius, M.D. *The Homeopathic World* XVIII. pp. 25–26.

Burton, J. H. (1845) T*he Law of Bankruptcy, Insolvency, and Mercantile Sequestration, in Scotland.* W. Tait.

Burton, P. F. (2003) An Occupational Analysis of the Society of Friends in Nineteenth-Century Scotland. *Quaker Studies* 7(2). pp. 145–164.

Butler, A. (2020) *A Unique Type of Loneliness: Infertility in Nineteenth-Century America.* Master of Arts thesis, Arkansas Tech University.

Cabot, H. R. The Early Years of William Ropes & Company in St. Petersburg. *The American Neptune* 23(1). p. 131–39.

Cage, R. A. (1983) The Standard of Living Debate: Glasgow, 1800–1850. *The Journal of Economic History* 43(1). pp. 175–82.

Cameron, A.(2007) The Establishment of Civil Registration in Scotland. *The Historical Journal* 50(2). pp. 377–395.

Campbell, I. (1974) Carlyle and the Secession. *Records of the Scottish Church History Society* 18. pp. 48–64.

Canton, W. (1904) *A History of the British and Foreign Bible Society*. Vol. 1. John Murray.

Carlsson, B. (1984) The Development and Use of Machine Tools in Historical Perspective. *Journal of Economic Behavior & Organization* 5(1). pp. 91–114.

Carmichael, P. and Gauldie. E. (1969) *The Dundee Textile Industry, 1790–1885 from the Papers of Peter Carmichael of Arthurstone.* Fourth. Edinburgh.

Carnie, R. H. (1978) Working Class Readers in Eighteenth-Century Scotland: The Evidence from Subscription Lists. *The International Review of Scottish Studies* 8. pp. 77–94.

Chadkirk, J. W. C. (1994) *An Investigation into Quaker Famine Relief in the Samara Province of Russia 1916 – 1923.* Honours degree in History, University of North London.

Chambers, J. D. (1972) *Population, Economy and Society in Pre-Industrial England.* London: Oxford University Press.

Chambers, W. (1864) *A History of Peeblesshire.* Dalcassian Publishing Company.

Clark, D. L. (1979) The Reverend Andrew Lothian, 1763–1831, United Secession Minister. *Scottish Church History Society* 20(2). pp. 143–162.

Clark, G. (2005) The British Industrial Revolution, 1760–1860. In: Roderick Floud and Donald McCloskey, *World Economic History*, pp. 1–65.

Clark, J. (1830) *The Influence of Climate in the Prevention and Cure of Chronic Diseases, More Particularly of the Chest and Digestive Organs: Comprising an Account of the Principal Places Resorted to by Invalids in England, the South of Europe, &c.; a Comparative Estimate of Their Respective Merits in Particular Diseases; and*

General Directions for Invalids While Travelling and Residing Abroad. With an Appendix, Containing a Series of Tables on Climates. 2nd ed. London: J. Murray.

Clark, S. (1984) A Survey of Early Paisley Engineers'. *Scottish Industrial History* 6.2. pp. 2–30.

Clow, A. and Clow, N. L. (1945) Vitriol in the Industrial Revolution. *The Economic History Review* 15. pp. 44–55.

Cohen, M. (2003) The Dynamics of Capitalism in the Irish Linen Industry: A "Space-Time Structuration" Analysis. *Journal of Historical Sociology* 16. pp. 432–59.

Conway, S. (1995) Britain and the Impact of the American War, 1775–1783 *War in History* 2(2). pp. 127–50.

Conway, S. (2001) War and National Identity in the Mid-Eighteenth-Century British Isles'. *The English Historical Review* 116(468). pp. 863–893.

Cook, T. (2011) *Clio's Warriors: Canadian Historians and the Writing of the World Wars.* Vancouver: UBC Press.

Cooke, A. (2009) The Scottish Cotton Masters, 1780–1914. *Textile History.* 40(1). pp. 29–50.

Cooke, A. (2010) *The Rise and Fall of the Scottish Cotton Industry, 1778–1914: 'The Secret Spring'.* Manchester: Manchester University Press.

Cookson, G. (1994) *The West Yorkshire Textile Engineering Industry, 1780–1850.* PhD Thesis, University of York.

Cookson, G. (2018) *The Age of Machinery: Engineering the Industrial Revolution, 1750–1850.* Vol. 12. People, Markets, Goods: Economies and Societies in History. Woodbridge: The Boydell Press.

Corfield, P. J. (1989) Dress for Deference and Dissent: Hats and the Decline of Hat Honour. *Costume* 23(1). pp. 64–79.

Cowan, R. (1840) Vital Statistics of Glasgow, Illustrating the Sanatory Condition of the Population. *Journal of the Statistical Society of London* 3(3). pp. 257–292.

Crawford, J. C. (2014) The High State of Culture to Which This Part of the Country Has Attained': Libraries, Reading, and Society in Paisley, 1760–1830'. *Library & Information History* 30,(3) pp. 172–94.

Crawford, J. M., (ed). (1893) *The Industries of Russia: Manufactures and Trade with a General Industrial Map*. Vol. 1. St Petersburg, Russia: Trenke and Fusnot.

Crawford, K. (2013) *The Law and Economics of Orderly and Effective Insolvency*. PhD thesis, University of Nottingham.

Croix, D. de la,; Schneider, E. B. and Weisdorf, J. (2019) Childlessness, Celibacy and Net Fertility in Pre-Industrial England: The Middle-Class Evolutionary Advantage. *Journal of Economic Growth* 24(3) pp. 223–256.

Crosby, A. W. (1961) *America, Russia, Hemp, and Napoleon: A Study of Trade between the United States and Russia, 1783–1814*. PhD thesis, Boston University Graduate School.

Cross, A. G. (1972) Chaplains to the British Factory in St Petersburg, 1723–1813. *European Studies Review* 2(2). pp. 125–142.

Cross, A. G. (1997) *By the Banks of the Neva: Chapters from the Lives and Careers of the British in Eighteenth-Century Russia*. Cambridge and New York: Cambridge University Press.

Cross, A. G. (2014) *In the Lands of the Romanovs: An Annotated Bibliography of First-Hand English-Language Accounts of the Russian Empire (1613–1917)*. Cambridge, UK: Open Book Publishers.

Daniel, W. (1995) Entrepreneurship and the Russian Textile Industry: From Peter the Great to Catherine the Great. *The Russian Review* 54(1) pp. 1–25.

Delahaye, A.; Booth, C.; Clark, P.; Procter, S. and Rowlinson, M. (2009) The Genre of Corporate History. *Journal of Organizational Change Management* 22(1). pp. 27–48.

Denoon, B. (1991) James Finlayson of Penicuik 1772–1852: Industrial Founder of Finland's Second City. *Aberdeen University Review* 65, (Autumn).

Denoon, B. (1992) Mysterious Man of the Future. *Scottish Field*, February. pp. 46–47.

Denoon, B. (2004) Finlayson, James (1772?–1852?), Engineer and Cotton Manufacturer. Oxford Dictionary of National Biography.

Denoon, B. (2020) James Finlayson of Penicuik, Founder of Tampere, Finland. *University of Edinburgh Journal* 49(4). pp. 279–284.

Denzel, M. A. (2010) *Handbook of World Exchange Rates, 1590–1914*. Ashgate Publishing,

Devine, T. M. (1976) The Colonial Trades and Industrial Investment in Scotland, c. 1700–1815. *The Economic History Review* 29(1). pp. 1–13.

Devine, T. M. (1988) Urbanisation. In: T. M. Devine and R. Mitchison (eds) *People and Society in Scotland, 1760–1830*. pp. 27–52.

Devine, T. M. (2005) The Modern Economy: Scotland and the Act of Union. In: *The Transformation of Scotland: The Economy since 1700*. Edinburgh: Edinburgh University Press. pp. 13–33.

Devine, T. M. (2008) *Scotland and the Union 1707–2007*. Edinburgh University Press.

Dixon, M. (1986) The Common Laws of Organizational Stupidity: How Organizations Lose Touch with Reality. *Jobs Column, Financial Times*. 3 April; 4 September; and 10 December.

DRBs Scottish Women's History Group. (2014) *Women on the Platform: DRB Scottish Women's History Group.*

Dribe, M.; Olsson, M. and Svensson, P. (2015) *Famines in the Nordic Countries, AD 536 – 1875*. Lund Papers in Economic History. General Issues, No. 138.

Dukes, P. (1987) *The Caledonian Phalanx: Scots in Russia*. Edinburgh: National Library of Scotland.

Durie, A. (1975) Textile Bleaching: A Note on the Scottish Experience. *The Business History Review* 49(3) pp. 337–345.

Economakis, E. G. (1998) *From Peasant to Petersburger*. Basingstoke: Macmillan Press.

Egorova, K. and Zubacheva, K. (2020) The Ruble's Journey through Time, from the Middle Ages to the Present Day *Russia Beyond: Business*, 14 May.

Eichthal, G. d'. (1977) *A French Sociologist Looks at Britain: Gustave d'Eichthal and British Society in 1828*. In: Barrie M. Ratcliffe and William Henry Chaloner (eds). Manchester: Manchester University Press.

Eilittä, L. (2017) British Travellers Visiting Finland: From "Enlightened" Expectations to "Romantic" Fulfilment. In: Cian Duffy (ed) *Romantic Norths: Anglo-Nordic Exchanges, 1770–1842*, Cham, Switzerland: Springer International Publishing. pp. 53–73.

Ellison, H. J. (1965) Economic Modernization in Imperial Russia: Purposes and Achievements. *The Journal of Economic History* 25(4). pp. 523–540.

Evangelical Magazine and Missionary Chronicle (1839) Laying of the Foundation Stone of the British and American Chapel, St Petersburg. *Evangelical Magazine and Missionary Chronicle* 17. pp. 446–47.

Evans, E. J. (1994) *The Great Reform Act of 1832*. 2nd ed. London: Routledge.

Fagerstrom, D. I. (1954) Scottish Opinion and the American Revolution. *The William and Mary Quarterly* 11(2). pp. 252–275.

Fairholm, M. (2013) *Mothers, Wives, Housekeepers and More? Maria Feodorovna and Women's Education in Russia, 1796–1828*. PhD Thesis, University of Alberta.

Fedosov, D. (2000) Scotland and Russia: A Boundless Bond. In *Russia and the Wider World in Historical Perspective*. London: Palgrave Macmillan, 2000.

Fedosov, D. (n.d.) *The Caledonian Connection: Scotland-Russia Ties: Middle Ages to Early Twentieth Century a Concise Biographical List*. www.scalan.co.uk/scotsinrussia.htm.

Fewster, F. A. (1970) *Finlayson 1820–1970*. Tampere, Finland: Oy Finlayson Ab.

Finden, W. and Bartlett, W. H. (1840) *The Ports, Harbours, Watering-Places and Picturesque Scenery of Great Britain*. Vol. 1. London: Virtue & Co.

Findlay, A. M. (2022) *The Wilkies of Knowehead*. Uddingston: Rectory Press.

Finlay, R. J. (1999) Keeping the Covenant: Scottish National Identity. In: T. M. Devine and J. R. Young (eds) *Eighteenth-Century Scotland: New Perspectives*, East Linton: Tuckwell Press. pp. 121–133.

Fitton, R. S. (1989) *The Arkwrights: Spinners of Fortune*. Manchester: Manchester University Press.

Fitzpatrick, S. (2015) Impact of the Opening of Soviet Archives on Western Scholarship on Soviet Social History. *The Russian Review* 74(3). pp. 377–400.

Flint, M. (2020) Cash Flow Management & Small Business Financial Strategy. *Financial Strategy, Preferred CFO* (blog), 8 June 2020.

Floud, R. (1976) *The British Machine Tool Industry, 1850–1914.* Cambridge: Cambridge University Press.

Foreman, C. (2007) *Glasgow Street Names.* 2nd ed. Edinburgh: Birlinn.

Forssell, P. (2014) *Augusta Lundahl.* Biografiskt Lexikon för Finland.

Foyster, E. and Whatley, C. A. (eds) (2010) *A History of Everyday Life in Scotland, 1600 to 1800.* Edinburgh University Press.

Frankland, C. C. (1832) *Narrative of a Visit: To the Courts of Russia and Sweden, in the Years 1830 and 1831.* Vol. 2. Henry Colburn and Richard Bentley.

Freytag, G. (1895) *Technique of the Drama: An Exposition of Dramatic Composition and Art.* S. Griggs.

Frigren, P.; Hemminki, T. and Nummela, I. (2017) Experiencing and Encountering Impoverishment in Nineteenth-Century Finland. *Journal of Finnish Studies* 20(1) pp. 5–37.

Garfield, E. (n.d.) Drycleaning. Part 1. The Process and Its History: From Starch to Finish. *Essays of an Information Scientist* 8(22). pp. 213–222.

Garmon, F. (2014) Economic Independence and the Encouragement of Manufactures: Technology Transfer in the Textile Industry, 1783–96. *Melbourne Historical Journal,* 42(1). pp. 107–146.

Gifford, J.; McWilliam, C.; Walker, D. and Wilson, C. (2003) *The Buildings of Scotland: Edinburgh.* Pevsner Architectural Guides: Buildings of Scotland. London: Yale University Press.

Gilbert, J. (2005) Failing and Flying. In: *Refusing Heaven: Poems by Jack Gilbert.* New York: Alfred A. Knopf

Ginsburg, M. (1972) The Tailoring and Dressmaking Trades, 1700–1850'. *Costume* 6(1). pp. 64–71.

Glover, G. (2018) *The Two Battles of Copenhagen, 1801 and 1807: Britain and Denmark in the Napoleonic Wars.* Casemate Publishers.

Glover, K. (2007) *Elite Women and the Change of Manners in Mid-Eighteenth-Century Scotland.* The University of Edinburgh.

Gompert, D. C., Hans Binnendijk, and Bonny Lin. (2014) Napoleon's Invasion of Russia, 1812. In: *Blinders, Blunders, and Wars: What America and China Can Learn* Santa Monica, CA: Rand Corporation. pp. 41–52.

Goodman, J. (2000) Languages of Female Colonial Authority: The Educational Network of the Ladies Committee of the British and Foreign School Society, 1813–1837. *Compare: A Journal of Comparative and International Education,* 30(1). pp. 7–19.

Goodwin, G. (n.d.) William Dunn (1770–1849). In: *Dictionary of National Biography 1885–1900.*

Gorshkov, B. B. (2000) Serfs on the Move: Peasant Seasonal Migration in Pre-Reform Russia, 1800–61. *Kritika: Explorations in Russian and Eurasian History* 1(4). pp. 627–656.

Gorshkov, B. B. (2009) *Russia's Factory Children: State, Society, and Law, 1800–1917.* Google Books. Pittsburgh, PA: University of Pittsburgh Press.

Gowland, R. L.; Caffell, A. C.; Quade, L.; Levene, A.; Millard, A. R.; Holst, M.; Yapp, P. et al. (2023) The Expendables: Bioarchaeological Evidence for Pauper Apprentices in 19th Century England and the Health Consequences of Child Labour. Edited by Siân E. Halcrow. *PLOS ONE* 18(5).

Graham, P. L. (1963) *Speech to the Newsweek Foreign Correspondents.* London.

Grainger, J. D. (2014) *The British Navy in the Baltic. Vol. 49.* Woodbridge: Boydell & Brewer Ltd.

Granville, A. B. (1829) *St. Petersburgh, A Journal of Travels to and from That Capital; through Flanders, the Rhenich Provinces, Prussia, Russia, Poland, Silesia, Saxony, the Federated States of Germany, and France.* Vol. 2. London: Henry Colburn.

Griffiths, T.; Hunt, P. and O'Brien, P. (2008) Scottish, Irish, and Imperial Connections: Parliament, the Three Kingdoms, and the Mechanization of Cotton Spinning in Eighteenth-Century Britain. *The Economic History Review* 61(3). pp. 625–650.

Grimsted, P. K. (1997) Increasing Reference Access to Post-1991 Russian Archives. *Slavic Review* 56(4). pp. 718–759.

Gripenberg, L. (1929) James Finlayson. In: *Teoksessa Tampere. Tutkimuksia Ja Kuvauksia I. (Tampere: Studies and Descriptions I.).* Tampere [Finland]: Tampereen Historiallinen Seura (Tampere Historical Society). pp. 173–90.

Guest, R. (1823) *A Compendious History of the Cotton-Manufacture: With a Disproval of the Claim of Sir Richard Arkwright to the Invention of Its Ingenious machinery.* Printed by J. Pratt, and Sold by E. Thomson [and 3 Others] Manchester, [Greater Manchester].

Gulvin, C. (1984) *The Scottish Hosiery and Knitwear Industry: 1680–1980.* Edinburgh: John Donald Publishers Ltd.

Haapala, P. (1986) Tehtaan valossa: Teollistuminen ja työväestön muodostuminen Tampereella 1820-1920 (In the light of the factory: industrialization and the formation of the working population in Tampere 1820-1920) (Historiallisia tutkimuksia). Tampere, Finland: Osuuskunta Vastapaino.

Haapala, P. (2005) History of Tampere: The Very Long Road to Informational City' In: Antti Kasvio and Ari-Veikko Anttiroiko, (eds) *E-City: Analysing Efforts to Generate Local Dynamism in the City of Tampere.* Tampere: Tampere University Press. pp. 163–181.

Haapala, P. (2011) Tampere: A History of Industrial Society. In: Miia Hinnerichsen (ed) *Reusing the Industrial Past by the Tammerkoski Rapids: Discussions on the Value of Industrial Heritage,* Tampere [Finland]: City of Tampere, Museum Services, Pirkanmaa Provincial Museum. pp. 9–19.

Hakala, E. (2015) James Finlayson. *Avainsijoitus* (blog), 31 October.

Halkerston, P. (1819) *A Compendium or General Abridgement, of the Faculty Collection of Decisions of the Lords of Council and Session, from February 4, 1752 to the Session of 1817.* Google Books.

Hall, D. J. (1969) Membership Statistics of the Society of Friends, 1800–1850. *The Journal of the Friends' Historical Society* 52(2). pp. 97–100.

Hammermen of Glasgow. (n.d.) *Early History.* http:www.hammermenofglasgow.org.

Hansen, M.; Smith, D. J. and Carruthers, G. (2018) Mood Disorder in the Personal Correspondence of Robert Burns: Testing a Novel Interdisciplinary Approach. *Journal of the Royal College of Physicians of Edinburgh* 48(2). pp. 165–74.

Hartley, J. M. (1995) "It is the Festival of the Crown and Sceptres": The Diplomatic, Commercial and Domestic Significance of the Visit of Alexander I to England in 1814. *The Slavonic and East European Review* 73 (2). pp. 246–68.

Hartog, F. (2015) *Regimes of Historicity: Presentism and Experiences of Time*. Columbia University Press.

Heckscher, E. F. (1922) *The Continental System: An Economic Interpretation*. Clarendon Press.

Henderson, T. S. (1859) *Memoir of the Rev. E. Henderson Including His Labours in Denmark, Iceland, Russia, Etc., Etc.* London: Knight & Son.

Henderson, W. O. (1968) *Industrial Britain under the Regency: The Diaries of Escher, Bodmer, May and de Gallois*. London: Cass.

Hietala, M. and Kaarninen, M. '(2005) The Foundation of an Information City: Education and Culture in the Development of Tampere. In: Antti Kasvio and Ari-Veikko Anttiroiko (eds) *E-City : Analysing Efforts to Generate Local Dynamism in the City of Tampere*. Tampere, Finland: Tampere University Press. pp. 183–215.

Hine, W. C. (1975) American Slavery and Russian Serfdom: A Preliminary Comparison'. *Phylon* 36(4). pp. 378–384.

Hinnerichsen, M., (ed.) (2011) *Reusing the Industrial Past by the Tammerkoski Rapids: Discussions on the Value of Industrial Heritage*. Tampere [Finland]: City of Tampere, Museum Services, Pirkanmaa Provincial Museum.

Hirvonen, Y. (1943) 'Herätysajan Henkilöitä Tampereella (Revivalists, Tampere)'. *Tammerkoski-Lehdessä (Tampere Magazine)* 1. pp. 12–15.

Hirvonen, Y. (1943) Herätysajan Henkilöitä Tampereella (People of the Waking Hours). *Tammerkoski-Lehdessä (Tampere Magazine)* 2. pp. 42–43.

History of the Restoration Movement. (n.d.) Chronology on the Lives of Robert Haldane (1764–1842) And His Brother, James Alexander Haldane (1768–1851). http:// www.therestoration movement. com.

Hobsbawm, E. (1962) *Age of Revolution: 1789–1848* [Kindle] London: Phoenix Press.

Hodgetts, E. A. B. (1908) *The Court of Russia in the Nineteenth Century*. Vol. 1. London: Methuen.

Hodgetts, E. A. B. (1920) A Retrospect of the Personal Influence of Britons in Russia. *Journal of the Royal Society of Arts* 69: pp. 85–97.

Hoffman, L. W. (1975) The Value of Children to Parents and the Decrease in Family Size. *Proceedings of the American Philosophical Society* 119(6). pp. 430–438.

Holden, C. (1991) Information about Britons in Russia, from Church Archives in London. *Russian History* 18(1–4). pp. 65–75.

Holden, R. N. (2022) Cotton Mule Spinning after Richard Roberts. *The International Journal for the History of Engineering & Technology* 92(2). pp. 130–66.

Holmes, A. R. (2006) *The Shaping of Ulster Presbyterian Belief and Practice, 1770–1840*. Oxford: Oxford University Press.

Honeyman, Valerie. (2012) *"That Ye May Judge for Yourselves": The Contribution of Scottish Presbyterianism towards the Emergence of Political Awareness amongst Ordinary People in Scotland between 1746 and 1792*. PhD thesis, University of Stirling.

Hopkirk, J. (1816) *Account of the Forth and Clyde Canal Navigation, from Its Origin, to the Present Time*. Glasgow: John Smith and Son; Archibald Constable & Edinburgh; and Longman, Hurst, Rees, Orme, and Brown, London.

Horner, L (Factory Inspector) (1834). First Report to the Right Honourable Viscount Duncannon, H. M. Principal Secretary of State for the Home Department. In: *Factories Inspectors, Reports of Inspectors of Factories to the Secretary of State: Presented According to the Provisions of the Act of Parliament ; Ordered to Be Printed 11. Aug. 1834*. London, 1834. pp. 6–7.

Houston, R. A. (1982) The Literacy Myth? Illiteracy in Scotland 1630–1760. *Past and Present* 96(1). pp. 81–102.

Houston, R. A. (1988) The Demographic Regime. In: Devine, T. M. and Mitchison, R. (eds) *People and Society in Scotland*, Vol 1. A Social History of Modern Scotland. Edinburgh: John Donald. pp. 9–26.

Houston, R. A. (1998) Therapies for Mental Ailments in Eighteenth-Century Scotland. *Journal of the Royal College of Physicians of Edinburgh* 28(4). pp. 555–568.

Huhtala, L. (2012) The Bittersweet Pleasure of Self-Sacrifice [Online]. *The History of Nordic Women's Literature*. https://nordicwomensliterature.net.

Humphries, J. and Schneider, B. (2019) Spinning the Industrial Revolution. *The Economic History Review* 72(1). pp. 126–155.

Hynynen, A. (2006) Hard Networks of Regional Development. The Evolution of Technological Infrastructures and Urban Morphology in the Tampere Region. *Studia Regionalia* 18. pp. 269–276.

Innilä, K. (2008) *Augusta Lundahls Brev till Fredrika Runeberg 1829–1839*. Masters thesis, Tampere University.

Isle of Wight Hospitals (n.d) *The Royal National Hospital for Chest Diseases: A Victorian Hospital*. iowhospitals.org.uk/.

James, J. G. (2013) The Russian Iron Industry (Excluding Bridges) up to about 1850. *The International Journal for the History of Engineering & Technology* 83(1). pp. 22–61.

Jeremy, D. J. (1977) Damming the Flood: British Government Efforts to Check the Outflow of Technicians and Machinery, 1780–1843. *Business History Review* 51(1). pp. 1–34.

Jones, B. A. (2006) The American Revolution, Glasgow, and the Making of the Second City of the Empire. In: Simon P. Newman (ed) *Europe's American Revolution*, London: Palgrave Macmillan. pp. 1–25.

Jones, G. M. (1827) *Travels in Norway, Sweden, Finland, Russia, and Turkey [Electronic Resource] : Also on the Coasts of the Sea of Azof and of the Black Sea : With a Review of the Trade in Those Seas, and of the Systems Adopted to Man the Fleets of the Different Powers of Europe, Compared with That of England.* Vol. 1. London: John Murray.

Jones, P. M. (2011) Becoming an Engineer in Industrialising Great Britain *circa* 1760–1820. *Engineering Studies* 3(3). pp. 215–232.

Juhász, R. (2014) *Temporary Protection and Technology Adoption: Evidence from the Napoleonic Blockade.* CEP Discussion Paper No 1322 presented at the CEP/LSE International Economics Seminars.

Juuti, P. S. Mäki, H. R and. Rajala, R. P. (2011) Private Initiatives in Finland and South Africa: Proposals for Waterworks by von Nottbeck and Marks. *Water History* 3(1). pp. 29–43.

Kaarninen, M. (2019) Margaret Finlayson. In: P. Haapala, J. Peltola (eds) *Global Tampere: An Economic History of the City from the 18th Century to the Present.* Tampere [Finland]: Vapriikki Tampere Museums. pp. 30–31

Kaarninen, M. (2022) The Trials of Sarah Wheeler (1807–1867): Experiencing Submission. In: Katajala-Peltomaa, S., Toivo, R.M. (eds) Palgrave Macmillan, *Histories of Experience in the World of Lived Religion.* Palgrave Macmillan. pp. 195–217.

Karttunen, M-L. (2005) *The Making of Communal Worlds: English Merchants in Imperial St. Petersburg.* Doctoral Thesis, University of Helsinki.

Karttunen, M-L. (2006) The British Factory in Imperial St. Petersburg: English Civil Society in a Russian Context: A Discourse-Centred Perspective. *Suomen Antropologi* 30(3).

Kennedy, J. (2018) *Antiburghers to the End: Kilwinning Original Secession Church 1738–1956 and Baptismal Register 1772–1827.* Online. Kilwinning Heritage.

Kennedy, T. C. (2017) Quakers. In: Timothy Larsen and Michael Ledger-Lomas (eds) *The Oxford History of Protestant Dissenting Traditions, Volume III: The Nineteenth Century.* Oxford University Press. pp. 79-98.

Kinealy, C. and Moran, G. (eds) (2020). *Irish Famines before and after the Great Hunger.* Quinnipiac University Press.

Kiple, K. F. (1999) *Plague, Pox & Pestilence: Disease in History.* London: Phoenix Illustrated.

Knight, R. (2022) *Convoys: The British Struggle against Napoleonic Europe and America*. Yale University Press.

Knight, R. (2022) Safe Passage: Protecting Merchant Ships during the Napoleonic Wars. *History Today* 72(9). https://www.historytoday.com.

Knox, W. W. J. (2006) *Lives of Scottish Women: Women and Scottish Society, 1800–1980*. Edinburgh: Edinburgh University Press.

Kortekangas, P. (1969) The Church of Finland in a Changing Society. *Review of Religious Research* 10(2). pp. 88–99.

Koskinen, K. (2014) Tampere as a Translation Space. *Tranlation Studies* 7(2). pp. 186–202.

Kostiainen, J., and Sotarauta, M. (2002) *Finnish City Reinvented: Tampere's Path from Industrial to Knowledge Economy*. MIT IPC Local Innovation Systems Working Paper; No. 02-007.

Kostiainen, J., and Sotarauta, M. (2003) Great Leap or Long March to Knowledge Economy: Institutions, Actors and Resources in the Development of Tampere, Finland. *European Planning Studies* 11(4). pp. 415–38.

Kowalski, K.; Matera, . and Sokołowicz, M. E. (2020) The Role of Immigrants in the "Take-Offs" of Eastern European "Manchesters", Comparative Case Studies of Three Cities: Lodz, Tampere and Ivanovo. *Journal of Migration History* 6(3). pp. 269–299.

Kowalski, K.; Matera, R. and Sokołowicz, M. E. (2018) Cotton Matters. A Recognition and Comparison of the Cottonopolises in Central-Eastern Europe during the Industrial Revolution. *Fibres and Textiles in Eastern Europe* 26(6). pp. 16–23.

Krummel, D. and Siegfried, P. (2021) Child Labour Ethics through the Prism of Utilitarianism and Deontology. *Open Access Library Journal (OALJ)* 8(2). pp. 1–14.

Laqueur, W. Z. (1973) Rewriting History'. *Commentary* 55(3). pp. 53–63.

Lavanga, M. (2009) Culture and Cities: Urban Regeneration and Sustainable Urban Redevelopment. In: S. Ada (ed) *Cultural Policy and Management Yearbook*. pp. 63–75. Boekmanstudies [etc.].

Lawlor, H. C. The Genesis of the Linen Thread Trade. *Ulster Journal of Archaeology* 6. pp. 22–34.

Lefebvre, G. (1969) *Napoleon: From Brumaire to Tilsit: 1799–1807*. Vol. 1. London: Routledge & Paul.

Leveen, L. (2021) Best Guess or Worst Doubt: What the Role of Conjecture in Writing Biography and History. *H-CivWar Authors' Blog*. 17 August. https://networks.h-net.org/node/4113/blog/h-civwar-authors-blog/8089270/best-guess-or-worst-doubt-whats-role-conjecture.

Lindenmeyr, A. (1993) Public Life, Private Virtues: Women in Russian Charity, 1762–1914. *Signs* 18(3). pp. 562–591.

Lindfors, G. V. (1938) *Finlayson-Fabrikerna I Tammerfors Del 1: 1820 – 1907*. Helsingfors: Tilgmann.

Lloyd, A. J. (2007) *Emigration, Immigration and Migration in Nineteenth-Century Britain*. Contextual Essays from Gale Primary Sources: British Library Newspapers. Detroit: Gale, 2007.

Lobell, J. A. (2002) Digging Napoleon's Dead. *Archaeology* 55(5). pp. 40–43.

London Yearly Meeting (society of Friends) (1834) *Rules of Discipline of the Religious Society of Friends, with Advices: Being Extracts from the Minutes and Epistles of Their Yearly Meeting, Held in London, from Its First Institution*. Third. London: Darton and Harvey.

Longuinoff, Y. (2011) From Hull to Moscow. *The Sherwood Forest* 7(2). pp. 8–14.

Longuinoff, Y. (2017) Paleog Sherwood_family. http://www.sherwood-family.livejournal.com/26280.html.

Lumsden, C. C. (2012) *Class, Gender and Christianity in Edinburgh 1850–1905: A Study in Denominationalism*. PhD thesis, University of Edinburgh.

Lumsden, H., and Aitken, P. H. (1912). *History of the Hammermen of Glasgow: A Study Typical of Scottish Craft Life and Organisation*. Paisley: Alexander Gardner.

Määttanen, M. (2020) Finlaysonin Kukoistus Alkoi Salaperäisen Johtajan Komennossa – Lapsityövoima Ja Orjien Tuottamat Raaka-Aineet Olivat Tavallisia. (Finlayson's Heyday Began under the Command of a Mysterious Leader – Child Labor and Raw Materials Produced by Slaves Were Commonplace). *Kauppalehti*, 12 January. https://www.kauppalehti.fi/.

MacDougall, I. (1989) *The Prisoners at Penicuik*. Dalkeith: Midlothian District Council.

MacDougall, I. (2008) *All Men are Brethren: French, Scandinavian, Italian, German, Dutch, Belgian, Spanish, Polish, West Indian, American, and Other Prisoners of War in Scotland, 1803–1814*. Edinburgh: John Donald.

MacGillivray, N. (2003) *Food, Poverty and Epidemic Disease, Edinburgh: 1840–1850*. PhD Thesis, University of Edinburgh.

Mackelvie, W.; Young, D. and Blair, W. (1873) *Annals and Statistics of the United Presbyterian Church*. Edinburgh: Oliphant and A. Elliot.

Maclean, K. (2017) Finland, Finlayson and Finno-Scottish Links. *Royal Scottish Geographical Society Media Blog,* 5 December. http://www.rsgs.org/blog/.

MacLeod, J. (1944) Theology in the Early Days of the Secession. *Records of the Scottish Church History Society* 8. pp. 1–15.

Macmillan, D. S. (1975) Russo-British Trade Relations under Alexander I. *Canadian-American Slavic Studies* 9(4). pp. 437–448.

Maghenzani, S., and Villani, S. (eds.) (2021) *British Protestant Missions and the Conversion of Europe, 1600–1900*. Routledge, Taylor & Francis Group.

Marsden, R. (1884) *Cotton Spinning: Its Development, Principles, and Practice*. London: G. Bell.

Marwick, W. H. (1954) Friends in Nineteenth Century Scotland. *The Journal of the Friends Historical Society* 46(1). pp. 3–18.

Marwick, W. H. (1958) Some Quaker Firms of the Nineteenth Century I. *The Journal of the Friends Historical Society* 48(6). pp. 239–259.

Marwick, W. H. (1962) Some Quaker Firms of the Nineteenth Century II'. *The Journal of the Friends Historical Society* 50(1). pp. 239–259.

Marwick, W. H. (1969) Quakers in Victorian Scotland'. *The Journal of the Friends' Historical Society* 52(2). pp. 67–77.

Mason, B.; Brown, E. S. and Croarkin, P. E. (2016) Historical Underpinnings of Bipolar Disorder Diagnostic Criteria. *Behavioral Sciences* 6(3). pp. 1–19.

Massey, M. (1979) *The People Puzzle: Understanding Yourself and Others*. Reston Publishing Company.

Mathes, W. L. (1955) *The Influence of Napoleon's Continental System on Russian Economy, 1807–1811*. PhD Dissertation, The Ohio State University.

Mathieson, W. L. (1910) *The Awakening of Scotland: A History from 1747 to 1797*. J. Maclehose and Sons.

Maver, I. (2011) *18th Century Glasgow*. BBC History.

Maw, P.; Solar, P.; Kane, A. and Lyons., J. S. (2022) After the Great Inventions: Technological Change in UK Cotton Spinning, 1780-1835. *The Economic History Review* 75(1). pp. 22–55.

McCaffray, S. P. (2000) What Should Russia Be? Patriotism and Political Economy in the Thought of N. S. Mordvinov. *Slavic Review* 59(3). pp. 572–96.

McDowall, J. K. (1899) *The People's History of Glasgow: An Encyclopedic Record of the City from the Prehistoric Period to the Present Day*. 2nd ed. Glasgow: H. Nisbet.

McFarlane, E. A. (2015) *French Travellers to Scotland, 1780–1830: An Analysis of Some Travel Journals*. PhD Thesis, University of Stirling.

McKenzie Skene, D. W. (2015) Plus Ça Change, plus c'est La Même Chose? The Reform of Bankruptcy Law in Scotland. *Nottingham Insolvency and Business Law E-Journal* 3 NIBLeJ 15. pp. 285–300.

McKerrow, J. (1839) *History of the Secession Church*. Edinburgh: William Oliphant and Son.

McLaren, D. J. (2015) *David Dale: A Life*. Catrine: Stenlake Publishing.

McMillin, A. B. (1973) Quakers in Early Nineteenth-Century Russia. *The Slavonic and East European Review* 51. pp. 567–79.

Mead, W. R. (1963) 'The Adoption of Other Lands Experiences in a Finnish Context. *Geography* 48(3). pp. 241–54.

Mead, W. R. (1969) Britain in Scandinavia. *Geography* 54(3). pp. 271–83.

MeasuringWorth (2024) *Five ways to Compute the Relative Value of a UK Pound Amount 1270 to Present*. http://measuringworth.com.

Meisenzahl, R. R., and Mokyr, R. (2012) The Rate and Direction of Invention in the British Industrial Revolution Incentives and Institutions. In: Josh Lerner and Scott Stern (eds) *The Rate and Direction of Inventive Activity Revisited*, University of Chicago Press. pp. 443–479.

Metcalfe, W. M. (1909) *A History of Paisley 600–1908*. Paisley: Alexander Gardner.

Miller, W. F. (1913) Reminiscences of Some Old Edinburgh Friends. *The Journal of the Friends' Historical Society* 10(1). pp. 1–11.

Miller, W. F. (1913) Reminiscences of Some Old Edinburgh Friends. *The Journal of the Friends' Historical Society* 10(2). pp. 45–50.

Mitchell, G. M. (1925) The English and Scottish Cotton Industries: A Study in Interrelations. *The Scottish Historical Review* 22(86). pp. 101–114.

Mokyr, J. (2021) "The Holy Land of Industrialism": Rethinking the Industrial Revolution. *Journal of the British Academy* 9. pp. 223–247.

Mokyr, J.; Sarid, and Beek, K. van der. (2019) *The Wheels of Change: Human Capital, Millwrights, and Industrialization in Eighteenth-Century England*.

Morris, N. (2010) Timeline adapted by Concordia International School Shanghai from Industrial Revolution in Great Britain. http://www.library.concordiashanghai.org/.

Morton, V. (1991) *Quaker Politics and Industrial Change c.1800–1850: Jane Smeal Letter to Elizabeth Pease December 1836*. PhD Thesis, Open University.

Murray, D. B. (1977) *The Social and Religious Origins of Scottish Non-Presbyterian Protestant Dissent from 1730–1800*. PhD thesis, University of St Andrews.

Murray Thompson, (2015) P. *Matthew Murray 1765–1826 and the Firm of Fenton Murray and Co 1795–1844*. Paul Murray Thompson.

Musson, A. E. (1976) Industrial Motive Power in the United Kingdom, 1800–70. *The Economic History Review* 29(3). pp. 415–439.

Musson, A. E. and Robinson, E. (1959) The Early Growth of Steam Power. *The Economic History Review* 11(3). pp. 418–439.

Nantes, R. *English Bankrupts 1732–1831: A Social Account.* PhD thesis, University of Exeter, 2020.

Napier, D. D. (1912) *David Napier, Engineer, 1790–1869: [And] an Autobiographical Sketch, with Notes.* Glasgow: J. Maclehose.

Nenadic, S. S. (1986) *The Structures, Values and Influence of the Scottish Urban Middle Class, Glasgow 1800 to 1870.* PhD thesis, University of Glasgow.

Nenadic, S. (1994) Middle-Rank Consumers and Domestic Culture in Edinburgh and Glasgow 1720–1840. *Past and Present* 145(1). pp. 122–56.

Newington Necropolis. [A Brochure.]. Edinburgh, Print. Edinburgh, 1844.

Nisbet, S. M. (2003) *The Rise of the Cotton Factory in Eighteenth Century Renfrewshire.* PhD Thesis, University of Paisley.

Nisbet, S M. (2004) Early Cotton Spinning in the West of Scotland (1778–1799): Rothesay Cotton Mill. *Transactions of the Buteshire Natural History Society* 26. pp. 39–47.

Nisbet, S. M. (2009). The Development of the Cotton Industry in Paisley. *Renfrewshire Local History Forum (RLHF) Journal* 15.

Nisbet, S. M. (2009) The Making of Scotland's First Industrial Region: The Early Cotton Industry in Renfrewshire' *Journal of Scottish Historical Studies* 29(1). pp. 1–28.

Nisbet, S. M. and Foster, J. (2008) Protection, Inward Investment and the Early Irish Cotton Industry: The Experience of William and John Orr. *Irish Economic and Social History* 35(1). pp. 23–50.

Nykänen, P. (2000) Finlayson, James and Margaret: Founders of the Finlayson Cotton Spinning Mill. *Kansallisbiografia Online.* pp. 786–787.

Ó Grád, C. (2016) Did Science Cause the Industrial Revolution? *Journal of Economic Literature.* 54(1). pp. 224–239.

O'Brien, P. K. (1989) The Impact of the Revolutionary and Napoleonic Wars, 1793–1815, on the Long-Run Growth of the British Economy'. *Review (Fernand Braudel Center)* 12(3). pp. 335–95.

O'Brien, P. K. (2016) The Triumph and Denouement of the British Fiscal State: Taxation for the Wars against Revolutionary and Napoleonic France, 1793–1815. In: *The Fiscal-Military State in Eighteenth-Century Europe*. Routledge. pp. 167–200.

Oevermann, H.; Walczak, B. M. and Watson, M. (2022) *The Heritage of the Textile Industry: Thematic Study for TICCIH – The International Committee for the Conservation of the Industrial Heritage*. Lodz University of Technology Press.

Oren-Magidor, D. (2017) *Infertility in Early Modern England*. Palgrave Macmillan UK.

Owen, R. (1857) *The Life of Robert Owen Written by Himself: With Selections from His Writings and Correspondence*. Vol. 1. London: Effingham Wilson.

Pagan, J, ed. (1851) *Glasgow, Past and Present: Illustrated in Dean of Guild Court Reports, and in the Reminiscences and Communications of Senex, Aliquis, J. B., &c*. Glasgow: James Macnab.

Paisley Hammermen Society (n.d.) *History of Paisley*. http://paisley-hammermen.org.

Paloheimo, M. (2012) *Business Life in Pursuit of Economic and Political Advantages in Early-Nineteenth-Century Finland*. PhD Thesis, University of Jyväskylä.

Paterson, J. (1823) *A Letter to the Rev. H. H. Norris, A. M. Perpetual Curate of St John's Chapel, Hackney, &c. Containing Animadversions on His 'Respectful Letter to the Earl of Liverpool,' on the Subject of the Bible Society*. London: T. Hamilton.

Paterson, J. and Alexander, W. L. (Ed.) (1857) *The Book for Every Land: Reminiscences of Labour and Adventure in the Work of Bible Circulation in the North of Europe and in Russia*. London: John Snow.

Paton, C. (2016) *Discover Scottish Church Records*. 2nd ed. Ridgehaven Australia: Unlock the Past.

Paton, H. M. (1959) Some Secession Pamphlets. *Scottish Church History Society*.

Paul, K. T. (2013) Credit, Reputation, and Masculinity in British Urban Commerce: Edinburgh, c. 1710–70. *The Economic History Review* 66(1). pp. 226–248.

Pearson, R. (1990) Thrift or Dissipation? The Business of Life Assurance in the Early Nineteenth Century. *The Economic History Review* 43(2). pp. 236-254.

Peltola, J. (2019) The British Contribution to the Birth of the Finnish Cotton Industry (1820–1870). *Continuity and Change* 34. pp. 63–89.

Penicuik History Society (n.d.) *Penicuik Papermaking 300th Anniversary: Mill Conversion Penicuik*. http://www.penicuikpapermaking. org/.

Pennell, S. M. (1992) *The Quaker Domestic Interior, Philadelphia 1780–1830: An Artifactual Investigation of the "Quaker Esthetic" at Wyck House, Philadelphia and Collen Brook Farm, Upper Darby, Pennsylvania*. Masters thesis, University of Pennsylvania.

Penny Magazine (1836) Spinning Wheels and Jennies' *The Penny Magazine*, 9 July.

Pentikäinen, J. (1975) Revivalist Movements and Religious Contracultures in Finland. *Scripta Instituti Donneriani Aboensis* 7. pp. 92–122.

Peter, L. J., and Hull, R. (1970). *The Peter Principle*. London: Pan Books.

Phillips, C. (2019) Child Abandonment in England, 1741–1834: The Case of the London Foundling Hospital. *Genealogy* 3(3). 35.

Phillips, Z. (2018) *How to Get Your Sh!t Together*. [Kindle version]. Independently published.

Porter, R. K. (1809) *Travelling Sketches in Russia and Sweden, during the Years 1805, 1806, 1807, 1808*. Google Books. Vol. 1. Philadelphia: Hopkins and Earle.

Posselt (1907) The Bleaching, Dyeing and Finishing of Knit Goods. *Posselt's Textile Journal*, October. pp. 35–39.

Posselt (1911) Chronological Textile Events. *Posselt's Textile Journal*

Rahikainen, M. (2001) Children and "the Right to Factory Work": Child Labour Legislation in Nineteenth-Century Finland. *Scandinavian Economic History Review* 49(1). pp. 41–62.

Rahikainen, M. (2001) Historical and Present-Day Child Labour: Is There a Gap or a Bridge between Them?' *Continuity and Change* 16(1). pp. 137–156.

Rahikainen, M. (2002) First-Generation Factory Children: Child Labour in Textile Manufacturing in Nineteenth-Century Finland. *Scandinavian Economic History Review* 50(2). pp. 71–95.

Ramble, R. (1836) *Travelling Opinions and Sketches in Russia and Poland*. London: John Macrone.

Randall, I. M. (2018) "That the Progress of the Word Be Not Hindered": William Nicolson and the British and Foreign Bible Society in Russia, 1869–1897. *Baptistic Theologies* 10(2).

Reeves, D. (1973) *The Interaction of Scottish and English Evangelicals, 1790–1810*. M. Litt, University of Glasgow.

Reid, A.; Garrett, E.; Dibben, C.; and Williamson, L. (2015) "A Confession of Ignorance": Deaths from Old Age and Deciphering Cause-of-Death Statistics in Scotland, 1855–1949. *The History of the Family* 20(3). pp. 320–344.

Rek-Woźniak, M. and Woźniak, W. (2020) Working-Class and Memory Policy in Post-Industrial Cities: Łódź, Poland, and Tampere, Finland, Compared. *International Labor and Working-Class History* 98 pp. 5–21.

Rhodes, Rita. (1988) Women, Motherhood, and Infertility: The Social and Historical Context. In: Deborah P Valentine (ed) *Infertility and Adoption: A Guide for Social Work Practice*. Routledge. pp. 5–20.

Ricoeur, P. (2004) *Memory, History, Forgetting*. Translated by Kathleen Blamey and David Pellauer. Chicago and London: The University of Chicago Press.

Robb, S. (2014) The Public Washhouses of Edinburgh. In: *Book of the Old Edinburgh Club New Series*, 10. pp. 127–50.

Robertson, A. J. (1963) *The Growth of the Cotton Industry and Scottish Economic Development, 1780–1835*. M.A Thesis, University of Glasgow.

Robertson, M. L. (1956) Scottish Commerce and the American War of Independence. *The Economic History Review* 9(1). pp. 123–131.

Robertson, T. and Robertson, A. (2018) *Historical Journeys along Scottish Rivers. Appendix A2 Some Notes on Watermills*.

Robinson, E. (1975) The Transference of British Technology to Russia, 1760–1820. In: *Great Britain and Her World 1750–1870*. Manchester University Press. pp. 7–10.

Rodger, R. (2004) *The Transformation of Edinburgh: Land, Property and Trust in the Nineteenth Century. ,*. Cambridge: Cambridge University Press.

Ross, J. (1903) *A History of Congregational Independency in Scotland*. 2nd ed. Glasgow: Hay, Nisbet & Co.

Rosslyn, W. (2006) Benevolent Ladies and Their Exertions for the Good of Humankind: V. A. Repnina, S. S. Meshcherskaia, and the Origins of Female Philanthropy in Early Nineteenth-Century Russia. *The Slavonic and East European Review* 84(1). pp. 52–82.

Rosslyn, W. (2007) Women with a Mission: British Female Evangelicals in the Russian Empire in the Early Nineteenth Century. In: W. Rosslyn and A. Tosi (eds) *Women in Russian Culture and Society, 1700–1825*. London: Palgrave Macmillan.

Rothenberg, G. E. (1988) The Origins, Causes, and Extension of the Wars of the French Revolution and Napoleon. *The Journal of Interdisciplinary History* 18(4). (pp. 771–793).

Royal Museums of Greenwich. (2018) How Long Did It Take to Sail across the Atlantic?, 8 November. www.rmg.co.uk/stories/blog/library-archive/18th-century-sailing-times-between-english-channel-coast-america-how.

Rumball, H. F. (2016) *The Relinquishment of Plain Dress: British Quaker Women's Abandonment of Plain Quaker Attire, 1860–1914*. PhD thesis, University of Brighton.

Ryan, A. N. (1959) The Defence of British Trade with the Baltic, 1808–1813. *The English Historical Review* LXXIV, no: 292. pp. 443–66.

Ryan, A. N. (1962) Trade with the Enemy in the Scandinavian and Baltic Ports during the Napoleonic War: For and Against. *Transactions of the Royal Historical Society* 12. pp. 123–40.

Sampson, H. (2017) *A History of Advertising: From the Earliest Times*. anboco.

Sanderson, M. (1967) Education and the Factory in Industrial Lancashire, 1780–1840. *The Economic History Review* 20(2). pp. 266–279.

Särkkä, T.; Valtonen, M.; Turunen, O. and Valtonen, H. (2010) *The Economic and Social Networks of Business Leaders: Immigrant Businessmen in the Nineteenth Century Finnish Economy* (Revised Version). Glasgow.

Saxena, A. and Viberg, Å. (eds) (2009) *Multilingualism: Proceedings of the 23rd Scandinavian Conference of Linguistics, Uppsala University, 1–3 October 2008.* Acta Universitatis Upsaliensis. Studia Linguistica Upsaliensia. Uppsala: Uppsala Universitet.

Scott, R. (1964) *Quakers in Russia.* London: Michael Joseph.

Selleck, R. G. (1962) Quaker Pioneers in Finnish Economic Development: James Finlayson and the Wheeler Family. *Quaker History* 51(1). pp. 32–42.

Shaw, J. P. (1989) Water Power and Rural Industry in East Lothian'. *Transactions of the East Lothian Antiquarian and Field Naturalists' Society* 20. pp. 33–58.

Sibree, J. (1923) *A Register of Missionaries, Deputations, Etc.: From 1796 to 1923.* Fourth edition. London: London Missionary Society.

Sinclair, C. (2000) *Excerpt from Jock Tamson's Bairns: A History of the Records of the General Register Office for Scotland.* National Records of Scotland.

Singleton, F. and Upton, A. F. (1998) *A Short History of Finland.* 2nd ed. Cambridge University Press.

Sivula, A. (2014) Corporate History Culture and Useful Industrial Past: A Case Study on History Management in Finnish Cotton Company Porin Puuvilla Oy. *Folklore* 57. pp. 29–54.

Sloane, W. M. (1898) The Continental System of Napoleon. *Political Science Quarterly* 13(2). pp. 213–231.

Smith, A. (1776/2008)) *An Inquiry into the Nature and Causes of the Wealth of Nations.* Oxford World's Classics. 1776. Reprint, London: Oxford University Press.

Smith, C. J. (1978) *Historic South Edinburgh.* Vol. 1. Edinburgh: Charles Skilton Ltd.

Smith, C. J. (1986) *Historic South Edinburgh: People.* Vol. 3. Haddington: Charles Skilton Ltd.

Smith, M. (2009) The Church of Scotland and the Funeral Industry in Nineteenth-Century Edinburgh. *The Scottish Historical Review* 88(225). pp. 108–133.

Smith, R. M. (2019) The United Secession Church in Glasgow 1820–1847. *Scottish Church History* 34(1). pp. 48–90.

Smith, T. W. (1990) Classifying Protestant Denominations. *Review of Religious Research* 31(3). pp. 225–245.

Smoliarova, T. and Meyer, R. (2013) Words Turned to Spindles: Gavriil Derzhavin's Poetics of the Machine. *Ulbandus Review* 15. pp. 9–32.

Snowden, B. (2007) The Power of Ideas: Joel Mokyr on the Intellectual Origins of the Industrial Revolution and Modern Economic Growth. *World Economics – Henley on Thames* 8(3). 53.

Solar, P. M., and Lyons, J. S. (2011) The English Cotton Spinning Industry, 1780–1840, as Revealed in the Columns of the London Gazette. *Business History* 53(3). pp. 302–323.

Stallybrass, E. (1836) *Memoir of Mrs. Stallybrass, Wife of the Rev Edward Stallybrass, Missionary to Siberia.* London: Fisher, Son & Co.

Stark, J. (1874) *Sixteenth Detailed Annual Report of Registrar General of Births, Deaths and Marriages in Scotland BPP XIV [C.897] Xli.* General Register Office for Scotland. http://www.histpop.org.

Statutes, Great Britain. (1794) *The Statutes at Large: Part 1, From 32nd to 33rd Year of the Reign of King George III.* Edited by D. Pickering. Vol. 39. J. Bentham.

Stewart, R. W. (1976) *The Development of the Voluntary Principle and Practice in Scotland Particularly in the Antecedents of the United Presbyterian Church 1733–1847.* PhD thesis. University of Edinburgh.

Stradling, D. and Thorsheim, P. (1999) The Smoke of Great Cities: British and American Efforts to Control Air Pollution, 1860–1914. *Environmental History* 4(1). pp. 6–31.

Sullivan, J. (1929) Legend, Anecdote and History. *The Quarterly Journal of the New York State Historical Association* 10(1). pp.29–44.

Swan, W. (1823) *Memoir of the Late Mrs Paterson, Wife of the Rev. Dr Paterson, St Petersburg, Containing Extracts from Her Diary and Correspondence.* 2nd ed. Edinburgh: Waugh & Innes.

Swan, W. (1866) *Heart Musings: 'To Bring to Remembrance'*. Edinburgh: T. Constable.

Szreter, S. and Mooney, G. (1998). Urbanization, Mortality, and the Standard of Living Debate: New Estimates of the Expectation of Life at Birth in Nineteenth-Century British Cities. *The Economic History Review* 51(1). pp. 84–112.

Takei, A. (1994) The First Irish Linen Mills, 1800–1824. *Irish Economic and Social History* 21. pp. 28–38.

Tamm, M. (2014) Truth, Objectivity and Evidence in History Writing. *Journal of the Philosophy of History* 8(2). pp. 265–290.

Taylor, S.; Bell, E. and Cooke, B. (2009) Business History and the Historiographical Operation. *Management & Organizational History* 4(2). pp. 151–166.

Thompstone, S. (2002) *The Russian Technical Society and British Textile Machinery Imports*. Discussion paper. University of Nottingham.

Tiderman, F., Rayner, O. T. and Lyon, F. H. (eds) (1922) *Trade and Industry of Finland*. J. Simelius' Heirs Printing Company Limited.

Tilly, L. A.; Fuchs, R. G.; Kertzer, D. I. and Ransel, D. L. (1992) Child Abandonment in European History: A Symposium. *Journal of Family History* 17(1). pp. 1–23.

Timpson, T. (1841) *Memoirs of British Female Missionaries*. William Smith.

Tompkins, S. R. (1948) The Russian Bible Society: A Case of Religious Xenophobia. *The American Slavic and East European Review* 7(3). pp. 251–268.

Trouillot, M-R. (2015) *Silencing the Past: Power and the Production of History*. Beacon Press.

Trussell, J. and Wilson, C. (1985) Sterility in a Population with Natural Fertility. *Population Studies* 39(2). pp. 269–286.

Tucker, A. (2008) Historiographic Revision and Revisionism. In: Michal Kopeček (ed) *Past in the Making: Recent History and Historical Revisionism*, 15. Budapest: Central European University Press.

Twells, A. A. (1997) *The Heathen at Home and Overseas: The Middle Class and the Civilising Mission, Sheffield 1790–1843*. PhD thesis, University of York.

Uglow, J. (2014) *In These Times: Living in Britain through Napoleon's Wars, 1793–1815*. [Kindle]. Faber & Faber.

Uschanov, E.; Björklund, K. and Korkiasaari, J. (2014) *How to Trace Your Roots in Finland*. The Institute of Migration.

Vause, E. (2014) The Business of Reputations: Secrecy, Shame, and Social Standing in Nineteenth – Century French Debtors' and Creditors' Newspapers. *Journal of Social History* 48(1). pp. 47–71.

Venables, R. L. (1839) *Domestic Scenes in Russia: In a Series of Letters Describing a Year's Residence in That Country, Chiefly in the Interior*. John Murray.

Vincent, E. (1994) The Responses of Scottish Churchmen to the French Revolution, 1789–1802. *The Scottish Historical Review* 73(196). pp. 191–215.

Vincent, T. (2001) A Beginner's Guide to Finnish Genealogy'. *The Federation of East European Family History Societies (FEEFHS) Journal* 9. pp. 60–71.

Virrankoski, P. (1963) Replacement of Flax by Cotton in the Domestic Textile Industry of South-West Finland. *Scandinavian Economic History Review* 11(1). pp. 27–42.

Voionmaa (previously Wallin), V. (1907) *Tampereen Kaupungin Historia: III OSA Tampereen Historia Viime Vuosikymmeninä (1856–1905)(History of the City of Tampere: PART III History of Tampere in Recent Decades (1856–1905)*. Vol. Part 3. Tampere [Finland]: Tampere Kaupungin Kustantama.

Vries, M. F. R. de. (2019) The Icarus Syndrome: Execs Who Fly Too Close to the Sun. *Insead Knowledge: Leadership and Organisations*.

Walker, E. (2018) Preston Ranked in the UK Cities to See the Most Rain. *Preston Blog*, 21 March. www.blogpreston.co.uk/.

Walker, F. A. (1992) Enlightenment and Religion in Russian Education in the Reign of Tsar Alexander I'. *History of Education Quarterly* 32(3). pp. 343–360.

Walli, H. (1969) *Finnish Genealogical Research: Methods and Procedures*. Salt Lake City, Utah: Genealogical Society of Utah.

Wallin (later Voionmaa), V (1905). *Tampereen Kaupungin Historia: II OSA Tampereen Historia Aleksanteri I:n ja Nikolai I:n (History of the City of Tampere: PART II History of Tampere under Alexander Ist and Nicholas Ist)*. Vol. Part 2. Tampere [Finland]: Tampere Kaupungin Kustantama.

Wardin, A. W. (2013) *On the Edge: Baptists and Other Free Church Evangelicals in Tsarist Russia, 1855–1917*. Eugene Oregon: Wipf & Stock.

Watkins, S. W. (2014) Hat Honour, Self-Identity and Commitment in Early Quakerism. *Quaker History* 103(1). pp. 1–16.

Watson, M. (2011) Cotton Mill Cities and Power Canals in Scotland, America, Finland and Estonia' In: Miia Hinnerichsen(ed) *Reusing the Industrial Past by the Tammerkoski Rapids: Discussions on the Value of Industrial Heritage*. Tampere [Finland]: City of Tampere, Museum Services, Pirkanmaa Provincial Museum.

Watson, N. (n.d.) *Maritime Science and Technology: Changing Our World*. Lloyd's Register Foundation,

Watson, T. (1894) *Kirkintilloch: Town and Parish*. Glasgow: John Smith and Sons.

Watters, F. (1994) The Night of the Big Wind, 1839. *'Before I Forget...': Journal of the Poyntzpass and District Local History Society* 7. pp. 73–82.

Wheeler, D. (1842) *Memoirs of the Life and Gospel Labors of the Late Daniel Wheeler: A Minister of the Society of Friends*. Harvey and Darton.

Whittemore, C.; Marwick; MacDonald, A.; Waugh, W. and Quigley,I (2014) *Stories from an Edinburghshire Village: Howgate*. Whittemore, West Linton.

Whyman, S. E. (2007) Letter Writing and the Rise of the Novel: The Epistolary Literacy of Jane Johnson and Samuel Richardson. *Huntington Library Quarterly* 70(4). pp. 577–606.

Whyman, S. E. (2009) *The Pen and the People: English Letter Writers 1660–1800*. Oxford: Oxford University Press.

Widdicombe, J. H. (2020) A Brief History of Bronchitis in England and Wales. *Chronic Obstructive Pulmonary Diseases* 7(4). pp. 303–14.

Wikipedia contributors (n.d.) James Finlayson (industrialist). *Wikipedia, The Free Encyclopedia.*

Wilcox, R. W. (1900) Senile Bronchitis (1827–1924). *The American Journal of the Medical Sciences* 119(5). pp. 520

Wilson, J. J. (1891) *Annals of Penicuik.* Edinburgh: T. & A. Constable.

Wolff, K. H. (1974) Textile Bleaching and the Birth of the Chemical Industry. *The Business History Review* 48(2). pp. 143–163.

Wood, A. (2016) The Historical Treatment and Perception of Bankrupts. *The Gazette.*

Wood, J. T. (1822) *A Voyage to St. Petersburg in 1814 with Remarks on the Imperial Russian Navy by a Surgeon in the British Navy.* London: Sir Richard Phillips & Co.

Woodcroft, B. (1854) *Titles of Patents of Invention, Chronologically Arranged: From March 2, 1617 (14 James I.) to October 1, 1852 (16 Victoriae).* Vol. Part 1. London: G.E. Eyre & W. Spottiswoode.

Wrightson, K. (1994) "Sorts of People" in Tudor and Stuart England. In: *The Middling Sort of People: Culture, Society and Politics in England, 1550–1800*, pp. 28–51. Basingstoke: Macmillan.

Yli-Hinkkala, H. (2015) *"Per Angusta Ad Augusta." Ferdinand Uhde Finlaysonin Tehtaan Johtajana 1836-1844.* Masters thesis, Tampere University.

You, I. S. (2011) *The Contribution of British Entrepreneurs to the Spread of the Industrial Revolution to the European Continent.* Student Research Paper, AP European History Class. Korean Minjok Leadership Academy, International Program.

Young, C. (1991) An Assessment of Scottish Sequestrations as a Source in Historical Analysis. *Journal of the Society of Archivists* 12(2). pp. 127–135.

Young, S. (2008) *The Wielobycki Brothers and Homeopathy*, 26 October. www.sueyounghistories.com/.

Zeev, N. B., and Mokyr, J. (2015) *Flexible Supply of Apprenticeship in the British Industrial Revolution.* Preliminary version.

Zeitlin, E. A. (1934) Iz Istorii Machinogo Proizvodstva v Rossii: Pervonachal'noe Tecknicheskoe Oborudovanie Aleksandrovskoi Manufactury (Contribution to the History of the Machine Industry in Russia. The First Technical Equipment of Aleksandrovsk Manufactory'. In: *Academy of Sciences, U.S.S.R., Trudy Instituta Istorii Nauki i Tekhniki (Proceedings of the Institute of Science and Technology.* 3(1). pp. 263–272.

Index

M

N

Naiper, John. *See* Napier, John (1752-1813)

Napier, John (1752-1813), 11, 129–31, 136, 301

Napoleon's Russian campaign, 153

nemesis, 10, 12

New Lanark Mills, 83, 92, 96, 297–99

Newington Necropolis. *See* cemeteries, Newington Cemetery, Edinburgh

Nicolson Square, Edinburgh, 26

    description, 224

    public baths, 225–26

    residents, 230

    Wesleyan Methodist chapel, 177, 225

Night of the Big Wind, Ireland, 219

Nordenskiöld, Niilo (1792-1866), 202, 204, 284

Nottbeck, Carl Samuel (1779-1847), 208–10, 216, 302

O

Ochta, 153, 167, 176

Okta. *See* Ochta

Old Scotch Independents, 92

orphanages

    Alexandrovsk, 157–58

    benefactors, 297

    economic model, 297–98

    Imperial Foundling Hospital of Saint Petersburg, 158

    Tampere, 200–201, 203, 296, 299

Orr, W. & J. (Paisley and Ireland), 217

Oxenham, Hugh, mangle maker, 95

ISBN 978-1-7384792-0-7

9 781738 479207 >

£11.79